——*THE STATE OF THE ART*——

THE
STA
OF TH
AF

DAVID LEHMAN

A CHRONICLE OF AMERICAN POETRY, 1988–2014

UNIVERSITY OF PITTSBURGH PRESS

Published by the University of Pittsburgh Press, Pittsburgh, Pa., 15260

Manufactured in the United States of America
Printed on acid-free paper
10 9 8 7 6 5 4 3 2 1

ISBN 13: 978-0-8229-4439-3
ISBN 10: 0-8229-4439-1

Library of Congress Cataloging-in-Publication Data

Lehman, David, 1948–
The State of the Art: A Chronicle of American Poetry, 1988–2014 / David Lehman.
   pages cm. — (Pitt Poetry Series)
Includes bibliographical references and index.
ISBN 978-0-8229-4439-3 (hardback: acid-free paper)
1. American poetry—20th century—History and criticism. 2. American poetry—21st
century—History and criticism. 3. Poetics. I. Title.
PS325.L44 2015
811'.5409—dc23   2015004047

In memory of Archie Ammons, Bob Creeley,
Adrienne Rich, John Hollander, and Mark Strand

———————

And death shall have no dominion.
DYLAN THOMAS

—— CONTENTS ——

FOREWORD *by Denise Duhamel*   ix

ACKNOWLEDGMENTS   xv

INTRODUCTION   xvii

1988   *"like dropping a rose petal down the Grand Canyon and waiting for the echo"*   1

1989   *in an unlit alcove where bookstore patrons fear to tread*   4

1990   *to inflame passions, disturb the complacent, and arouse the anxiety of despots*   7

1991   *a poem entitled "Cigarettes" by a poet named Ash*   11

1992   *The question of poetry and its audience*   14

1993   *the gust of fresh air that turned into the blizzard of '93*   17

1994   *It's safe to say that the inaugural was the best-attended poetry reading of the decade*   21

1995   *At least somebody played ball in 1994*   26

1996   *a given volume in this series might hang question marks over all three terms in the title*   31

1997   *As a gimmick, if that's what it is, National Poetry Month worked*   36

THE BEST OF THE BEST AMERICAN POETRY, 1988–1997 (1998)
The debate is joined   43

1998	The president spoke of having had to memorize 100 lines of Macbeth	48
1999	"Whitman rocks"	53
2000	"Now I know how poems feel"	62
2001	"Everybody else was analog and Nietzsche was digital"	69
2002	The day now marks a boundary	76
2003	"How many people have to die before you can become president?"	83
2004	canons do not remain fixed for long	92
2005	the creative writing workshop [and] the fall of civilization	99
2006	Accessibility—as a term and, implicitly, as a value	108
2007	Undoubtedly the most parodied of all poems	113
2008	Who says that hot poems can't get you into trouble in 2008?	120
2009	"that is how I should talk if I could talk poetry"	127
2010	McChrystal sent copies of "The Second Coming" to his special operators	140
2011	in Dickinson's brain, "wider than the sky"	147
2012	the "uncanny" is a category too little invoked	158

THE BEST OF THE BEST AMERICAN POETRY, 25TH ANNIVERSARY EDITION (2013)
"Every time I read Pessoa I think" — 163

| 2013 | It was his poetry that kept him going | 172 |
| 2014 | In the antagonism between science and the humanities | 180 |

INDEX OF NAMES — 193

FOREWORD

by *Denise Duhamel*

In May 1987, I graduated from Sarah Lawrence College with an MFA. In
September 1988, I bought my first copy of *The Best American Poetry* series
(guest edited by John Ashbery). It never occurred to me that I was reading
the inaugural volume. I assumed the series had been waiting for me all along.
Maybe it was my earnest involvement with the world of poetry—everything
from "slamming" at the Nuyorican Poets Café to spending lunch hours reading
chapbooks at Poets House—that made me take David Lehman's enormous
endeavor for granted. For me, such an anthology was a most natural thing to
behold. Maybe it was my youthful exuberance—I'd just Xeroxed one hundred
copies of one of my own poems for the collaboratively self-published *The Na-
tional Poetry Magazine of the Lower East Side*—that made me believe every-
one loved good poems. I remember sitting in ABC No Rio, reading *The Best
American Poetry* selections by Bernadette Mayer and Ruth Stone, while waiting
for latecomer contributors to arrive. I showed the book to a few new friends
who all agreed I should check out Kenneth Koch, David Lehman, and John
Ashbery. I tucked the anthology in my backpack as we all gathered in a circle
then passed around our Xeroxes so that each copy of our literary endeavor
would have the same order. Some selfless soul (a visual artist who'd designed
one hundred covers) placed our efforts between cardstock and leaned down

hard on a three-hole punch. While I knew *The Best American Poetry 1988* and *The National Poetry Magazine of the Lower East Side* (which would be sold on consignment at St. Mark's Bookstore) were two very different enterprises, I could at least metaphorically see David Lehman and John Ashbery passing their favorite poems back and forth.

At the time I lived in an extremely dicey apartment on East 5th Street and Avenue B. From my barred window my pink neon sign flashed "poet." Poetry was what got me through my adjunct teaching gigs, my tedious temp agency desk jobs, the crack vials and vile smells in the hallway. I was living a dangerous life, and poetry was dangerous. Dangerous, exciting. I couldn't get enough. Though I was poor in terms of money and possessions, I reminded myself that I was living in Alphabet City—how could I not make my life about words? Like Samuel Taylor Coleridge, I found poetry "its own exceeding great reward."

David Lehman is a first-class poet and his sestina "Operation Memory" was the first poem of his I came upon through *The Best American Poetry*. Though I was a decade younger than the speaker in his poem, I felt a kinship to those last three lines:

> It happened, I was asleep in bed, and when I woke up,
> It was over: I was 38, on the brink of middle age,
> A succession of stupid jobs behind me, a loaded gun on my lap.

I remember thinking I'd be fine should the same thing happen to me. The "loaded gun" in my mind was a book of poems that could trigger anything. In 1990, I bought a copy of David's book for which this sestina became its title. I could write a foreword about David's brilliant gestures and stances as a poet, but I am here on a different mission. One called "Operation Foreword."

> I was weeding my garden when
> The phone rang. Operation Foreword. My flowerbeds
> Would have to wait. David had planted hundreds,
> No thousands, of poems in BAP! And there I was, in the middle
> Of my milkweed, my periwinkles, when my job
> Changed. A foreword to David's forewords. I downloaded
>
> A PDF, printed it out, and read. Each essay was loaded
> With charm and smarts. David defended poetry when
> The naysayers held a gun to its head. A vigilante, David's job

———— *DENISE DUHAMEL* ————

Was to disarm critics who'd woken up on the wrong side of the bed.
What more could I add? I felt like I was in middle
School again, annotating with my yellow no. 2

Pencil. It all came back—magnetic poetry for the fridge, 1996
And the advent of National Poetry Month. David's mother lode
Of poetry news. On New York subways, poems popped up amid
Ads for hemorrhoid cream and banks. When
Sheryl Crow turned Wyn Cooper's poem "Fun" into a song, bedfellows
Of pop music and poetry were made. My jojoba

Would have to flourish without me. I was entrusted with the job
To write a foreword to all of David's forewords. In 2001,
We all turned to Auden, and in 2002, David made his bedazzling
Case for "September 1, 1939," the loaded
Last line of the penultimate stanza. When
Poetry popped up on TV, David was the middleman

To *ER*, *Felicity*, *Party of Five*, sophisticated *Mad Men* and the middlebrow
Sports Night, *Bull*, and *Law and Order: Criminal Intent*. His job
Was to find poetry where we'd be least likely to look. When
David went to the movies, he found verse there too—
Ten Things I Hate About You fully loaded
With references to *The Taming of the Shrew*. Kat beds

Joey (a disaster), so little sister Bianca can't bed
Cameron—or even go to the prom. She gives the middle
Finger to conformity. But I digress. Better to take a load
Off your feet and read David, entrepreneur as savvy as Steve Jobs.
Think about it—David made *Best American Poetry*, a one-
In-a-million, soaring enterprise. When

You're looking for poetry's bedrock, when you want to read
Seventy-five great poems on everything from the Middle East
To Job, you know where to go. And don't forget each exploding foreword.

———————

A confession. When the series was new and I was a new reader to the series, I'd
often skipped or skimmed David's forewords and each guest poet's introduction,

so anxious was I to get to the poems. It was only as I grew more vigilant that I became obsessed with the front matter in *The Best American Poetry*. *The State of the Art* is vital, the collected forewords (so far, that is) of a distinguished man of letters and arguably the most important tastemaker of contemporary American poetry.

David's wit and sublime reasoning infuse the forewords you are about to read. (Or that you have already read and will reread as a whole.) He has been known to turn to his own playful poetry in his forewords (1990, 1997, 2001), as I have done here. David loves homage, imitation, and poems that talk to other poems. He often makes connections between the historical and the present, between current editions of *The Best American Poetry* and past ones. He takes his cue from Charles Baudelaire who advised, "Always be a poet, even in prose." David's deep knowledge of poetry and its history are evident on each page, as is his keen cultural analysis. In his prescient first foreword, David anticipates the growing number of MFA programs creating a wider poetry readership. There I was, along with many others back in 1988, excited that such an anthology existed. Terrance Hayes (guest editor of *The Best American Poetry 2014*) bought his first copy in 1990. And the readership grows every year. MFA alums are not the only readers David has cultivated. *The Best American Poetry* series, ushered in with David's wise and elucidated commentary, has garnered readers from all walks of life.

Throughout his forewords, David also chronicles the rise of critical theory, deconstruction, New Historicism, and the decreasing number of actual poetry critics. American poets (not unlike sisters) came to be "doin' it for themselves." In a 1985 pop song, Annie Lennox and Aretha Franklin sang that sisters are "ringin' on their own bells." And to a large extent, *The Best American Poetry* series is ringing poetry's bells, shaping the discourse of American poetry. Poets, through each guest editor's choices and the contributors' notes, provide important dialogue and invite debate.

Most of all, David's forewords are exceedingly insightful about the state of contemporary poetry and serve as minicourses in what poets have said about poetry and the times in which they lived. He writes about the impact of A. R. Ammons, W. H. Auden, Elizabeth Bishop, Joseph Brodsky, Hart Crane, Emily Dickinson, T. S. Eliot, Louise Erdrich, Allen Ginsberg, Dana Gioia, Václav Havel, Seamus Heaney, John Milton, Marianne Moore, Frank O'Hara, Marge Piercy, Rainer Maria Rilke, Percy Bysshe Shelley, Gertrude Stein, Wallace Stevens, Wisława Szymborska, Walt Whitman, Oscar Wilde, William Wordsworth, and others. David discusses these poets through anecdote and analysis, for the benefit of the general reader as well as poetry lovers. Molly Peacock has noted that "A poem is an instant, lightning across the sky. Prose is before the storm, the storm, after the storm." And David's prose is just that—the history of poetry, the contextualizing of poetry, and the predictions for its future. Through his forewords, David foresaw not only the rise in the number of poetry readers but also the adaptation of poetry to various new technologies, including the wildly successful *The Best American Poetry* blog. He writes eloquently about the "dumbing down" of culture without ever "dumbing down" poetry for us. He is illuminating, provocative, and ecumenical. American poets couldn't have asked for a better advocate.

In addition to all David does for poets and their readers through the series, these forewords remind us of his efforts to popularize poetry while retaining its dignity. David developed the Poetry Olympics in 1997. I remember attending the Poetry Game Show in which David hosted a hilarious segment called "What's That Line?" If I remember correctly, there were bonus points given to any contestant who could correctly spell Szymborska. That took place in 1996. Three years later, David went to a symposium in Rotterdam, a sort of world summit on poetry, and came back to report the findings on the state of poetry in other countries. David has been an ambassador of American poetry, and he has always done us proud. In his forewords, he reminds us of our privilege, our freedom of speech. While some American poets may grouse about their invisibility, David points out the real danger poets can face elsewhere, paying tribute to imprisoned and tortured poets in Burma, Hungary, Vietnam, and Qatar.

David's influence has been tremendous. When *The Best American Poetry* series started, only two other "best" anthologies existed—one for short stories (compiled since 1978) and another for essays (compiled since 1986). Since that time many others have come along. *The Best American Crime Writing, The Best American Crime Reporting, The Best American Infographics, The Best American Magazine Writing, The Best American Mystery Stories, The Best American Science Writing, The Best American Science and Nature Writing, The Best American Sports Writing, The Best American Travel Writing,* and *The Best American Nonrequired Reading* (which appeals to high school readers) line bookstore shelves and Amazon pages. Other "best" anthologies include *The Best Food Writing, The Best Horror of the Year, The Year's Best Dark Fantasy and Horror, The Best Music Writing,* and *The Best Writing on Mathematics.* Some of these anthologies have endured while others lasted only a few years. There are now "best of" poetry anthologies in Australia, Canada, Great Britain, Ireland, and New Zealand that all use *The Best American Poetry* as their model.

I met David in person in 1993 and we became fast friends. We have had the pleasure of collaborating on poems and plays and even *The Best American Poetry 2013*. I did think back to those days of collating *The National Poetry Magazine of the Lower East Side* as David and I discussed which poems to include in the volume I guest-edited. David has an enthusiasm for poetry that informs his opinions and optimism, making him a delightful collaborator in every way. Though he publishes his poetry primarily with Scribner, he also undertakes small press projects such as *Poetry Forum: A Play Poem: A Pl'em* (with Judith Hall) and his collaborative book *Jim Cummins and David Lehman Defeat the Masked Man* for which I wrote the foreword. David's productivity is simply awe-inspiring. While he is arguably the most impressive person in his field, he retains a sense of fun and wonder. He takes poetry seriously and has serious fun with his craft. In addition to writing these forewords, he is always at some stage of compiling or editing or proofing *The Best American Poetry*. Lucille Ball once said, "If you want something done, ask a busy person to do it. The more things you do, the more you can do." She could have been talking about David.

———ACKNOWLEDGMENTS———

Heartfelt thanks go to Glen Hartley and Lynn Chu, whose agency has represented me since I started writing books more than thirty years ago. I tell people that I have enjoyed working with many editors. But I add that I have always had just one agent. *The Best of the Best* retrospective that appeared in 2013 was dedicated to Glen Hartley.

I owe a debt to the men and women of Scribner, the firm that has published *The Best American Poetry* from the start. My editors there have included John Glusman, the very first, who signed up the book when it was deemed a risky thing to do. He was followed by Erika Goldman, Hamilton Cain, Gillian Blake, Alexis Gargagliano, Daniel Burgess, and Ashley Gilliam, who worked under the editorial direction of Nan Graham.

The contributions of Howard Altmann, Mark Bibbins, Nora Brooks, Danielle Chin, Denise Duhamel, Amy Gerstler, Stacey Harwood, Ron Horning, Jamie Katz, and Stephanie Paterik were many and varied. When you do a book like this, you benefit from all manner of help—on everything from prepping the manuscript to finding a winning title, arguing a point, supporting the effort.

Great thanks to Peter Kracht, Ed Ochester, and their able team at the University of Pittsburgh Press.

——— INTRODUCTION ———

I wrote this book almost without knowing it. Since 1988, when *The Best American Poetry* made its maiden voyage, I have written a foreword for each year's volume. The first year the task was relatively easy. I needed to announce our existence, to state the rationale for the book, to say a few words about the year's guest editor, and to summarize such rules as we provisionally adopted. While we had a two-year commitment from the publisher, no one expected the series to last. It took us all by surprise when it did. By the time Bill Clinton challenged George Bush for the presidency, we had become—as reviewers put it—an "institution," even an "annual rite of autumn." Poets and their readers awaited the book with enthusiasm or apprehension, with hands ready either to clap or to don boxing gloves.

It occurred to me then that if you set aside the important utilitarian functions that the foreword must continue to perform—introducing the year's guest editor, for example—this piece of writing might be as free in its movement and as capacious as a verse essay. And by trial and error, the annual foreword evolved into a form, harder to summarize than a sestina or villanelle with their strict rules but a form nevertheless. Gradually the pieces grew longer and more ambitious.

I have now written twenty-nine—one for each volume in the series plus preambles to the two retrospective *Best of the Best* collections that have appeared, the hotly debated selection edited by Harold Bloom in 1998 and the twenty-fifth anniversary volume that Robert Pinsky assembled in 2013. I am not alone in believing that the forewords, gathered into a book of their own, might constitute something other, something more, than the chronicle of a single anthology series, however influential. Do they help annotate a history of American poetry in the last quarter of a century, as we went from a familiar reality (typewriters, the Cold War) to a brand-new set of coordinates (smart phones, global terrorism)? I would like to think that these annual reports reflect some of the changes as they registered on our poets—and some of the innovative strategies that poets and their advocates have developed. I would like to think that they collectively convey a multi-reel picture of American poetry—its practitioners, its audience, its place in our culture as a whole, the issues that confront us, the timeless questions, the surprises—as the old century expired and a new one speedily took its place.

When I wrote chapter one of this book, the president was Ronald Reagan and the Berlin Wall was still up. Not even Al Gore had heard of the Internet. The poetry slam was a new phenomenon. Poetry readings were taking place not only in the familiar venues but also in bars, breweries, and even hardware or other stores not customarily associated with verse. The beats were back, or had never left, and the doors of bohemia had swung open. We had, without knowing it, heard the first rap poems when Muhammad Ali, then still Cassius Clay, improvised his rhyming battle cries in the early 1960s, but the genre had yet to establish itself. The consultant in poetry to the Library of Congress had just been rechristened the poet laureate of the United States, and some who were tapped for the post made the most of the opportunity to celebrate modern poetry, combat illiteracy, promote the recital of favorite poems, and enlarge our audience. States, cities, boroughs, and even museums and TV networks got into the act, appointing their own poets laureate. In the universities, the poets of the language school, convinced of the impossibility of unmediated discourse, were in the process of supplanting an older generation of formalists who doubled as practitioners of the New Criticism. The New Criticism went old hat, and perhaps for the first time ever the poetry party that identified itself as avant-garde was embraced by an establishment that had once been allergic to radical change. The borders between academic poetry and popular poetry, which was suddenly not an oxymoron, dissolved somewhat in this period that suspended value judgments in concert with a Nietzschean imperative. Nothing is true. Everything is permitted.

That is one version, abbreviated and partial, of what has happened in (or to) poetry at a time of vast technological upheaval, a global reconfiguring of political actuality, and constant change. Some of the change is generational. We have lost the voices of many esteemed individuals: Ai, Ali, Ammons, Arnold, Baraka, Berg, Brodsky, Bukowski, Carruth, Cassity, Clampitt, Coleman, Creeley, Davison, Dickey, Digges, Disch, Edson, Emerson, Gilbert, Ginsberg, Grossman, Guest, Gunn, Heaney, Hecht, Henry, Hine, Hollander, Hull, Justice, Kenyon, Kinnell, Kizer, Knott, Koch, Kumin, Kunitz, Lamantia, Levertov, Levis, Merrill, Rector, Rich, Scalapino, Schuyler, Shapiro (Harvey), Shapiro (Karl), Shinder, Simpson, Snodgrass, Stafford, Starbuck, Stone, Strand, Swenson, Updike, Van Duyn, Vazirani, Violi, Wetzsteon, and I'm afraid this is an incomplete list. On the other hand, poets have appeared in *The Best American Poetry* who were infants when the series came into existence. Terrance Hayes, the guest editor of the 2014 edition, opens his introduction to the volume with the statement that the first book of poetry he ever purchased was the 1990 volume edited by Jorie Graham.

There are trends that are undeniable. Our demographics have changed. Many more women, persons of color, Asian Americans, Hispanic Americans, Native Americans, and so forth, are engaged in writing and publishing poetry, and what they produce does not necessarily conform to the imperatives of identity politics. Poets are writing with candor about formerly taboo subjects; nothing is off limits, especially when the subject is the writer's personal, social, and sexual life. Experimentation with ad hoc forms continues apace, and the prose poem has achieved a level of acceptance that is unprecedented in American poetry. A poem posted on a blog or website may go viral, giving rise to thousands of tweets—a sentence that would have made no sense whatever to a reader back in 1988 when leveraged buyouts were the rage on Wall Street and the magic word was glasnost.

In my forewords, I was writing not for future readers but for an immediate audience of persons who were presumably engaged enough with American poetry to want to follow its progress—to read and judge for themselves a group of the year's poems that had earned the approbation of a distinguished practitioner of the art. I wrote about the way poetry figured in the culture at large—how it entered television shows and movies; where it had become newsworthy and why; how the very word was an honorific when applied to statesmen or rock stars if not to poets. I wrote about the series itself and its history after we had compiled a notable track record, but I was always more focused on the major transitions of our time, some of them gradual, some of them hitting with the force and horror of the atrocities of September 11, 2001. When, in W. H. Auden's words, the "unmentionable odor of death" spread itself across the city of New York, accompanied by anger, fear, and the expiration of "clever hopes," many of us turned instinctively to poems: Auden's "September 1, 1939," Marianne Moore's "What Are Years?"

Unsung heroes and lamented victims from around the world claimed my attention: the Afghani poet Nadia Anjuman, whose husband beat her to death because she not only wrote poetry but also joined an undercover group defying the Taliban's decrees prohibiting women from reading, writing, and engaging in studies; Gyorgy Faludy, the Hungarian poet who survived the punishments of the Stalinist concentration camp in Recsk; the Burmese poet Saw Wai, who was sent to prison for publishing a love poem said to bear a secret message critical of Burma's military dictator; the Vietnamese poet Nguyen Chi Thien, who survived torture and imprisonment and memorized the scores of poems he had composed despite his oppressors' refusal to let him have pen and paper. Each is a reminder of our own good fortune, which we sometimes take for granted. Each also dramatizes that much depends on our poems. They cannot do the living for us, but they can help us endure disappointments, hardships, and loss. They keep the chaos and madness at bay.

Inevitably I found myself tangling with the really big important questions that poets and their proponents have always confronted. What is a poet, and where does inspiration come from? If from within, is it something that one can generate or must it arise unbidden, as if the poet were himself or herself surprised? If from without, is it like a divine visitation, or is the stimulus something painful and even cruel, like the wound that accompanied the fabled archer's bow, which ended the Trojan War triumphantly for the Greeks? What makes a poem great? Are poems in dialogue with other poems, usually but not always by poets long since deceased? Can we understand parody as a species of literary criticism? If we adapted W. H. Auden's idea of a "daydream College for Bards" to the many undergraduate and graduate writing programs that have emerged in the last thirty years, what would the result look like? Can we balance the rival claims of populism and elitism in an anthology that calls itself "the best" and seeks a large audience? Was Tocqueville right when he predicted that in a democracy invariably "the number of works grows rapidly, while the merit of each diminishes"? Can poems be said to have a political dimension, by intention or in spite of it? Is the public value of the art measured more accurately in ceremonies and medals—an inaugural ode, a poem read before a joint session of Congress, an inspired public initiative—or, on the contrary, in acts of protest, resistance to the pressures of reality, writing that set its teeth on edge against the prevailing order, wars and government failures?

Or would poets be wise to separate the aesthetic from the political? Is poetry an analog art in a digital age? What accounts for the mean-spiritedness of much poetry criticism? How has the widely discussed crisis in the humanities made itself felt in creative writing programs? Does the future of poetry depend on the health of such programs? Will the book exist or will computer screens consign the physical object to museums or reliquaries? How has the publishing industry adjusted to the new dispensation?

Reading through this volume, I encountered more off-the-cuff literary analysis than I expected. On three separate occasions I was moved to write a poem and embed it in the foreword. To make a point or to enter a contested space, I managed to quote and talk about Milton's "Lycidas," Wordsworth's "Tintern Abbey," Shelley's "Mask of Anarchy," Dickinson's "There's a Certain Slant of Light," Arnold's "Dover Beach," Hart Crane's "Chaplinesque," Auden's "September 1, 1939." Certain novels—Ian McEwan's *Saturday*, Nicholson Baker's *The Anthologist*—entered the discussion. I seem always to have kept an eye out for closet poets—such as J.Lo and Saddam Hussein, who may have had nothing else in common—and for unusual developments, including the day that *Haaretz*, the oldest Hebrew-language daily in Israel, had its entire newspaper, from headlines and news summary to sports and weather, written by poets.

When I recall working with the twenty-nine poets I've recruited as guest editors—Ashbery, Hall, Graham, Strand, Simic, Glück, Ammons, Howard, Rich, Tate, Bloom, Hollander, Bly, Dove, Hass, Creeley, Komunyakaa, Hejinian, Muldoon, Collins, McHugh, Wright, Wagoner, Gerstler, Young, Doty, Pinsky, Duhamel, and Hayes—I count myself as fortunate more than twice over. In writing this introduction, I thought of incorporating sentences culled not entirely at random from each of the introductory essays written by this distinguished roster. I will present them here in no particular order, and without a key. You may want to turn this list into a guessing game, but I would hope that you would also consider these remarks on their own terms, without reference to names and dates:

"The alphabetical order of poets, a convention of this series, creates a structure of its own."

"The present is notoriously blind to itself."

"I am your untrustworthy guide."

"In each generation, the practitioners for their own purposes revise that forever shape-shifting and evolving organism, the canon."

"As the deadline approached, I changed the final lineup over a dozen times, just as I find myself repeatedly removing and reinserting lines when writing a poem."

"Too many poems seemed content to convey an experience followed by a reaction to it without factoring in the reader's presumed indifference to the inner lives of strangers."

"Genuine originality is born and works in private, and art of any kind is solitary, and often lonely, work."

"Do even poets read poetry?"

"It is ironical that, in this bad time, American poetry is of a higher quality than our criticism or teaching of poetry."

"It seems that poetry is more often than not *bad* news that stays news."

"Writing a poem is like traversing an obstacle course or negotiating a maze."

"We poets love to parade as victims; we love the romance of alienation and insult."

"When voices that were based on experience began to rise from the fringes of our society, the new avant-garde, armed with critical theory, began to make 'pre-emptive strikes' at those who saw content as a reflection of their lives and vision."

"The thing that got me was when the critics began to encourage the view of themselves as no longer subject to or dependent on poems but in a higher register of influx than poets or poems."

"The most frequent accusation leveled against contemporary poetry is its difficulty or inaccessibility."

"Poetry was not something my parents found themselves reading for pleasure. It was the enemy."

"The language of the chat rooms is empty."

"To engage with art as the artist has done is to take an active and activist role rather than a passive and consumerist one."

"Art is not a service."

"Poetry mustn't try to compete with the sound bites of politics or the vapidity of popular culture. Rather it should serve as an antidote for them."

"If some new manifestation of a literary dictator would appear on the scene, many of today's poets would be extremely grateful to him or her and would set about breaking the new strictures and decrees as soon and as thoroughly as possible."

"My lifelong romance with literary objects began not with the wish to say some*thing*, but with the hope to say some*how*."

——— *DAVID LEHMAN* ———

"I love the moment of 'not knowing' more than the moment of 'knowing' in a poem."

"Baudelaire, who coined the Tradition of the New, once said that if the greatest of all pleasures is to be surprised, the only other pleasure nearly as great is to *give* surprise."

"I went into poetry for the money."

"We need a kraken to rise up and scare the piss out of us into what's in our hearts and whatever Urge it is that constitutes the Soul."

"Where there are no words, poetry springs into being."

"I think of Robert Duncan's saying, 'I can't remember if I wrote it or if I read it!'"

"There's nothing more American and more hopeful than our poetry."

All of these sentences are, in some sense, valid. Do they, these five hundred and forty words, constitute a coherent statement? Perhaps, if "The Waste Land" is your model—though in that case we would need footnotes, whether capricious like Eliot's or punctilious, a task for another day. I present these quotations rather as one would present aphorisms on the last page of a literary journal—in the hope that they will trigger an association of thoughts that may prove useful, may awaken curiosity, may even stimulate the imagination.

A shibboleth that I set out annually to demolish is the assumption that no one reads a book's introduction, foreword, or preface. Denise Duhamel, a wonderful poet with whom I have collaborated on a variety of projects, has contributed a foreword here that strengthens my belief that it is an underrated form that can beautifully serve the aims of a writer of ingenuity and wit.

A second and more pernicious shibboleth is that poetry is dying or is already ripe for burial. Obituaries for poetry are perishable. So are many poems that will slide into oblivion without needing a push. But the activity of writing them redeems itself even if it is only a gesture toward what we continue to need from literature and the humanities: an experience of mind—mediated by memorable speech—that feeds and sustains the imagination and helps us make sense of our lives.

THE STATE OF THE ART

"like dropping a rose petal down the Grand Canyon and waiting for the echo"

The poet Don Marquis proposed a lovely simile for a perennial problem. "Publishing a volume of verse," he observed, "is like dropping a rose petal down the Grand Canyon and waiting for the echo."

But bringing out a new poetry anthology—with plans to make it an annual event—isn't simply a quixotic gesture or a defiant one. It is also the product of a calculation. Given the popularity of creative writing programs in the United States today, isn't it reasonable to suppose that the potential audience for poetry is much wider than defeatists would think? There are annual anthologies devoted to the short story, and there is one that selects among the year's best essays. Why not do the same with poetry, a genre of literature that continues to flourish despite unfavorable conditions? We might find that many readers are prepared to embrace contemporary poetry—if only a discriminating editor showed them what to look for.

That possibility is one of the reasons behind *The Best American Poetry*. A second is practical. Poetry of high quality is appearing in a dizzying range of publications; not even the most dedicated reader can keep up with it all. An annual anthology seems the obvious solution—so obvious that one wonders why it hasn't been tried before. There is certainly abundance enough to fuel a *Best American Poetry* annual, and make it live up to its name.

The basic idea is simple. Each year a different guest editor—a poet of distinguished stature—will select the poems and write an introduction to the volume. John Ashbery, the guest editor of our initial volume, helped me improvise the way toward a set of structural principles. I wanted to make sure that the guest editor would have maximum flexibility within defined limits. We decided that each year there will be no fewer than fifty poems and no more than seventy-five, that all selections will come from works published in the previous calendar year, and that no individual poet will be represented by more than three poems. Mr. Ashbery, who favors eclecticism and diversity as guiding virtues, chose seventy-five poems by as many different poets. It is entirely possible that next year's guest editor may, for example, settle on sixty poems—three by each of twenty poets.

Because audiences find helpful the incidental remarks that poets make between poems at poetry readings, I thought it might be interesting to try to produce a similar effect in an enlarged section of contributors' notes. Each poet was asked to write, in addition to biographical information, a comment on his or her poem—about its form or its occasion or the method of composition or any other feature worth remarking on. This was strictly optional; poets are entitled to their reticence. But I was pleased that so many took the time and trouble to meet my request. Their comments seemed invariably to enhance the pleasures of their work.

Other "rules" sound like compromises hammered out in congressional subcommittees. There was the question of sources. We elected to concentrate on magazines, big circulation periodicals as well as small press productions. But we stopped short of excluding books by individual poets. It is, after all, impossible to get a true measure of the state of contemporary poetry without appealing to poetry collections as well as to magazines. What about a poem that appeared in a magazine four years ago and was reprinted in a collection last year? To such questions, the anthologist's ever-ready response is: you just play it by ear.

Then there was the question of eligibility. How about foreign poets in residence in the United States or on long-term academic appointments at American universities? Did the "American" in our title have to mean "made in the U.S.A."? We worried about it but in the end decided it was foolish to be strict constructionists, especially in cases where the poet has come to seem a vital presence in a particular American community. Thus readers will note the work of John Ash and Seamus Heaney and Derek Walcott in this anthology. It, like Walt Whitman, is large enough to contradict itself with impunity.

DAVID LEHMAN

As the series editor of *The Best American Poetry*, I have assigned a number of tasks to myself. In addition to maintaining continuity from year to year, enforcing such rules as there are, the series editor is expected to support and assist the guest editor, in part by scanning the world of magazines and making preliminary recommendations. But probably the series editor has no function more important than that of determining who the guest editor will be. I was lucky this year. John Ashbery is, in a phrase he once applied to Elizabeth Bishop, a "poet's poet's poet." It's irresistible to read over his shoulders, to get some sense of his taste and values and predilections. My thanks go to him; to my editor at Scribner's and Collier, John Glusman; and to a true friend of the project, Glen Hartley.

in an unlit alcove where bookstore patrons fear to tread

A little while ago in Ithaca, New York, the university town where I live, two good bookstores decided to merge and relocate. With some fanfare, after inevitable delays, the new store opened. I headed straight for the poetry section. It was impressive: an alcove with tall bookcases on facing walls. There were easily twice as many shelves than at either of the former locations. There was only one problem. Something was wrong with the lighting system, making it difficult to read the titles on the spines of the books.

That seems an apt metaphor for the condition of contemporary poetry. There's plenty of it, and plenty of it is good, but it seems to be located in an unlit alcove where bookstore patrons fear to tread. Everyone who loves poetry must sometimes wonder whether it will languish for lack of a lightbulb. An optimist, of course, would phrase that differently. An optimist would say: Our poets operate in the dark, like surefooted jewel thieves. The wonder is that the incandescence around them is so bright.

The Best American Poetry is a publishing experiment conducted in the spirit of a wager. The experiment is to see whether a single annual volume can accurately reflect the diversity of American poetry—can reflect it with enthusiasm but also with the need to make critical discriminations—and honor excellence regardless of what form it takes, or what idiom it favors, or from which region of the country it comes. The wager is over the question of poetry's audience. Everyone complains that poetry doesn't have one. We bet the opposite—that there are more than enough readers around who would seriously like to know what the poets in America are up to these days.

The rules of this anthology series are few and flexible. Each January a different guest editor, a poet of distinguished stature, makes the selections based on works published in the previous calendar year. No volume in the series will have fewer than fifty poems or more than seventy-five; there is a limit of three poems by an individual poet in any given year; the guest editor is asked to include a poem of his or her own. The series editor is expected to support and assist the guest editor, in part by scanning the world of magazines and making preliminary recommendations. Translations are ineligible, but prose poems are as welcome as playful pantoums, "avant-garde plays," narratives, elegies, exotic formal arrangements, erotic lyrics, musings on taboo subjects, satire, "cinematic" poems, and blank verse—all of which the reader will find in the pages that follow.[1]

Last year *The Best American Poetry* made its debut, with John Ashbery serving as guest editor. The response to that volume has been exhilarating. Appreciative reviewers noted Mr. Ashbery's ecumenical spirit. As he put it in his introduction to the volume, "I like things that seem to me good of their kind, and don't especially care what the kind is." He chose seventy-five poems by as many poets; Donald Hall, guest editor of the 1989 volume, has elected to follow suit and has done so with equal generosity and savvy. Mr. Hall is an indefatigable correspondent, and I know I will miss the frequent exchanges between us as we shipped each other poems, compared judgments, and traded ardors and bêtes noires during the six-month period in which a hill of photocopies evolved inexorably into *The Best American Poetry 1989*. By a happy coincidence, Donald Hall was working on the anthology at the time he published *The One Day*, which won him the National Book Critics Circle Prize for poetry this year—and which may be, as Olympians are taught to say, his "personal best."

Critics periodically take swipes at poetry—not at specific poets or movements but at American poetry itself, as though it were monolithic (when in fact it is diverse) and moribund (when in fact it is vital). "Contemporary poetry in the United States flourishes in a vacuum," writes one such essayist. It is possible to assent to this broad thesis—*flourishes* is the right word—without reaching the dire conclusion that poetry is finished. Consider the number, the

---

1. Variants of this paragraph have appeared in subsequent volumes in the series, with differences in detail, but have been omitted from the book at hand after this instance.

quality, and the range of magazines that publish poetry—not grudgingly, not out of obligation, but with pleasure and conviction. Nearly three dozen are represented in *The Best American Poetry 1989*, ranging from *The New Yorker* to the *Reaper*, from *Boulevard* to *Grand Street*, from flamboyant gadflies like *Exquisite Corpse* to classy campus-based quarterlies like the *Gettysburg Review*, not to mention the quarterly reviews with states in their names, Ohio and Iowa, Michigan and Georgia.

Yet it would be foolish to deny that poetry in America today has its share of problems. One vexing matter is the vacuum of genuine critical response. Many brainy assistant professors and graduate students, from whose ranks critics of poetry used to emerge, prefer the autotelic world of critical theory: criticism without an object outside of itself. I wish we could get these potential readers to see what they're missing. Not all but many critical theorists regard the making of evaluative aesthetic judgments as either irrelevant or downright pernicious. Given this dismal state of academic affairs, poets may have little choice but to act as their own critics, and to try to create the taste by which their works will be enjoyed. The expanded section of contributors' notes in *The Best American Poetry* is a modest step in this direction. The poets were encouraged to comment on their work, and the majority of them did so, helping us see how poems get written.

"Poetry is a pheasant disappearing in the brush," wrote Wallace Stevens. But it is also, he wrote, "a search for the inexplicable," "a renovation of experience," and "a purging of the world's poverty and change and evil and death." Critical neglect cannot defeat the impulse to make something imperishable out of the transitory words of our days.

to inflame passions, disturb the complacent, and arouse the anxiety of despots

*T*he Best American Poetry, now in its third year, has already gone far to debunk some popular misconceptions. Poetry doesn't sell—yet the 1989 volume appeared last fall on a best-seller list compiled from independent bookstores. Poets are supposed to be the only audience poets can count on having—yet *The Best American Poetry* has been thoughtfully and generously reviewed by critics who do not themselves write poetry. The many positive responses to this series have helped to prove a point and to challenge a glib supposition. Poetry in the United States today does have a vital readership; rumors regarding the death of the reader have been greatly exaggerated.

Contemporary American poetry is said to be rife with sectarianism, though this book stands as evidence that the poets of rival sects may consort to their mutual enhancement. *The Best American Poetry* can't negotiate a truce among all the movements and schools and modes of writing poetry—there are simply too many of them, and the competitive impulse is as natural in an artist as in an athlete. But we can try to glean the best work being done today, irrespective of the biases of this man's region and that woman's literary allegiances. We can try to promote a more magnanimous spirit of response to the genuine article, wherever it may be found.

I asked Jorie Graham to serve as this year's guest editor for several reasons

—chief among them my admiration for her work. Though I could not prevail upon her to include a poem of her own in this volume, I was fascinated from start to finish by her profoundly ecumenical taste and could only marvel at her energy. It was clear to both of us that no two readers can realistically expect to keep up with all the poetry that is published in any given year. But we did our best—and the telephone company's records attest to our zeal for the project. Toward the end of the year, not a week went by without three or four long phone conversations during which fresh discoveries were read aloud and notes were compared on a new batch of periodicals. Nearly three dozen magazines are represented in *The Best American Poetry 1990*. We found our poems in *The New Yorker*, *The Atlantic*, and *The New Republic*; in campus quarterlies from Yale and Utah, Virginia and Denver, the University of the South and SMU; in *Antaeus*, *Ploughshares*, and other sturdy mavericks; and in the numerous magazines with the singular names *How(ever)*, *Fine Madness*, *Hanging Loose*, *O.blek*, *Avec*, and *Hambone*.

Jorie Graham is on the permanent faculty of the University of Iowa's Writers' Workshop, the oldest and arguably the most prestigious writing program in the country. To many, Iowa is regarded as the very heartland of creative writing—against which some polemicists have railed. We read about the "workshop" poem, the "perishable" poem that "didn't need to be written," the "safe" exercise in a fashionable idiom. This volume helps demolish that stereotype. Some of the most genuinely innovative poets in *The Best American Poetry 1990* attended creative writing programs at one time or another. At their best, it would seem, such programs offer young writers an extended parenthesis in their lives—a time to *live* poetry, if they wish, before they return to the diaspora of the working world.

In the pages that follow, the reader will encounter a plentiful amount of prose poetry, a pair of eclogues, "an old-fashioned song" and a sequence of "hermetic" ones, elegies, narratives, some fiercely religious lyrics, and several works that elevate punctuation marks to agents of poetic invention. The range of subject matter is broad, extending from Klaus Barbie to the Barbie doll; a meditation on Orpheus may segue into a telephone dialogue between a mother and son, to be followed in turn by the verbal encounter of "aurora Borealis and the Body Louse." The variety of styles on display in this book is striking—and should combat the negative press that experimentalism too often receives. A number of the poems opt for unusual, seemingly improvised formal arrangements. Far from gratuitous, this emphasis on play seems bound up with a restless investigative spirit, and it helps give the poems their surface dazzle—they're fresh as paint.

——— *DAVID LEHMAN* ———

Our seventy-five contributors range from a college freshman to the current poet laureate of the United States. As in the previous volumes in the series, all were asked to comment on their poems, and many agreed to do so. The expansive section of contributors' notes in *The Best American Poetry* is intended not only to inform but to aid in fostering a direct relation between the reader and the voices behind the voices of the poems.

As this year's anthology headed into production, I wrote a poem to celebrate the completion of the book. The idea was to incorporate as many of the poets' names as possible, either directly or through homophones, echoes, and bilingual puns:

OUR REVELS

Walking along the strand, hand in hand,
We saw a cabin with the sign Lux et Veritas
Over the portal. The bearded man inside
Was eating graham crackers and reading Howards End.
A woman in Victorian garb bearing a dish of plums
Appeared out of nowhere. A bell tolled, sounding
Like the opening measures of Wagner's Flying Dutchman.

Down the hall (for the cabin was larger than it looked)
Children were speaking German. They exchanged little myths,
Wandering birds, magic mountains, and morning stars,
While the berry king, looking for an ash tray,
Announced that our revels were still in progress.
Then he quoted the divine opening of St. John's Gospel.
Love was the lever that lifted us above the amen corner.

We felt rich. And when we looked out the window,
We saw the spires of a medieval university
And Sherlock Holmes shadowing Professor Moriarty
Across a misty meadow. One hill, one man;
One gardener, one strip of galvanized steel;
One loaded shotgun, one moss-gathering stone;
A mill, a mule, a pin, a palm, a wading bather, a music stand.

And how would we know what to write
When we returned to our warren of offices

And gave up trying to keep up with the Joneses
And their kin, melting with ruth as we carved their names
On Birnam Wood, on the outskirts of the estate?
Dubious but determined, we gave up there for here:
Merrily, merrily, we welcomed in the year.

Walt Whitman is the bewhiskered gent, and Emily Dickinson the bearer of ripe fruit, in the poem's first stanza. They are invoked as the tutelary figures of American poetry.

In the course of 1989, the Berlin Wall came down, and the leaders of the United States and the Soviet Union declared the Cold War over. Americans were exhilarated by the speed of political change in the nations of Eastern Europe. Few things can be as heartening as the spectacle of a totalitarian state yielding, however grudgingly, some of its power to a popular democratic movement. In Czechoslovakia a poet and playwright, Václav Havel, became a national hero for his part in the Civic Forum mass movement. Early in the year he spent four months in jail; by year's end he was the president of a nation suddenly liberated from its forty-one-year-old Communist regime. But 1989 was also a year in which a head of state called for the assassination of a prominent novelist; and for writers and publishers closer to home, it seemed a year of threats, overt or camouflaged, to their freedom of expression. A tyrannical edict, proposed though happily not executed, concentrates the mind wonderfully—it makes us realize how fragile a thing is a writer's liberty. How good it is to celebrate the freedom of the word, knowing that art still has the ability to inflame passions, disturb the complacent, and arouse the anxiety of despots.

a poem entitled "Cigarettes"
by a poet named Ash

Conventional wisdom has it that most of the poetry written in an era is fated to be minor. In the cosmic view of things, this proposition seems self-evident. Judged by the standards of Shakespeare and Milton, how many contemporaries will strike future generations as major? Critics, whose job it is to make discriminations, are not the only ones who put poets in their place. The poets themselves do it unconsciously. It may help motivate us—some of us anyway—to adopt Hemingway's metaphor and imagine that we are getting into the ring with Rilke when we write our next poem. Reading, however, as lovers of poetry rather than as pugnacious aspirants to personal greatness, we are bound to be less severe in our judgment, more generous with our hearts. Reading for the pure pleasure of it, we find abundance.

Tracking the poetry published in the United States in any one year is an instructive experience. The first time you do it, you might begin with a cool skepticism. You can't imagine coming across seventy-five poems worthy of acclaim. What you realize soon enough is that it's a difficult task just to keep up with what's out there—there is so much of it, and so much of it is good. One constant in this anthology series is that each of the four guest editors to date has admired more works than could be included in even a capacious volume. The hardest part in the making of this book occurs in those late December days when five or ten or fifteen poems must finally be dropped from an ever-burgeoning manuscript. For the editors, the thrill of discovery may be the most pleasurable part of the enterprise. Thirty-six of the poets represented in *The Best American Poetry 1991* have appeared in none of the three previous volumes, eclectic though these were. A mere handful of names have turned up four years running.

The reader of these pages will find sonnets and songs, elegies, verse essays, dramatic monologues, narratives. The subjects range from nature (woods and gardens, flowers and leaves) to second nature (myths, dreams, memories). The settings include a hospital ward, a beauty parlor, a playground, a lunch counter, the Metropolitan Opera, a country fair. Seemingly by accident some titles appear to pair off. A number of poems treat sexual themes with sensitivity and candor; two are entitled "Desire." Two poems that have "evidence" in their titles are narratives of an investigative character. Of the two sets of haiku, one is oriented in the traditional direction while the other features pop icons from the Hollywood Hills. We have an acrostic, a cento, a villanelle, a self-described "entertainment," and an ad hoc form whose only rule is that each line must consist of five words. We also have a poem entitled "Cigarettes" by a poet named Ash.

Mark Strand, my choice to edit this year's anthology, is an experienced anthologist who put together an influential selection of *Contemporary American Poets* two decades ago. *The Best American Poetry* is designed to reflect the taste and values of the guest editor, and it is a pleasure to work with someone as definite in his judgments as is Mr. Strand. Moreover, he is highly respected by poets who transcend the usual sectarian boundaries, and he happens to be writing the finest poetry of his life. In 1990 he published *The Continuous Life*, a brilliant book. He was also appointed the nation's poet laureate, proving that not every government decision affecting the arts is wrong.

Mr. Strand and I decided to enforce very strictly the rule limiting eligibility to poems that appeared in magazines in the year 1990. This seems a good place to salute those magazines—and the editors who are the unsung heroes and heroines of American letters. With sadness I note the passing of the *Yale Review* and with gladness the rumor that the administration of that university has reconsidered its decision to jettison the venerable journal, an exemplary model of a literary quarterly.

Another campus-based periodical, *Mississippi Review*, wrote to a number of poets recently asking us to comment on the allegation that contemporary poetry lacks "vision." It occurred to me that there may be some unwritten rule of lit-crit discourse that presumes an invisible but highly questionable link between the pulse of poetry on the one side and the agents of presidential power on the other. Seven or eight years ago, when the New Formalism was new, I remember seeing it smeared as "Reaganetics." Now, evidently, all of contemporary poetry has been accused of being Bush League—victim of that "vision thing." On the face of it, the knock is absurd. Read the poems in this book in good faith and then tell me that our poets lack a power of vision commensurate with their mastery of invention and craft.

But discussion of the "vision thing" may produce some good if it causes us to take stock of our first premises and reexamine our practice in the light of our principles. W. H. Auden remarked that a young poet who liked tinkering with words had a better chance of getting somewhere than a young poet who wrote because he or she had something to say. I think that's true. But something further needs to be said. If verse without some kind of formal restraint is like playing tennis without a net, poetry that is short on statement conjures up an image out of the movie *Blow-Up*: tennis without the ball. The work on display in *The Best American Poetry 1991* demonstrates that an athletic metaphor is often very much to the point. These are poems of dexterity, speed, and power; of lyric grace under imaginative pressure.

The question of poetry and its audience

I remember when the Carter administration invited several hundred poets to the White House for a celebration of American poetry. There was a reception, handshakes with the president, the pop of flashbulbs. Concurrent poetry readings in various White House rooms capped off the festivities. In each room a few poets had been asked to read. The rest of the poets, the ones who hadn't been asked to read, could attend the reading of their choice. A year later, Jimmy Carter lost the presidency.

I used to think that this incident was a parable for poetry in our time. It seemed to make the point that poets were the only real audience poetry had and that they were implicitly in different camps, having to contend with one another for what little audience there was. I no longer feel so defeatist about poetry's prospects. I believe that American poetry has a true readership beyond its own practitioners and that furthermore it would be impertinent to behave as though this readership were necessarily restricted to an academic ghetto. This is not to deny the existence of a problem but to suggest that perhaps the problem has been ill defined. It is not that American poetry lacks distinction or variety or potential readers; it is that the task of reaching this readership requires a plan as imaginative in its way as the verse on the pages of the books that publishers continue to publish, with reluctance in some cases and with something like ardor in others.

The question of poetry and its audience—with the implicit nagging undertone that maybe poetry doesn't have readers because it doesn't deserve them—has certainly become a hot item in the popular press. Every couple of years an article in a national magazine arouses a good deal of comment by alleging that poetry is dead or by countering this claim with a list of helpful suggestions for improving poetry's public image. In May 1991 Dana Gioia asked readers of the *Atlantic Monthly*, "Can Poetry Matter?" (Gioia recommended that poets recite other poets' works at public readings.) Joseph Brodsky, the nation's new poet laureate, fired off "An Immodest Proposal" in *The New Republic* on Veteran's Day. (Brodsky proposed that an anthology of American poetry be found beside the Bible and the telephone directory in every hotel room across the land.) At Columbia University, three eminent critics pondered "An Audience for Poetry?" with its pointed question mark, while a panel of five poets convened at Adelphi University to discuss "Is Poetry a Dying Art?" On the latter occasion, the moderator ruefully recalled that his title echoed that of Edmund Wilson's famous essay "Is Verse a Dying Technique?" Wilson published his piece in 1928. Many noble technicians of verse have written since then, and many more will survive the articles and symposia of today, which may even have a salutary effect if they remind people that poetry is, for some of us, a burning issue. Still, all this talk does lead one to wonder whether Oscar Wilde was wrong to suppose that it is easier to do a thing than to talk about it.

It has been a pleasure working with Charles Simic on *The Best American Poetry 1992*. A marvelous poet writing at the height of his powers, Mr. Simic is also an accomplished essayist, and at the time he and I were collaborating on this project he was working on a monograph about Joseph Cornell—a telling choice, for a Simic poem and a Cornell box illustrate similar principles of juxtaposition and surprise. Both are hospitable to all manner of object and event, and the same may be said about the makeup of this anthology. *The Best American Poetry 1992* includes a "Midwestern Villanelle" and a "Saga" built on sonnet variations, a poem for the New Year and another for All Hallows' Eve, a poem about the jazz trumpeter and singer Chet Baker and one about the fate of eyeglasses in Auschwitz. There is a prose poem by the author of the nation's number-one nonfiction best seller and a meditation on the color green by a nineteen-year-old writer living in Vancouver. More than half of the poets in *The Best American Poetry 1992* have not previously appeared in the series. Over three dozen magazines are represented (and numerous others were consulted). Seven titles came from *The New Yorker*, topping the list, and it was a banner year also for the *Paris Review* and *Ploughshares* (six titles each) and for those stalwart campus quarterlies the *Iowa Review* (five) and the *Michigan Quarterly Review* and *Field* (four each). The settings range from a women's jail in Rome to the back rooms of a fast-food joint in downtown Milwaukee. And then there are the poems that unabashedly declare their subjects in their titles, such as "Nostalgia" and "Sex," which seem to be our idiomatic equivalents for what T. S. Eliot called "memory and desire."

No critic will ever have the effect on our poets that certain of their grade school teachers had—the ones often credited by the poets themselves for their lifelong devotion to the art. But criticism done right, not vindictively or meanly but with generosity and amplitude, with a respect for the reader's intelligence and the writer's intentions, can help teach us *how* as well as *what* to read, by example rather than by precept. There is no substitute for the sort of poetry criticism that we have so little of at the present time. The contributors' notes in this book—many of which include the poet's comments on his or her poem—are meant not in place of interpretive criticism but as a way of assisting such an effort, and as a bonus for the reader.

From the start, the editors and publishers of *The Best American Poetry* have gone on the assumption that readers equal to the best poetry of the day do exist and will stand up and be counted. It pleases me to report that this seemingly quixotic article of faith has turned out to be a simple statement of fact.

the gust of fresh air that turned
into the blizzard of '93

E ven an optimist on the subject of American poetry has days when he
wonders whether it's a losing cause—which for a romantic may be the
noblest cause worth fighting for. There are also days when, in the words
of Frank O'Hara, "I am ashamed of my century / for being so entertaining /
but I have to smile." One Wednesday last May, Esther B. Fein of the *New York
Times* reported in her "Book Notes" column that John Ashbery had won the
1992 Ruth Lilly Poetry Prize from *Poetry* magazine. On the same day, in the
same column, Fein passed along the news that Barbara Taylor Bradford, a
best-selling author of blockbuster fiction, had defected from Random House
to HarperCollins, a switch that—one wag later exclaimed—"simultaneously
raises the literary stature of both publishers." The thing that caught my eye
in this juxtaposition of publishing items was that Ashbery's prize included a
purse of $25,000, making it "one of the largest poetry awards in the United
States," while in spectacular contrast Bradford's new contract with Harper-
Collins guaranteed her more than $20 million for her next three poshlust pot-
boilers. It was, in this context, refreshing to hear what Ashbery told the *Times*
reporter when she called him for a quote. "Not that many people in this country
like poetry," he said matter-of-factly, "and in fact, many people hate it."

There is no need to deny the simple truth of this observation even when affirming that, all in all, the climate for poetry in 1992 was more lovely and more temperate than the fickle weather of Florida in August. There was even the occasional exception to the rule that poetry and big bucks are mutually exclusive. The Nobel Prize in literature—worth more than a million dollars—went to a Caribbean poet, who divides his time between Boston and Trinidad. The announcement of Derek Walcott's good fortune, timed perfectly to coincide with the quincentennial of Columbus's expedition, raised to three the number of Nobel laureates who are primarily poets, were born elsewhere, live in the United States at least part of the time, and are published by Farrar, Straus and Giroux. More anomalous was the announcement, a few weeks before the Nobel news, that the same publisher had just sold the film rights to Elizabeth Bishop's "The Man-Moth." It's hard to predict what Columbia Pictures will do with its new property, since this terrific poem—which is based on a newspaper misprint—has no plot. Evidently, that is something the studio can provide. The producer and screenwriter are excited about the poem's atmosphere, which seems to them suggestive of "expressionist cinema." If the film is made, Bishop's forty-eight line poem could fetch as much as $75,000, or $1,562.50 per line.

Like cigarettes in fashion ads, poems are turning up in places where we stopped expecting to find them. At funkier-than-thou bars and cafés in cities from Boston to Los Angeles, teams of scruffy versifiers are slugging it out in mock competitions known as poetry "slams." The poems aren't so much read as performed, like acts in a variety show, and the poet may be a bad-boy rapper, or a bad-girl tap dancer, or an unkempt bard with a goatee and a black turtleneck sweater playing the bass and howling. Are the beats back? No, the "wannabeats" have arrived. It is easy to mock the literary efforts on display, or to rue the transformation of the art into a species of nightclub infotainment suitable for MTV. But the whole "downtown" poetry phenomenon has felt a little like the gust of fresh air that turned into the blizzard of '93: a lot of noise, a lot of excitement, a lot of hype, and some rattling of the windows in stuffy rooms where another high-minded symposium on the future of poetry had been threatening to kill Pegasus and then beat the winged horse all over again.

Most of the good news concerning the publication of poetry has a modest pecuniary dimension. Given the economic conditions governing the book business during an extended recession, the wonder is not that some trade houses have abandoned poetry—which is the lamentable case—but that others have resolutely stayed with it and done reasonably well by it. But, then, the bottom line in this case is not financial at all. It is rather akin to the surprising last line in a sonnet of reversed expectations. It is the very plausible possibility that

American poetry is, and should be, the envy of the English-speaking world—a statement made not with nationalistic fervor but with the pleasure and excitement that accompany creative ferment.

It may never be fashionable to admit this, but American poetry is not only in a state of high vitality but also is reaching a wider public audience than pessimists ever thought possible. Ours may be a small audience by the standards of Barbara Taylor Bradford, a tiny audience by the standards of *Batman Returns* (which is, I think, what Hollywood means by "expressionist cinema"). But the audience for poetry is knowledgeable and discriminating, avid to the point of love and dedication. It is also underrated in size. It is certainly an audience big enough to sustain the annual *Best American Poetry* anthology series, which is now six editions strong. Poetry, to paraphrase W. H. Auden, not only survives; it thrives in the valley of its saying.

The Best American Poetry is meant to be, in several senses, a state-of-the-art anthology. The selections are made each year by a different guest editor— in each case, a distinguished American poet—who reads many hundreds of poems culled from dozens of periodicals. John Ashbery, the guest editor of the inaugural volume, has been succeeded by Donald Hall, Jorie Graham, Mark Strand, Charles Simic, and this year, Louise Glück. Since she burst onto the scene with her first book *Firstborn* in 1968, when she was twenty-five years old, Ms. Glück has garnered accolades from the critics and honors and prizes from the institutions that award them. Her work holds a particular interest for other poets and for students of poetry. The poems in her last two books, *Ararat* and *The Wild Iris*, are dissimilar in style, subject matter, and focus. What they have in common is their urgency, their intensity, and the genuineness of their inspiration, which may be a hard quality to define but is an easy one to discern in poems that have a real authority.

The guest editors in this series have, without exception, been loyal to their lights and steadfast in their standards while ranging far afield in surveying the poetry of our time. People are curious about how the process works. It varies from year to year, but as a partner in the deliberations, I can attest that for the editors it is an awesome task to try to keep up with all the poetry out there— and it is always an educational experience. Both the guest editor and I find that we are constantly reading, and rereading, for the anthology. (Except for translations, all poems appearing in magazines in the year under survey are eligible.) Periodically, and with greater urgency as the year goes by, we compare notes, discoveries, enthusiasms, opinions. With some of the editors, the brunt of this work was done by phone; the letter was the medium of choice for Louise Glück, as it was for Donald Hall. Ms. Glück applied herself with vigor to the task of reading and evaluating poems. As the year began she could be heard clamoring for literary magazines "like a person in a restaurant banging the table for service." Devour them she did. Nearly four dozen magazines are represented in *The Best American Poetry 1993,* far more than in any previous year.

Putting the anthology together is a huge undertaking. The guest editor makes her final selections on New Year's Eve, revising the "yes list" (as we called it) for the last time that day. Now that the nucleus of the book is in place, we can go on to prepare the book's "back matter." Each of the seventy-five poets has to be located, then asked (in some cases, cajoled) to supply biographical information and to comment on the chosen poem. Permissions have to be obtained. The editor's introduction and the series editor's foreword have to be written. The manuscript must be copyedited, the galleys proofread with care. The cover art for the book must be chosen. And all this must be done in a great hurry, since our target date for finished books is Labor Day. It is a backbreaking production schedule, and this seems an opportune moment to thank the unheralded people—at the Macmillan Publishing Company and outside it—who collaborate on the project annually, making sure that no deadline is missed.

The Best American Poetry has a primary purpose, announced in its title—to honor poems of immediate interest and enduring value—but also several subsidiary purposes, such as the desire to feed the interest that readers of poetry are bound to have in the taste and judgment of our leading poets. It is true, as several persons have said, that the title of this book makes an aggressive claim. That is one reason why I like it. I like the idea of risking an unequivocal opinion. (As former president Jimmy Carter—who published three of his poems last year in *New Letters*—put it: Why not the best?) Working on the book generates an almost palpable sense of excitement as each year's guest editor begins with a certain healthy skepticism—are there really as many as seventy-five poems out there worthy of inclusion?—and concludes the task complaining that seventy-five is too low a limit. Though the hours are long and the labor sometimes wearying, there is a special pleasure in challenging a shibboleth, and it continues to be fun praying that poets of various camps, schools, movements, and regions can consort to their mutual advantage, to the reader's edification, to the editors' delight, and to everyone's profit. Long may it be so.

—— 1994 ——

It's safe to say that the inaugural was the best-attended poetry reading of the decade

One of the few persons associated with the Clinton administration whose stock has never stopped rising is the poet Maya Angelou, who presented her inaugural ode with all the splendor of ceremony on January 20, 1993. Not everyone thought "On the Pulse of Morning" was a wonderful poem, but it was good theater and shrewd politics. Ms. Angelou rhymed *Sioux* and *Jew*, *Greek* and *Sheik*, sweetly opposed war and "cynicism," and ended wishing everyone "good morning." People were deeply moved by her performance. The novelist Louise Erdrich enthusiastically declared she "felt that this woman could have read the side of a cereal box," which was meant to be a compliment though it sort of backfires when you realize that it compares the inaugural ode to the side of a cereal box. Erdrich's point, however, was that Angelou's presence was "powerful and momentous." And so it was for most of the thousands in attendance and the millions watching on TV. It's safe to say that the inaugural was the best-attended poetry reading of the decade. The boost to Ms. Angelou's market value was immediate. *Wouldn't Take Nothing for My Journey Now*, her latest book of essays, quickly made it onto the best-seller list. Half the colleges in the country would give almost anything to have her grace their commencement exercises. The poet has become a symbol of unity in multicultural diversity, and a national role model for young African American women.

In the road movie *Poetic Justice*, released in the summer of 1993, Janet Jackson gets to write, and recite, the poems of Maya Angelou—which I cite as evidence not only of Ms. Angelou's personal ascendancy but also of the current unanticipated prestige that surrounds poetry generically in the culture at large. Verse has suddenly become ubiquitous. There are poems on placards for straphangers to ponder in New York City's buses and subway trains: I've spotted works by Charles Reznikoff, Gwendolyn Brooks, Robert Frost, and William Carlos Williams. Out West, cowboy poetry festivals, like the one held annually in Elko, Nevada, proclaim that a major revival of cowboy verse is in progress. In Beverly Hills the actor Mickey Rourke recently cleared sixteen thousand dollars on the sale of eight framed, poster-size poems he had written. For example: "I Should Have Been Born / A Statue of Stone, / I'd Have No Pain / No Place to Call Home." In Florida, poetry enabled a skillful defense attorney named Roy Black to get his client, a Miami cop, acquitted in a widely publicized murder trial concluding on Memorial Day weekend. Mr. Black moved the jury—and caused his client to weep—when he declaimed a poem, which he characterized as an anonymous policeman's soliloquy, most of which he lifted from chapter sixty-two of *Blue Truth*, a detective novel by a maverick ex-cop from Fort Lauderdale named Cherokee Paul McDonald. A paragraph: "When you were violated, I was violated. When you were dying on the hard pavement, I knelt over you to keep the sun from your eyes. I wore your powerful tin badge on my chest, and it gave me reason. I took out my sword and hurled myself against those who had hurt you."

When Elizabeth Holtzman, the former comptroller of the city of New York, faced defeat in the Democratic senatorial primary, she gamely tried to rally her supporters by quoting this grotesque image from a Marge Piercy poem: "A strong woman is a woman who is straining. / A strong woman is a woman standing / On tiptoe and lifting a barbell / While trying to sing Boris Godunov." (No wonder she lost.) The *New York Times* put it on the front page. Not to be outdone, the *New York Post* treated its readers to a tabloid seminar on geek verse: a two-page spread on the terrible teenage poems written by Joel Rifkin, the accused slayer of seventeen prostitutes.

About all this we are entitled to feel at least a little ambivalent. There is the question of quality. People who love poetry, this poorly paid nonprofession, love it so much they hate to see it adulterated, and surely much of the poetry in the news in 1993 was adulterated verse, trite, forgettable, bogus. The Gap commercial with Max Blagg's elegy for his blue jeans, the unkempt bards of downtown bars who became the overnight darlings of the media, the poems of MTV—these may all be events in the history of publicity, rather than that of poetry.

Even so, such developments may have a heartening effect on those of us who never doubted that American poetry is healthier and more vital, fresher and more various than it is alleged to be. It is good to have that feeling confirmed in the wider populace. But if the world of poetry is spacious enough to accommodate the spurious as well as the genuine article, and if it is only to be expected that exuberance and delight are dealt out in ampler portions than is lasting talent, the need to make critical discriminations has never been greater. And in the absence of reliable, disinterested, intellectually strenuous criticism of poetry, much of this function must be performed by anthologies.

That is one rationale for *The Best American Poetry,* now seven editions strong. Each volume is implicitly an act of criticism as well as of celebration. The anthology is frankly elitist in that we hope to honor the poems of our moment that are worthiest of attention and acclaim. At the same time there is a decidedly populist cast to our enterprise since we who collaborate on it try to make the book as inclusive as possible. It is important to keep the claims of elitism and those of populism in some sort of balance. Poetry was never meant to be the handmaiden of politics or to have its values dictated by politicians. Harm can come from well-meaning efforts to turn poetry into an instrument for social change. But we should also bear in mind Walt Whitman's declaration that "the United States is the greatest poem."

A. R. ("Archie") Ammons, who made the selections for *The Best American Poetry 1994,* is one of America's best-loved poets. He has always been a maverick, and his long poems *Tape for the Turn of the Year* in the 1960s, *Sphere* and *The Snow Poems* in the 1970s, and *Garbage,* which was published in 1993, are extraordinary for their ambition, sweep, and inclusiveness. They are highly innovative without making a fetish of innovation as a value. And they are accompanied by a large body of shorter poems notable for their lyric intensity. For his works, Mr. Ammons has won a whole shelf of poetry prizes, fellowships, and awards. Archie and I are longtime neighbors in Ithaca, New York, and we talk about poetry regularly and often, so the work on this anthology was as if continuous with a conversation that began many years ago. Readers will discover in *The Best American Poetry 1994* a wealth of long poems, including a controversial verse play. There is a sestina, a phantom elegy, a sequence of "cinematic" prose poems and one of "unholy" sonnets. The remarkable frankness with which American poets, both male and female, write about sex and romance is reflected here. Other subjects that provoke our poets include baseball, death, science, nature, alcoholism, AIDS, childbirth, snow, the human anatomy, Greek mythology, Leni Riefenstahl, and John Cage. A year ago *Harper's* put *The Best American Poetry* on its Index, revealing that "the number of poems that rhyme" in the 1993 edition was "one." I trust this rhymewatch will be a regular feature in the magazine.

For me, an attraction of the series is the sense that we are making a record of the taste of our leading poets. And there is a second critical function that the anthology performs, since each of the seventy-five poets represented in the book is encouraged to write a comment on the chosen poem. (Some decline —three poets represented in the 1993 edition of *The Best American Poetry* even used their space to denounce the idea—but most are happy to oblige.) Readers seem to like this feature a good deal, as do students in writing workshops; the disclosures tend to be less academic, and are almost always more revealing, than the stuff you get in the quarterlies. The prose of articulate poets is a delight.

But in the end there is no substitute for real honest-to-goodness criticism— criticism without fear or favor—preferably written by people who are not themselves poets. It is highly possible that the perennial crisis in poetry is really a crisis in the criticism of poetry. The poems in America are as various and as fresh and as new as they ever were in the land of dreams. It is indeed likely that someday someone will look back on our much maligned era and pronounce it a golden age for American poetry. People will say: Ashbery was in his prime, and Ammons, and Merrill, and Merwin, and Strand, and Glück, and Rich, and Wilbur, and . . . a dozen other names. It is a pity that the professors responsible for responding to the poems have largely abandoned the field, preferring the ethereal realms of literary theory: deconstruction in the 1980s, the New Historicism now. But perhaps the English department is the wrong place to look for the sort of vigorous, generous, spirited criticism that a healthy art form needs. It could be that a better hope lies with independent scholars, scholars without an academic affiliation: a noble category that has emerged in the last decade. And perhaps we should be expecting more from high school teachers, that vast underrated army, who have traditionally inspired young people with the lifelong love of poetry.

Given the natural enmity that is supposed to govern relations between the poet as a type and the critic as a type, it is awkward for me as a poet to stand up and say, "We need better critics"—it's a bit like an old-line liberal standing up and saying, "We need better conservatives." But the facts point to this conclusion. Until and unless there are critics to help educate the taste of our readership, separating the good from the bad, and propounding the principles of aesthetic judgment, we will run the risk of expanding that readership at the expense of the art itself. In the meantime we may take solace in the way the art has been flourishing, against the odds, and in defiance of the gloom-sayers. We may rejoice in the abundances of our common poetic heritage and try to add our own indelible contributions.

At least somebody played ball in 1994

A recent survey of Americans indicates that many are suspicious of art. "I'm glad it exists," one woman said. "But I don't necessarily like it in my house." That may sum up a current attitude toward painting. With poetry, however, it's a different story—the opposite story. Everyone seems to be writing the stuff or talking about poetry's resurgence. The very word *poet* remains an honorific, if only when applied to singers and politicians. New York governor Mario Cuomo, on the eve of electoral defeat, struck *Newsweek*'s Joe Klein as "A Public Poet in Autumn." The same magazine's headline writers hailed Bruce Springsteen and Merle Haggard as "Two Poets of the Common Man." And when Kurt Cobain of the rock group Nirvana blew his brains out, the *New York Times* put the news on the front page, declaring the passing of the "Hesitant Poet of 'Grunge Rock.'" Journalism's herd of independent minds immediately picked up the poetic spin, and the newsweeklies chimed in with obits of "The Poet of Alienation."

All through 1994 the evidence continued to mount. Either there really is a big new boom in poetry, or there has been one all along and the media have just caught on. Daily newspapers and Sunday supplements tirelessly recycle their obligatory features on the proliferation of poetry readings across America. The spoken word is in the spotlight at dank cellar bars, reminding the reporter on the beat of late-1950s visions of ecstatic transcendence, incense, bongo drums, and the meaning of life.

Allen Ginsberg in particular has quickened the ardor of the fourth estate. You can tell that the khaki-clad author of *Howl*—and of the new book *Cosmopolitan Greetings*—is back in the press's good graces by the sudden fixation on his finances. One week last September, *New York* magazine reported that Ginsberg's teaching salary at Brooklyn College is just shy of six figures, and the next week the *Times* disclosed that the poet had sold his papers to Stanford University for a million dollars. Whether the conjunction of Allen Ginsberg and Mammon proves that the fates are ironists, or that capitalism and the counterculture always could coexist, or that being an English major needn't be the career disaster feared by a college student's anxious parents, who can say? Not Allen, who is cheerfully up to his old tricks: he chanted a protest poem entitled "Hum Bom" from the pitcher's mound in Candlestick Park in June. At least somebody played ball in 1994.

The success of *Dead Poets Society* a few years ago confounded Hollywood insiders, who felt that the movie's title consisted of the three least attractive words in the language. In Hollywood, one successful picture kicks off a trend, and in 1994, Dorothy Parker's poems punctuated *Mrs. Parker and the Vicious Circle*. In *Four Weddings and a Funeral*, a poem by W. H. Auden is recited at the most dour of the eponymous events, and it so moved audiences that Random House published a slender paperback with "Funeral Blues" plus nine other Auden poems in a hot-selling edition of forty thousand copies. At Jackie Kennedy's funeral, Maurice Tempelsman, her longtime companion, read C. P. Cavafy's poem "Ithaka," a wonderful choice; Cavafy's American readership tripled overnight. On Halloween, fifteen thousand copies of a book containing "The Raven" were distributed free at public libraries. They made an event of it in Austin, Texas, where someone from the coroner's office and someone from the department of taxation gave a "death-and-taxes" reading of Poe's haunting poem. "Fun," a poem by Vermont poet Wyn Cooper, became the nation's number one rock hit, "All I Wanna Do," by Sheryl Crow, which reached the double platinum mark in sales. (When the song won the 1995 Grammy Award for Record of the Year, Crow said backstage that she had written "five different sets of lyrics for that song, and all of them sucked," before Cooper's poem saved the day.) Meanwhile, *Cats* continues on Broadway, which means that T. S. Eliot's volume of feline light verse has made more money for the Eliot estate than the rest of his writings combined.

Some would argue that all this activity obscures the point, which is that poetry is at a serious disadvantage in the culture of celebrity. The idea of lasting fame, as Milton wrote about it in "Lycidas," is as fundamental to poetry as it is anomalous in the era of the abbreviated attention span. "Fame is the spur that the clear spirit doth raise / (That last infirmity of noble mind) / To scorn delights, and live laborious days," Milton wrote. The desire for fame has always motivated poets. But the fame that Milton had in mind is not the fabrication of "broad rumour," the product of buzz and hype. It is the serene judgment of immortality:

> Fame is no plant that grows on mortal soil,
> Not in the glistering foil
> Set off to the world, nor in broad rumour lies,
> But lives and spreads aloft by those pure eyes,
> And perfect witness of all-judging Jove;
> As he pronounces lastly on each deed,
> Of so much fame in heaven expect thy meed.

Fame thus nobly conceived remains the poet's spur. But fame conceived as fifteen minutes of media attention, in which intense exposure is followed by erasure, is hospitable not to poetry but to an image or representation of it, a simulacrum.

The reading public doesn't always recognize the real thing. "We complain that it doesn't sound like the way we talk," the columnist Anna Quindlen observed, "but if it sounds like the way we talk, we complain that it doesn't rhyme." When Yusef Komunyakaa's *Neon Vernacular* won the 1994 Pulitzer Prize, Quindlen noted that the book's first printing amounted to 2,500 copies, "which is fairly large for poetry but a joke to the folks who stock those racks at the airport." It is a truism that the only time a poem can reach America's huge moviegoing audience is when it is read aloud in a movie. But this scarcely means that poetry lacks a sizable constituency of its own. It means rather that poetry stands in the same relation to literary culture that jazz and classical music stand in relation to the culture of noise. The audience is there in significant numbers, and you will not overlook it unless your frame of reference is the national TV audience for a celebrity murder trial.

The Best American Poetry depends on the vitality of the art on the one hand, and on the attentions of a receptive readership on the other. We are lucky to have both. We are lucky also to have Richard Howard as the year's guest editor. *Like Most Revelations* (1994), Mr. Howard's latest collection of poems, was short-listed for the National Book Award; he won the 1970 Pulitzer Prize in poetry and the 1983 American Book Award in translation for his complete version of Baudelaire's *Les Fleurs du mal*. Not only is he a translator of renown but also an important teacher and literary editor, who has a great history of discovering and nurturing poets and publishing them in one or another of the fine magazines he has served as poetry editor. (The list includes *New American Review*, *Shenandoah*, *The New Republic*, the *Paris Review*, and *Western Humanities Review*; he remains poetry editor of the last two named.) Editing *The Best American Poetry 1995* seemed like a natural extension of his customary exertions.

It is characteristic of Richard that early on he laid down several laws governing this year's book. No poet would be eligible who had served as a guest editor in this series. Moreover, no poet would be eligible who had appeared in three or more previous volumes. At a stroke these edicts eliminated the work of Ammons, Ashbery, Bradley, Clampitt, Creeley, Fulton, Glück, Graham, Hall, Hass, Hollander, Howard, Koch, Levine, Merrill, Merwin, Mitchell, Moss, Pinsky, Rich, Simic, St. John, Strand, Tate, and Wilbur, among others—a formidable list. But that was the point. The limitation would mean that for this particular year the aim would be, in Mr. Howard's words, "not an anthology of confirmation but an anthology of surprise, even astonishment."

The accent is on discovery. We have come up with many new poets; forty-nine have never previously appeared in *The Best American Poetry*. It says something about the depth of American poetry that such notables as Margaret Atwood, Irving Feldman, Allen Ginsberg, Heather McHugh, Grace Schulman, and David Wagoner appear this year for the first time. Poems were chosen from fifty magazines, more than ever before. The proportion of poems from little magazines (as opposed to wide-circulation periodicals such as *The New Yorker* and *The Atlantic*) went way up. There were more poems in verse forms, intricate or homemade: the book contains two villanelles, two sestinas, three sonnet chains, and a poem in the shape of history's widening gyre. Some of the poems exemplify the idea that poets keep the conscience of society. There are poems here about Bosnia, urban violence, political injustice, French collaborationism, and gays in the military. Other poems treat the hardboiled romance of film noir, the landscape of New Mexico or that of a scruffy suburban hill, fairy tales and Zen Buddhist koans, Frank O'Hara and Miles Davis, Tarzan and *Citizen Kane*, but also language and its properties, birth, childhood, brotherhood, masturbation, sex, friendship, marriage, children, childlessness, and death.

Last winter the poet who goes by the name of Sparrow went with some downtown friends to the offices of *The New Yorker*, where they staged a sit-in to protest the poetry published in that magazine. "Personally, I think our poets are just as bad as their poets, but at least we have a sense of humor," said

Sparrow. "We demand to get published in *The New Yorker*—because we're just as bad as they are." Knowing there are places where the word *bad* means its opposite, I want to assure Sparrow that our doors are open and that the best bad poems of the year stand a fighting chance of getting in. To honor "the best" in any field is perhaps a daring thing to do at a time when many cultural institutions are full of doubt and self-doubt. But it is a dare one may confidently take up. Modern American poetry is a cultural glory on the level of jazz and abstract expressionism. It is constantly renewing and refreshing itself, and so the spirit of discovery will always play as great a part in the making of this anthology as the pleasures of abundance.

a given volume in this series might hang question marks over all three terms in the title

Americal poetry sometimes seems to be split down the middle. In the summer of 1995, half the crowd cheered Bill Moyers's latest TV extravaganza, *The Language of Life,* documenting a poetry festival in New Jersey that drew thousands of enthusiastic fans. The other half roared their approval when Helen Vendler ripped Moyers to shreds in the *New York Times Book Review.* "It is never a service to a complex practice to dumb it down," Vendler argued. The division between those who regard Moyers as a hero and those who cordially despise what he does seems suggestive of deeper conflicts and some larger cultural ambivalence about poetry in the United States today.

There are, on the one hand, the many signs of poetry's resurgence. Subway riders in New York like having poems by Sappho and Richard Wilbur next to the hemorrhoid ads. Three times in 1995—on New Year's Day, the Fourth of July, and Labor Day—the nation's newspaper of record devoted its entire op-ed page to poems. The Minneapolis man who invented "Magnetic Poetry" kits for crafting poems on refrigerator doors said his company is selling 40,000 of them a month. The Whitney Museum in New York mounted a major show devoted to the cultural implications of the Beat movement in poetry. Twice now in four years, the world's most lucrative and exclusive literary prize, the Nobel, has gone to a poet and part-time resident of Boston. The choice of Seamus

Heaney seems to have met with universal acclaim. The poetry that matters the most to us can "touch the base of our sympathetic nature while taking in at the same time the unsympathetic reality of the world to which that nature is constantly exposed," Heaney declared in his Nobel address. Poetry has power —"the power to persuade the vulnerable part of our consciousness of its rightness in spite of the evidence of wrongness all around it."

In May of this year, I participated in a "poetry game show" held at a theater in New York City as a benefit for the Poetry Calendar, the city's free monthly guide to poetry readings and performances, listing some 350 events on average, plus workshops and broadcasts. The host was Bob Holman, the porkpie-hat wearing author of *The Collect Call of the Wild*, a maestro of the poetry slam, who explained that the judging of poems would be conducted on a scale from zero to ten, "zero for a poem that should never have been written, ten for one that causes simultaneous mutual orgasm." Five poetry organizations fielded teams. In the Dead Poets' Slam, Siobhan Reagan of the Academy of American Poets wowed the judges by donning a bikini and a hat the shape of a wedge of Swiss cheese before reciting a Stevie Smith poem about wearing an odd hat on a desert isle. In the Instant Haiku round, Jennifer Cahill of the Poetry Society of America read the haiku she made up on the spot—a poem in Japanese about the summer vacation of a snake. As quizmaster of What's That Line?, I did a slow double take when Lord Byron's recipe for a hangover ("I say—the future is a serious matter— / And so—for God's sake—hock and soda water!") was incorrectly attributed to Charles Bukowski. But I was impressed with the *Paris Review* staffer who knew that the two-line poem entitled "Their Sex Life" ("One failure on / Top of another") was written by A. R. Ammons. The entire evening furnished compelling proof that poetry as a form of intellectual entertainment can please an audience that is wider, wilder, and more vocal than the audience for poetry is generally thought to be.

On the other hand . . . it sometimes seems as if poetry has been alotted a fifteen-second spot on the philistine national consciousness. Poetry is *The Battle Hymn of the Republic* on Memorial Day, or it is a rhymed injunction to the jury of a celebrated murder case, or maybe it is something in the air of a hip dark underground café that can help sell blue jeans. I recently saw a commercial for cheap trousers in which the American slob, male of the species, defiantly says, "I have no inner child, do not read poetry, and am not politically correct." A dissertation could be written on the conception of poetry that informs this sentence.

Thrillers, too, inform us about popular conceptions and misconceptions, and so I eagerly read Michael Connelly's new novel, *The Poet*, which is what book critics call a popcorn read, very enjoyable. It's about a psychopath who specializes in killing homicide cops while making the murders look like suicides. The spurious suicide notes have one thing in common: each contains a suitably morbid phrase from the poems of Edgar Allan Poe. In addition to being diabolically clever, the killer is cruel, sadistic, and very sick. The FBI's nickname for him is "The Poet."

The Best American Poetry can help clarify some of the confusions of the moment by invoking the standards of our leading poets. Each year a different guest editor—a poet of major reputation—chooses seventy-five poems to be honored. For *The Best American Poetry 1996* we have had the benefit of Adrienne Rich's sustained attention. Ms. Rich has long had a devoted following. Her first book, *A Change of World*, was chosen by W. H. Auden for the Yale Younger Poets Series, then as now our most prestigious first-book contest, when she was still a Radcliffe undergraduate, in 1951. More than fifteen books of poems have appeared since then. The title of one of them—*The Will to Change*—announces her poetic mandate. The National Book Award, the Ruth Lilly Poetry Prize, the Lambda Book Award for lesbian poetry, and the Lenore Marshall Prize are among the prizes she has received. The poems in *Dark Fields of the Republic*, her latest book, manage the difficult feat of wedding the unyielding voice of protest to the lyric cry, whose action is no stronger than a flower.

In January 1992 I received a letter from Ms. Rich saying she felt honored that Charles Simic, the guest editor of *The Best American Poetry 1992*, had chosen a poem of hers. She took an additional moment to comment on the series, in which four volumes had appeared to date. "The quality of the work in the series thus far is very high, and the poems diverse in certain ways," she wrote, "but they don't as yet, to my sense of it, reflect the richness and range of the best American poetry." In our subsequent correspondence she wrote warmly about the resurgence of American poetry, which she elsewhere described as a "pulsing, racing convergence of tributaries—regional, ethnic, racial, social, sexual." She was especially keen on the poetry surfacing outside of mainstream journals. "I am with you wholeheartedly in your belief that a wider readership exists for poetry than is commonly assumed, and I consider *The Best American Poetry* one of the hopeful signs in recent years," she wrote me. But "for all its inclusiveness," there are "still exclusions that reflect the deep segregations of our society, the mental suburbs in which many mainstream editors do their work, the artistic ghettoes to which too many of the best poets in the United States are relocated."

As a result of our correspondence I was determined to persuade Ms. Rich to guest-edit a volume in the series. Ms. Rich agreed on condition that I would guarantee her editorial autonomy and that the decision to include or exclude any given poem would be made by her. I readily consented to this condition, which is in fact a governing condition of the series. The final say in each volume is always the guest editor's.

In her book *What Is Found There: Notebooks on Poetry and Politics* (1993), Adrienne Rich describes the "revolutionary" power of poetry. "A revolutionary poem will not tell you who or when to kill, what and when to burn, or even how to theorize," she writes. A revolutionary poem is, rather, "a wick of desire" that "may do its work in the language and images of dreams, lists, love letters, prison letters, chants, filmic jump cuts, meditations, cries of pain, documentary fragments, blues, late-night long-distance calls. It is not programmatic: it searches for words amid the jamming of unfree, free-market idiom, for images that will burn true outside the emotional theme parks." The tradition she uses as a point of departure in her own work is that of Bertolt Brecht and Pablo Neruda and Muriel Rukeyser: poetry committed to a vision of social justice or radical change; poetry dedicated to keeping the conscience of society, affirming the ideals of human community.

With unflagging energy, Adrienne Rich pursued her vision of the "richness and range of the best American poetry" when she was reading for this volume. She was especially intent on discovering work that might otherwise go undiscovered, and she considered as many magazines as she could get hold of, including all the usual suspects plus a number of publications never before represented in this series, such as *The Americas Review, Bamboo Ridge, Cream City Review, Farmer's Market, Lingo, Many Mountains Moving,* and *River City.* Leading the honor roll this year are *Poetry,* with six selections, and *Prairie Schooner,* with five; *TriQuarterly,* the *Southern Review, Callaloo,* and *Hanging Loose* contributed four poems apiece. Only nineteen of the poets selected for this volume have appeared in a previous edition of *The Best American Poetry.*

Publishing poetry is almost by definition a Sisyphean task, and the wonder is that the boulder pushed with such struggle up the hill does sometimes reach the apex and roll down the other side, triumphantly. Heroic efforts are routinely made. This is the right moment to acknowledge the publishing team at Scribner, who have renewed their commitment to *The Best American Poetry* in the cheerful faith that what is past is prologue. I think, too, of the tremendous vitality of literary magazines, whose editors must work overtime just to keep up with the unsolicited manuscripts that arrive each day. *Michigan Quarterly Review* receives thirty to fifty poems daily; the editors at *Agni* estimate that they consider ten thousand poems a year. One might expect that it takes a lot of running just to stay in place, yet it's still possible to come up with a fresh approach, as *Hanging Loose* has demonstrated with its outstanding coverage of writers of high school age. And I would say a word for the small presses that have contributed so strongly to the decentralization of American poetry—presses such as Coffee House and Graywolf in the Twin Cities area of Minnesota, and Sun & Moon in Los Angeles, and Copper Canyon in Port Townsend, Washington. They do important work, as do the independent bookstores where poetry is prized out of all proportion to its commercial worth.

The *Best American Poetry* cannot settle all the quarrels in the poetry world. Nor is that its aim. In fact, it is possible that a given volume in this series might hang question marks over all three terms in the title: *best* (which "privileges an elite"), *American* (when "English-speaking North American" would be more nearly correct), and *poetry* (what is poetry?). *The Best American Poetry 1996* thus enters a contested site. But it does so with an olive branch in its mouth, like the dove announcing the end of the deluge to Noah. Representing women and gays and Latinos and poets outside the mainstream more amply than any previous book in the series, this is a bid not to discard canons but to add to them, to enlarge our poetic community, and to honor the many forms and motions of American poetry in our time.

As a gimmick, if that's what it is,
National Poetry Month worked

E very force creates a counterforce, and the ballyhooed recent resurgence of American poetry has been no exception. For every CNN report touting the "spoken word" scene, hip-hop poems, and poetry slams, a dour voice has piped up that it is not amused. There are those, there have always been those, who contend that what is new is meretricious and what is old, irrelevant. A vague dissatisfaction with what contemporary American poetry has to offer is a staple of Sunday book supplements. Rather than printing a review of a new poetry book each week, the editors salve their consciences by running a semiannual story about the uncertain fate of poetry in the era of the Internet or about how writing programs make for mediocre verse. The more self-examining of the plaintiffs wonder whether poetry is a thing of youth, and it is the poetry of their youth—the poetry they read in college—to which they pledge their fealty. It's as if a teenage crush on Mickey Mantle had incapacitated the fan from appreciating the skills of Ken Griffey Jr.

The standard-issue article about poetry's problems is a temptation for essayists who realize that few actual poems need to be read in order to accomplish the task. They can vent their nostalgia for the Romantic period, when poets had the good sense to die young, and their annoyance with versifiers who refuse to shut up though they have sixty or more winters on their heads. A new volume every three years is seen not as heartening evidence of poetic longevity but as the unfortunate side effect of academic necessity. Too many poems are "competent"—an odd complaint, and one that nobody would think to apply disdainfully to short stories or essays. But then perhaps we expect better, a higher standard of excellence, and not only excellence but also inspiration, from poets than we do from our other writers.

It is the nature of most criticism to be sour. John Updike publishes a book every season? The critics say he writes too much. Thomas Pynchon writes too little. Poets, however, can't write little enough. No one held it against Philip Larkin that he wrote one good poem in his last dry decade. (There were complaints enough about his xenophobia and sexism.) Poetry is too personal, or it is not personal enough. Rhyme and meter are old hat, yet poems lacking them are slack. More people are writing poetry than ever before, but little of it will last. More than twelve hundred poetry titles have been published annually in the United States since 1993, but that merely reverses a precipitous decline—from nearly thirteen hundred a year to just under nine hundred—in the aftermath of the stock market crash in October 1987. Poetry's ghetto is in the back of the bookshop far from the cash register. But poetry had better not pitch its tent where there are lights and cameras, since popular poetry is a contradiction in terms.

Critics inveigh against poetry writing programs on the grounds that they turn out mostly poetasters and epigones. The same critics forget that the fruits of an arts education begin with the ability to appreciate the art in question. If the lampooned institution of the creative writing workshop creates the readership of the future, more power to it. We do not consider the student of Plato to be a failure if he does not produce a dialogue of the quality of the *Symposium*. Nor should the likelihood of failure stand in the way of making the effort. Sometimes a spectacular failure is worth any number of modest successes. The study of writing would seem as important an experience for the professional scholar or general reader as for the aspiring writer, and it would be difficult to exaggerate the part that workshops can play, for good or ill, in creating the taste by which our poetry will be enjoyed. It is a profound irony that skills at reading poetry, which once were taught in English departments, now owe their existence to writing workshops, where literature rather than metatextual theorizing remains in favor.

For the second straight year, a poet won the Nobel Prize for literature. The announcement on October 3 that Wisława Szymborska of Poland had won the 1996 award vaulted her from obscurity to international prominence overnight. Editors and journalists scrambled to find Szymborska's work and commissioned translators to render it into English. By a splendid coincidence that illustrated Gertrude Stein's sense of the word ("a coincidence is something that is going to happen, and does"), both *The New Republic* and *The New Yorker* printed the same Szymborska poem on the same October week in two different translations. "Some People Like Poetry," as translated by Stanisław Barańczak and Clare Cavanagh, was the version that ran in *The New Republic*. It ended this way:

> Poetry—
> but what is poetry anyway?
> More than one rickety answer
> has tumbled since that question first was raised.
> But I just keep on not knowing, and I cling to that
> like a redemptive handrail.

"Some Like Poetry," Joanna Trzeciak's version in *The New Yorker*, arrived at a different conclusion:

> Poetry—
> but what sort of thing is poetry?
> More than one shaky answer
> has been given to this question.
> But I do not know and do not know and clutch on to it,
> as to a saving bannister.

In Trzeciak's translation, poetry is the bannister that helps the poet keep her balance on the vertiginous staircase of unknowing. In the Barańczak and Cavanagh translation, not poetry but the poet's determination to persist in the absence of certainties and facts is what is redemptive. So profound is the difference that the concurrent appearance of the two translations seemed itself to constitute a literary event—an ambiguous parable that could yield lessons ranging from the familiar ("poetry is what is lost in translation") to the paradoxical ("poetry is mistranslation"). What was not in dispute was the fact that Szymborska's work had begun to attract the attention and admiration that may not be essential to the writing of poetry but are surely a grace for all who read and love it.

Perhaps because of the official presidential designation of April as National Poetry Month, the first line of "The Waste Land" provided the lead for more soft-news stories in 1996 than in any past year, and the rest of the poem received its due when the Irish actress Fiona Shaw presented it in a one-woman show at a suitably dilapidated off-Broadway theater in November. In general, National Poetry Month received good notices, though some of the articles mixed their metaphors with wince-provoking abandon ("Poetry is a bomb that frags you with metaphor, explodes in your head where it heals rather than harms," wrote one enthusiast). As a gimmick, if that's what it is, National Poetry Month worked, stimulating a proliferation of readings, lectures, and bookstore events related to poetry. Sales were up by 35 percent at Borders and 25 percent at Barnes & Noble. Independent bookstores like the Hungry Mind in Saint Paul, Minnesota, did even better. In Los Angeles, the UCLA Bookstore reported an increase of "at least 600 percent" with $3,500 in poetry receipts in the first week of April alone. To mark the second appearance of National Poetry Month, in 1997, thousands of free copies of "The Waste Land" were distributed at U.S. post offices on April 15, the cruelest day of all.

Not everyone was charmed, however. Richard Howard, a chancellor of the Academy of American Poets, the organization that initiated National Poetry Month, said, "I was never before so certain why April was declared by a poet to be the cruelest month; now I know." He had "no hesitation" in calling National Poetry Month "the worst thing to have happened to poetry since the advent of the camera and the internal combustion engine, two inventions which the poet Wystan Auden once declared to be the bane of our modernity." In Mr. Howard's view, such a ploy as National Poetry Month cannot but contribute to the commodification of poetry, putting the art on a par with the chocolates and flowers customarily purchased on Valentine's Day. The workings of capitalism have sanitized poetry when the thing to do is to eroticize it. "So wretched, and so absurd, has the position of poetry writing become in our polity—unread though occasionally exhibited, despised though invariably ritualized, as at certain inaugurations—that not only are we determined to put the poor thing out of its agony, but we have made it a patriotic duty to do so." Publicity, in an age of publicity, was an enemy. Let us, Mr. Howard urged, "make poetry, once again, a secret."

Poetry always was a secret pleasure, indulged in alone, the self communing with a book as the writer of that book once communed alone with the cosmos. Something has changed, as Mr. Howard notes, in an age of consumerism, so-phisticated marketing techniques, communications technology, and television's vast wasteland. Poetry readings have, to an extent unforeseen when Dylan Thomas and Allen Ginsberg were the rage, replaced the solitary act of reading. Poetry is more of a group event than it used to be. At least that is the public aspect of poetry—the poetry that is most visible and audible. Compare the poetry of today with that of a quarter century ago and you see a sharp rise in the number of public poems: not that they necessarily deal with public issues, just that they seem to have been written with a live audience, ready to sigh on cue, in the poet's mind.

But it is the nature of secrets to avoid being found out, and the clamor and din surrounding poetry do not deny that something important may be happening far from the spotlight. What is this news, and how is it to be found out? If it is up to posterity to determine the lasting value of works of art, on what basis can we anticipate the process today? If we are to begin to judge, however tentatively and falteringly, who is to do the selecting?

The Best American Poetry has, since its inception nine volumes ago, made available to an increasing readership a wide and generous sampling of the poems of our time. From the start we have felt that an annual winnowing was essential, since no casual reader can possibly keep up with all the poetry that is published annually in periodicals and since a surprisingly high proportion of those poems are worth reading more than once. A test of good poetry is that it compels multiple rereadings, and that is certainly a test that the editors of *The Best American Poetry* have taken to heart. Our period, as even cranky critics note, is rich in poets who have had long and productive careers. The guest editors of this anthology come from these distinguished ranks. They are asked to be as ecumenical as they can be, but it is always understood that each will honor his or her own lights. The result is, in effect, a work in progress, for *The Best American Poetry* is meant to provide a continuing record of the taste and judgment of our leading poets. It is also meant to heed the imperative articulated by Wallace Stevens: "It must give pleasure."

I asked James Tate to edit *The Best American Poetry 1997*, not only because I admire his writing but also because I know him to be a discriminating reader and I was curious to see what poems he would deem fittest to survive. Born in Kansas City, Missouri, in 1943, Mr. Tate burst on the poetry scene in 1966 when his book *The Lost Pilot* was chosen for the Yale Younger Poets Series. He was among the youngest ever to achieve that distinction. His *Selected Poems*, a distillation of his first nine volumes, won the Pulitzer Prize for poetry in 1992. In 1995 he received the Dorothea Tanning Award from the Academy of American Poets. In addition to his poems, he has written short stories, and he is the coauthor, with Bill Knott, of a terrific book of collaborative poems improbably titled *Are You Ready, Mary Baker Eddy?* (1970).

While *The Best American Poetry 1997* naturally reflects Mr. Tate's predilections as a poet, I think the reader will find that the contents are as unpredictable as the plot twists in a French prose poem. Poems were selected from thirty-nine magazines, with *Poetry* topping the list (eight selections), followed by *American Poetry Review* (six), *Ploughshares* and *The New Republic* (five apiece). The book is strong on narrative—what one poet calls the "stories in poetry." There are a number of prose poems, but there are also prayers and meditations and chants, a poem in the form of a fan letter and a sui generis poem in the form of haiku-like bumper stickers. The music in the background is provided by Mozart, Beethoven, Wagner, Gershwin, Mick Jagger, Janis Joplin, Bob Dylan, and the Sex Pistols. Among the subjects addressed are "the problem of anxiety," "the exaggeration of despair," and whether History to the survivors may say alas but cannot help or pardon. In one poem we find Jesus, Mary, and Joseph and in the next one Groucho, Beppo, and Harpo. Little Red Riding Hood, Clytemnestra, and Sisyphus put in appearances. The poets think about thinking, smoking, bourbon, heroin, California, death, and the sexes, their chronic conflicts and periodic acts of reconciliation. The anthology includes the work of four recently deceased poets—Joseph Brodsky, William Dickey, Allen Ginsberg, and Larry Levis—mourned and honored here.

When James Tate's most recent collection, *Worshipful Company of Fletchers* (Ecco Press), won the 1994 National Book Award in poetry, the citation began as follows: "A reader of James Tate's poetry, laughing out loud, said, 'I didn't know that poetry was allowed to be so much fun.'" We hope that the poems in this volume will provoke a similarly delighted response. If poetry is its own excuse for being, as Emerson said of beauty, there can be no defense of it more eloquent than verse.

> Articles about the dismal state of poetry
> Bemoan the absence of form and meter or,
> Conversely, the products of "forms workshop":
> Dream sonnets, sestinas based on childhood photographs,
> Eclogues set in Third Avenue bars,
> Forms contrived to suit an emergent occasion.
> God knows it's easy enough to mock our enterprise,
> Hard, though, to succeed at it, since
> It sometimes seems predicated on failure.
> Just when the vision appears, an importunate
> Knock on the door banishes it, and you
> Lethe-wards have sunk, or when a sweet
> Melancholic fit should transport you to a
> North Pole of absolute concentration,

Obligations intrude, putting an end to the day's
Poem. Poetry like luck is the residue of
Quirky design, and it
Refreshes like a soft drink full of bubbles
Sipped in a stadium on a lazy August afternoon
That was supposed to be spent at a boring job.
Ultimately poetry is
Virtue if it is our lot to choose, err, regret and
Wonder why in speech that would melt the stars.
X marks the spot of
Your latest attempt. Point at a map, blindfolded:
Zanzibar. Shall we go there, you and I?

The Best of the
Best American Poetry,
1988–1997

——1998——

The debate is joined

W hen *The Best American Poetry* was conceived ten years ago, it seemed to me an idea so inevitable that I wondered that no one else had acted on it. I had the vision of an annual anthology that would chronicle the taste of our leading poets and would reflect the vigor and variety of an art that refuses to go quietly into that good night to which one or another commentator is forever consigning it. I had been reading literary magazines by the dozens and was impressed by the quality of the poetry that regularly appeared in print to little fanfare. Not only were Ashbery and Merrill and Ammons and other masters writing in peak form, but extraordinary specimens by poets I'd never heard of were turning up every day in remote periodicals, experimental journals, staid old quarterlies, flashy new ones, and desktop broadsides from Maine to Alaska. Wouldn't it make sense—and perhaps dollars, too—to cull the year's most compelling works and perpetuate them in a handsome volume? Done right, the anthology would transcend sectarian differences and tribal conflicts in a spirit of generosity and ecumenicism, but with the firm insistence that aesthetic excellence must be the paramount imperative. We would honor the notion that poems from rival traditions can consort together to their mutual advantage. Each year's book would represent the predilections of a different guest editor, himself or herself an eminent practitioner. We would ask the poets selected for inclusion to provide comments about the poems, how they had been written or what had occasioned them. The magazines in which the poems appeared would be listed, their editors named, their addresses given, to aid the potential subscribers and prospective contributors in our audience. We were bound to have one. Readers hungry for poetry would respond with ardor.

Or would they? Book publishers, with their customary air of noble irresolution, did their best to disabuse me. "You'll be lucky to sell two thousand copies," one executive said sympathetically. I could see her point. It was a truth universally acknowledged that the book trade now functioned within a vast literary-industrial complex whose corporate masters were ruled by an unforgiving bottom line. Would we please and excite readers in sufficient quantities to pay our own freight? I couldn't help recalling the analogy that Don Marquis, the creator of *archy and mehitabel*, had spun when the century was young. Publishing a book of verse, he observed, was like dropping a rose petal in the Grand Canyon and waiting for the echo. What made me think that the gesture would be less futile now? If someone had forecast that *The Best American Poetry* would still be going strong ten years later—with a readership that grows wider each year—even I, with my unreasonable attachment to the project, would have laughed. Yet that is what has happened.

The success of the series is due largely to the efforts of the ten poets who have served as guest editors: John Ashbery, Donald Hall, Jorie Graham, Mark Strand, Charles Simic, Louise Glück, A. R. Ammons, Richard Howard, Adrienne Rich, and James Tate. Each willingly took on the task of surveying the year's poetry, selecting seventy-five poems from a pool containing more than ten times as many candidates. Each contributed an introduction about his or her principles of selection, or about the state of American poetry, or about the process of writing a poem, or about the experience of reading for the anthology. There was never any presumption that the guest editors would substantially agree with one another or that their taste would necessarily overlap. In retrospect it seems to me that one might peruse the ten volumes, forge some sort of consensus view, and arrive at tentative conclusions regarding not only literary reputations, who's in, who's out, but also a host of critical questions having to do with the characteristic forms, styles, subject matter, and attitudes of poets in America today. But the purpose of this series is not to arrive at conclusions so much as to suggest a good starting point for readers preparing to embark on their own journey. *The Best American Poetry* does not set out each year to ratify a pantheon, and indeed the books in the series can be understood to be having a dialogue with one another—dialogue that sometimes turns into impassioned debate.

The debate is joined in *The Best of the Best American Poetry 1988–1997*. Now that ten years have gone by, it seems an opportune moment to return to the 750 poems that have been anthologized thus far and hazard an educated guess about which of them may endure into the next century. Since poets have done the selecting for the individual volumes, I thought to entrust this new task to a critic—preferably a fearless and influential one, with strong opinions, sophisticated taste, and a passion for poetry that matches any poet's. If the books in the series have lived up to their collective title, this anthology of anthologies might define a contemporary canon. Choosing the contents would therefore test any editor's nerve. Luckily, the one critic who has unabashedly and unapologetically committed himself to the idea of a literary canon, to the possibility of making one and to the necessity of having one, is a critic who long ago made a name for himself as a highly discriminating reader of the poetry of his time, whose provocative judgments have turned out often—remarkably often—to be right.

Harold Bloom has fascinated me since the September day in 1967 when I, a Columbia sophomore, drove up to Yale to visit a friend and sat in on Professor Bloom's modern poetry course. It was the first day of classes, and Bloom was going over his reading list, which consisted mainly if not exclusively of William Butler Yeats, Wallace Stevens, Hart Crane, and, I think, D. H. Lawrence. There was to be no Eliot, no Pound, no Auden, no William Carlos Williams. From memory Bloom recited Wordsworth and Emerson and Whitman and Stevens by the yard. He tossed off paradoxes worthy of Oscar Wilde and followed by quoting Wilde to the effect that all bad poetry was unfailingly sincere, a slogan that Bloom has since said he would like to see emblazoned on the gates of university campuses. I didn't know it then, but Bloom was still fighting Eliot's neoclassicism, royalism, and Anglo-Catholicism—still crusading for a "visionary company" of poets, such as Shelley, who had fallen into disfavor with the Eliot-inspired New Criticism—and he was not in the mood to give any quarter. Although the poets he excluded from his course were among those I loved the most, I was taken with his flamboyant manner and his idiosyncratic approach—not every professor was so candid or so sure of himself. And I found him to be wholly convincing when, in the early 1970s, he began to extend his "Romantic line" to the poets of the American present, championing Ammons and Ashbery and Merrill as our top bards.

This was the same time that Bloom propounded his theoretical model for the study of poetry. A quartet of studies, the first of which added a phrase to the lexicon ("the anxiety of influence"), made its author the most controversial critic of the period. The study of literary influence had once rested on naively benign premises; it was assumed that influence and inspiration were virtually indistinguishable, and literary history was seen as a series of successful baton exchanges in a marathon relay race. This understanding of how influence works was complicated by Walter Jackson Bate, who argued that the "burden" of the past can inhibit the new poet struggling to establish an original poetic voice. Bloom went further, advancing the thesis that "strong" poets manage to overcome the anxiety aroused by inevitable self-comparisons with their father figures. Proposing parallels between rhetorical tropes and psychological defense mechanisms, Bloom argued that poems always refer to (and "misread") antecedent poems, that poets wage Oedipal battles with their precursors, and that in a sense "all literature is plagiaristic." Bloom's efforts to "de-idealize" the study of literary influence aroused an anxiety equal to the one he had analyzed. Angry poets, resentful that he has overlooked them, have vilified and lampooned him. "I am the pariah of the profession," he told me when I interviewed him for a *Newsweek* profile in 1986.

Bloom has made few pronouncements about contemporary poetry in the last ten years. He has been absorbed by other subjects: Freud, Shakespeare, Genesis, indigenous American religions, and the making of a Western canon. As I write this, he is completing a magnum opus entitled *Shakespeare: The Invention of the Human*. An anomaly in a conformist's academy, he has risen to the defense of literature against the plethora of new ideologically inflected approaches that would subdue it. "I am," he writes in *The Western Canon*, "your true Marxist critic, following Groucho rather than Karl, and take as my motto Groucho's grand admonition, 'whatever it is, I'm against it.'" Bloom is eloquent in his defense of literature as an aesthetic realm, autonomous and unsponsored. "Reading deeply in the Canon will not make one a better or a worse person," he writes. "All that the Western Canon can bring one is the proper use of one's own solitude, that solitude whose final form is one's confrontation with one's own mortality."

In *The Best of the Best American Poetry 1988–1997*, Bloom has relied on what he has called "the only pragmatic test for the canonical"—he has chosen seventy-five poems that he thinks worthy of rereading. They are not the only poems of excellence to have been published in the last ten years; 675 others have appeared in this series alone; but they have passed the test of rereading, they have given pleasure more than twice over, and they demonstrate in their differing ways that something very important is going on in American poetry today. "The first thing that strikes a reader about the best American poets is how utterly unlike each other they are," W. H. Auden once observed. That was true of the generation of Pound, Williams, Stevens, Frost, Marianne Moore, e. e. cummings, and Laura Riding. It is equally true today, as readers of this anthology will see. The last ten years of American poetry have witnessed a continual widening of limits. Our poets have addressed themselves with un-precedented candor—and with wit and humor—to carnal knowledge and other taboo subjects. They have celebrated their freedom not only in their choice of subject matter but also in relentless formal innovation. Our poems range from the tightly controlled (sonnets, sestinas, villanelles) to the wild and seemingly lawless (prose poems, spontaneous oratory), with plenty of room for ad hoc forms (a poem in the form of a codicil to a will, a poem that plays fast and loose with the period as a punctuation mark). The diversity on display has little in common with a sense of diversity based on demographic properties. It is rather a diversity of means, metaphors, visions, and voices, and it occurs in response to the common challenge facing the modern poet. "Originality no longer means a slight modification in the style of one's immediate predecessors; it means a capacity to find in any work of any date or place a clue to finding one's authen-tic voice," Auden wrote. "The burden of choice and selection is put squarely upon the shoulders of each individual poet and it is a heavy one." The writer's burden, transmuted by the imagination, becomes the reader's gift. It is the grace of art that it conceals the struggle that went into its making.

The president spoke of having had to
memorize 100 lines of Macbeth

Not very long ago, the coverage of poetry in the national press was dominated by complaint and self-pity: the lament for a lost audience, the noise of interminable debate about the use of poetry in an age of technology, the growl of congressional disapproval. How quickly that has changed. Poets today still face major obstacles as they struggle to gain acceptance or even just to make ends meet. But the prestige of the art has steadily climbed since this decade began, and it has paralleled a growing public appetite for the best poems of our moment. The nation's hot romance with poetry shows no sign of cooling off.

When Ted Hughes's secretly written book about his marriage to Sylvia Plath was published, the *New York Times* carried the story on its front page. Within weeks, Hughes's *Birthday Letters* had displaced Toni Morrison's novel *Paradise* as the number one hardcover best seller at Colosseum Books in New York City. (Sales nationwide topped the 100,000 mark by the advent of spring.) Robert Hass, America's outgoing poet laureate, established the policy of choosing a poem from a new book every week and commenting on it for the *Washington Post Book World*. Robert Pinsky, Hass's successor as poet laureate, commenced work immediately on the "Favorite Poem Project," a kind of oral history of contemporary taste. A cross section of Americans from varied backgrounds will be asked to read and record their favorite poems for the Library of Congress. "If a thousand years from now anyone should ask who the Americans were, this archive might help give an answer," Pinsky said.

On the Internet, websites devoted to poetry are proliferating. *Poetry Daily*, true to its name, highlights a different poem every day; it also "reprints" articles on poetry from major newspapers. (When *Poetry Daily* learned that I was writing a poem a day as an experiment, they invited me to post my daily poem all through the month of April—a thrilling experience that left me more convinced than ever that poetry is conditioned by the fastest means of transmission available to the poet.) The Academy of American Poets' website offers the browser a brief course in modern poetry. The *Poetry Porch* provides poems, interviews, and links to university libraries. The Poetry Society of America has an online "peer workshop" and is planning to host an interactive cybersymposium this fall addressing the perennial question, "What is American about American poetry?" For the lively Electronic Poetry Center, the poet Charles Bernstein compiled a list of sixty useful experiments that poets might try. "Any profits accrued as a direct or indirect result of the uses of these formulas shall be redistributed to the language at large," the reader is advised. Visitors to the site are invited to participate in a group collaboration with other plugged-in poets.

Today, when shoe manufacturers plan a new ad campaign, they are liable to consider enlisting the help of poets, the way Ford asked Marianne Moore's help in naming the ill-fated car that management, ignoring Moore's recommendations, called the Edsel forty years ago. Poems are appearing on beer coasters and subway posters. In 1996 the Baltimore Ravens—named after Edgar Allan Poe's "grim, ungainly, ghastly, gaunt, and ominous 'bird of yore'"—replaced the Cleveland Browns ("Nevermore") in the National Football League. Ten pages of Barnes & Noble's 1996 annual report were devoted to poetry. There were quotes from John F. Kennedy and Claude Lévi-Strauss, photographs taken at readings, a list of the year's poetry best sellers (*The Odyssey* and *Canterbury Tales* were right up there with Maya Angelou), a poem by Nobel laureate Wisława Szymborska, and a letter to shareholders from Leonard Riggio, the firm's CEO, stating his determination to "broaden the marketplace for works of poetry and literature." On Valentine's Day 1997, passengers on Amtrak's Metroliner and guests at Doubletree hotels in Boston, Baltimore, and Atlanta were handed free copies—fifteen thousand in all—of a collection of famous love poems. In 1998 the American Poetry and Literacy Project planned to up the ante by giving away fifty thousand copies of *101 Great American Poems* to celebrate National Poetry Month in April. An aspect of this year's White House sex scandal not usually emphasized but of particular note in this context is that President Clinton gave Monica Lewinsky a copy of *Leaves of Grass*, a book he is said to present routinely to honored visitors and guests.

Whitman's immortal work was recited at the White House—Rita Dove reading from "Song of Myself" and Robert Pinsky from "Crossing Brooklyn Ferry"—when President and Mrs. Clinton hosted a "Millennium Evening" celebrating American poets and poetry. Hillary Clinton initiated the proceedings by quoting Howard Nemerov's poem "The Makers." The president spoke of having had to memorize 100 lines of *Macbeth* when he was in high school. He credited the experience with teaching him "about the dangers of blind ambitions, the fleeting nature of fame, the ultimate emptiness of power disconnected from higher purpose," with the result that "Mr. Shakespeare made me a better president." The event was beamed to 200 sites in forty-four states and was cybercast. A transcript was very quickly made available on the web, and it was no less pleasurable for the accidental transformations that hasty typing produced—as when Wallace Stevens's "the palm at the end of the mind" turned into "the pond at the end of the mine."

The Best American Poetry, now entering its second decade, has from the start committed itself to the idea that the enlargement of poetry's audience can be entirely consistent with uncompromising literary standards. We have wished to perpetuate excellence in any of the forms it may take. At the same time we have done our best to make this book as friendly and hospitable as possible to readers beyond the society of scribes. The poems in *The Best American Poetry 1998* were culled from big-circulation weeklies (*The New Yorker, The New Republic*), university quarterlies (the *Yale Review, Southwest Review*), and independent magazines (the *Threepenny Review*, the *Paris Review*). More than thirty periodicals are represented in these pages; many more than thirty were consulted (and, in future, we expect to add high-quality Internet magazines, such as *Slate* and *Jacket*, to the list). The seventy-five poems that made the editor's final cut faced stiff competition, and plenty of it. Most of the chosen poets have generously contributed comments on their poems, a section of this anthology that many readers prize—it has the salutary effect of demonstrating that modern poetry is by no means as inaccessible as advertised.

As the series editor of *The Best American Poetry*, I know that the most important decision I have to make every year involves the identity of the year's guest editor—himself or herself a major poet—who is asked to choose the poems and contribute an introduction assessing the state of the art. For the 1998 volume, I could think of no one better qualified than John Hollander. In a poetry culture in which the short, anecdotal, or confessional lyric is valued above all else, Hollander has, over the course of his career, given us brilliant examples of formal possibilities that we would be foolish to ignore: shaped verse, satirical epistles, songs, and meditations, as well as long poems and poetic sequences in forms devised by the poet himself. In addition to being a poet of remarkable resource and inventiveness, Hollander is an astute scholar (as readers of *The Figure of Echo* will see) and teacher (whose *Rhyme's Reason* ought to be a required manual for aspiring poets). He is also one of the most experienced anthologists of his generation. I knew that he would make his judgments carefully but confidently and that he would honor the diverse ways in which true poetry differs from what he calls the "canonical bad verse of our time."

To assist the year's guest editor, the series editor is obliged to read as many magazines as he can get his hands on. It is a tall task that is also, fortunately, a pleasure, for the reader of magazines encounters the new when it is truly new. Every year brings its share of discoveries and delights. In *American Poetry Review* I come across "The Winter of Our Discontents & Other Seasons" by Marcia Southwick, a poet previously unknown to me, who wants her poems "to be less Marcia-centric" and to this end decides to write about "*Star Trek*'s Seska the undercover Cardassian spy." The result is charming, as is Dina Ben-Lev's "Response to a Message of Hate on My Machine" in the impressive new magazine *Salt Hill*. In *Chain*, Peter Gizzi has an "Ode: Salute to the New York School 1950–1970 (A Libretto)," which turns out to be a wonderful cento (a poem consisting entirely of lines lifted from other poems) that doubles as an index to a chronological bibliography. The poem of the week in *The New Republic* is "Remembering My Visit to Martha's Vineyard Last Summer" by Ann Claremont Le Zotte. A note indicates that the poem has been "translated, from Sign Language, by the author." The effects of this maneuver are remarkable: "Plum cake tart eat I," the poem begins. Then I pick up *New American Writing* and read Paul Violi's "On an Acura Integra," which proves there is plenty of life left in the rhetorical gambit of the insincere apology. This hilarious poem is in the form of a note left on a wrecked car by the driver who crashed into it and then fled the scene. I mention these five poems, and could easily speak of five times as many, precisely because they did not make the final cut for this year's anthology—a fact that underscores just how bountiful American poetry is today.

One thing that is distinctive about American poetry is the largeness of spirit in which people raise the question, "What is American about American poetry?" The question is asked in earnestness, innocence, and generosity. Compare this to the rigorous and exclusionary procedures of the French Academy, for example. There are other aspects of American poetry that set it apart: a certain lawless energy, a native strain of celebration and self-celebration. American poetry can be said to have issued its literary declaration of independence from Britain when Emerson railed against conformism, Whitman said he could "resist anything better than my own diversity," and Dickinson gave everyone permission to be "Nobody." The history of our poetry seems a history of defiant individuality to the point of eccentricity, and who would want it otherwise? Poetry is freedom, and that includes freedom from social obligations and literary norms. At the same time, the idea of America remains an enthralling possibility for the imagination. "The United States themselves are essentially the greatest poem," Walt Whitman asserted in his prose introduction to the 1855 edition of *Leaves of Grass*. The genius of the United States, he wrote, rests not in its executives and legislatures but in the "unrhymed poetry" of the American people, which awaits "the gigantic and generous treatment worthy of it." The American poet in 1998 continues to find inspiration and sustenance in Whitman's words and in his vision of a country that absorbs its poets as affectionately as they have absorbed it.

"Whitman rocks"

"Not so long ago, the phrase 'California wine' belonged in the same book of oxymorons as, say, 'living poet' and 'Dutch cuisine.' You knew, on some level, that such things existed, but you didn't necessarily want any of them at your dinner table." Jay McInerney, who wrote these lines, thought them witty enough to serve as the lead of a *New Yorker* piece he recently wrote about California winemaker Robert Mondavi. The expulsion of poets from ideal republics is an old story, and what is most interesting in McInerney's formulation is the type of exclusion specified: the poet is barred from the socialite's banquet table, where French wine and French cuisine are served and conversation can be had with hip clever novelists, each a potential spokesperson for his or her generation.

Well, no one denies that poets receive fewer rewards than fiction writers. No poet can hope to enjoy as much fame, or as wide a readership, as a successful novelist. Even midlist fiction writers have a potential source of cash unavailable to the best poets, who waste little time praying that a Hollywood studio will take an option on their next book. (Martin Amis, in his recent story "Career Move," spins out the conceit, patently absurd, that sonnets are the vehicles of celebrity in our culture: "Don has a problem with the octet's first quatrain, Ron has a problem with the second quatrain, Jack and Jim have a problem with the first quatrain of the sestet, and I think we *all* have a problem with the final couplet.") Novelists are reviewed, moreover, while poets are largely ignored in the Sunday book supplements. Have a statistic. Between June 14, 1998, and September 27, 1998, five books of poetry were reviewed, and two others mentioned "in brief," in the *New York Times Book Review*. In the same period, ninety-six books of fiction were reviewed, with eighty-eight others treated "in brief." The ratio is even more comically one-sided when you factor in nonfiction books.

The irony is that American poetry today is not only, on its own terms, astonishingly vital and compelling, diverse and abundant, but also—though it is difficult to measure these things—probably in better shape altogether than contemporary American fiction. Indeed, the proliferation of memoirs written, in Oscar Wilde's words, "by people who have either entirely lost their memories, or have never done anything worth remembering," implies that narrative prose is stuck in that confessional box from which poetry moved on years ago. "But there is no competition," T. S. Eliot wrote in the biggest fib in his *Four Quartets*. "There is only the fight to recover what has been lost / And found and lost again and again."

Despite occasional reminders of its supposed second-class status, poetry today occupies a more honored place in the national consciousness than it has known since the 1960s, which was the last time in America that poets acted the part of heroes. The word *poetic* has long been an honorific when used to describe anything except poetry itself. (Example from the travel section: "In a corner of Lombardy, food is poetry.") But now poetry in the public imagination has acquired a dimension alien to the tradition of teacups and roses. In recent movies poetry is associated with liberation, truth-telling, and self-actualization. Life imitates *Bulworth* in which Warren Beatty, as a California senator running for reelection, sees the light and begins to tell it like it is—in the incessant rhymes and staccato rhythms of rap verse. In the movie's vocabulary the rapping ensures the speaker's authenticity and makes it possible for him to speak unpleasant truths in an insolent manner. (It may also signify the persistence of "the white negro" syndrome that Norman Mailer glamorized in an essay forty years ago.) *Bulworth* didn't do as well at the box office as advance hype had projected, but it had its effect on politics. As Election Day 1998 approached, Vice President Gore, stumping for the Democrats, tried to shed his wooden image by rapping his election slogans. "We say, 'legislate'; the Republicans say, 'investigate.'" And, "We say, 'make the decisions'; they take depositions. / We know our future is nearing; they hold more hearings. / We say, 'heal our nation'; they just say 'investigation.'"

———— *DAVID LEHMAN* ————

In his book on Muhammad Ali, David Remnick reminds us that the great champion was the original rap artist and performance poet, who improvised his verses into microphones held by relentless interviewers. The fighter composed what Remnick calls, only half in jest, his "Song of Myself" before the bout with Sonny Liston in which he won the crown. He was still known as Cassius Clay then:

> Now Clay swings with a right,
> What a beautiful swing,
> And the punch raises the bear
> Clear out of the ring.
>
> Liston is still rising
> And the ref wears a frown,
> For he can't start counting
> Till Sonny comes down.
>
> Now Liston disappears from view.
> The crowd is getting frantic,
> But our radar stations have picked him up,
> He's somewhere over the Atlantic.

Before his fight with the aging Archie Moore in 1962, Clay predicted the outcome: "When you come to the fight, don't block the aisle and don't block the door. You will all go home after Round Four." In one of the more surprising sentences I encountered in 1998, I learned from Remnick that Moore had slipped easily into the role of the professorial critic, duly finding fault with the younger fighter's literary style. "Sometimes he sounds humorous, but sometimes he sounds like Ezra Pound's poetry," Moore said. "He's like a man who can write beautifully but doesn't know how to punctuate. He has this twentieth-century exuberance, but there's bitterness in him somewhere." True to his word, Clay knocked him out in the fourth round.

In 1999 Clay's verses would get more respect. Poetry today is celebrated and often appropriated in everything from the marketing of perfume to the ice dancing of former U.S. Olympic skater Kristi Yamaguchi, who has been doing a solo program set to ten love poems by Komachi and Shikabu, "women of the ancient Japanese court," in translations by Jane Hirshfield and Mariko Aaratani. Poetry has also been used to wage a kind of counter-commercial campaign. In Los Angeles in January 1999 an outfit called Poets Anonymous spent roughly a million dollars to rent sixty billboards in prominent locations. For a month motorists were confronted with verse excerpts from a range of poets, including Pablo Neruda, Mark Strand, Charles Bukowski, and Lucille Clifton. I wondered what people made of the opening of Wallace Stevens's "The Well Dressed Man with a Beard," looming out at them at six major Los Angeles intersections: "After the final no there comes a yes / And on that yes the future world depends."

Bulworth isn't the only recent movie that capitalizes on the association of poetry with freedom, beauty, valor. *Life Is Beautiful*, Roberto Benigni's Oscar-winning movie, begins with a poet driving a car while declaiming verse. In his poem the brakes fail, and an instant later the brakes in the car fail, and the car careens off the road, and it is this accident that brings the movie's hero and heroine together for the first time. (According to the *New York Daily News*, Benigni spent the afternoon preceding his Oscar triumph reading William Blake's poetry.) The greatly celebrated *Shakespeare in Love*, which won this year's Academy Awards for best picture and best actress, is an irresistible fantasy about the author of *Romeo and Juliet* and the romance that is said to have inspired him to write the play and, for good measure, the sonnet comparing the beloved to a summer day. "I love poetry above all," the beautiful heroine (Gwyneth Paltrow) tells Queen Elizabeth. The Swan of Avon himself cuts a dashing figure, adept at both lovemaking and derring-do; not only does he write poetry but he speaks it as well, improvising as needed, no sweat. The coming attractions indicate that a new Hollywood production of *A Midsummer Night's Dream* is slated for summer release. A teen version of *The Taming of the Shrew*—renamed *10 Things I Hate About You*—has just opened. Can a resurgence of Bardolatry be under way? It is April as I write this, and I have just watched a commercial for the Seattle Mariners. In the commercial the Mariners' shortstop reads the "quality of mercy" passage from *The Merchant of Venice* to the runner on second base. The distracted runner is then picked off. "The hidden Shakespeare trick," a Mariner in the dugout muses.

Entertainment Weekly—which reports that Bruce Springsteen is a "huge fan" of *The Best American Poetry* series—also reveals that the actor Charlie Sheen is a poet. Sheen reads from his work throughout a just released straight-to-video movie, *Sisters*: "Did one depart with no remorse, / menstrual mood, unsigned divorce?" In one key respect Sheen is just like all other poets: he apparently failed to find a publisher for his manuscript when he completed it six years ago. Sultry songstress Jewel was luckier. *A Night Without Armor*, her first collection, was a pop sensation, with 300,000 copies in print. Critics invented new criteria to handle the phenomenon. "Jewel's book of poetry is solid by celeb-poet standards, and a fair bit of it is actually sort of readable in its own right," one noted. By mid-February 1999, *A Night Without Armor* had occupied a place on the *New York Times* best-seller list—where it was listed in fiction—for nineteen weeks.

Poems are popping up all over the place. On the Internet, literary "zines" with names like *Nerve* and *Pif* are multiplying. A new development is the interactive poetry chat room. According to Robin Travis, who runs several such chat rooms out of her Alabama home, 100,000 poets visit her site every month. In the twenty-four-hour reading room, people present their poems for public reaction. Critical debate divides pretty evenly. "There are academics who trash everything," Travis says. "And then there are those who say, 'Awesome!'"

On television, poetry has been punctuating sitcoms and drama series. The title character of *Felicity*, a poetry-loving first-year student at a New York university, corresponds with an older, wiser friend, who advises her on matters of the heart. She quotes Auden: "If equal affection cannot be, / Let the more loving one be me." On *Sports Night*, which is set behind the scenes of a cable TV sports show, one of the anchormen caps a defense of yachting by quoting a dimly recollected poem about a sailor's yearning for "the lonely sky and the sea." The lines ring a bell, and the guys proceed to debate whether Whitman, Byron, Thoreau, Wordsworth, or Dylan Thomas wrote the poem in question—which turns out to be John Masefield's "Sea Fever" ("And all I ask is a windy day with the white clouds flying, / And the flung spray and the blown spume, and the seagulls crying.") A college student in *Party of Five* complains about having to write a term paper on Madonna's second album. "It's Emily Dickinson we need help with," she very sensibly says. In an episode of *ER* the new chief of the emergency room has made a career out of impersonating top professionals: an architect in the past, now a surgeon. She has fallen in love with one of the doctors. Exposed and expelled, she sends him a good-bye note with some highly erotic verses, as if she were their author: "Because two bodies, naked and entwined, / leap over time, they are invulnerable, / nothing can touch them, they return to the source. / There is no you, no I, no tomorrow." The doctor's pal recognizes the lines as from Octavio Paz's "Sunstone"—she is an impersonator as a poet, too.

The impulse to versify the Starr Report or President Clinton's videotaped testimony or Monica Lewinsky's taped table talk seized many writers in 1998 and '99. *Harper's* published Daniel Radosh's "Ode to Monica," consisting entirely of descriptions of her voice gleaned from daily newspapers in one month (Sample: "Rapid-fire ramblings, more Buffy than Bacall / Vulnerable, sympathetic, honest, small / Much younger than her 24 years / Heartbreakingly sad, pathetic, near tears / Smarter and more strident than expected / Not that of a Valley Girl bubble head / Dumb, Valley Girl, starstruck, adolescent, little girl, teeny-bopper.") In *The New Yorker*, Rick Moody constructed a verse collage ("She wanted to have sexual intercourse with him at least once / Call me but love and I'll be new baptized / She told me I looked fat in the dress"), while John Updike, in "Country Music," sang of the girl in her "little black beret" who entranced the president and "led that creep astray." Monica Lewinsky disclosed that she had quoted *Romeo and Juliet* in a personal ad intended as an encrypted Valentine's Day appeal to her unnamed lover—a poignant detail. Bill Clinton turned to poetry in his most fulsome apology of the year, on December 11, quoting from Edward Fitzgerald's translation of *The Rubaiyat* of *Omar Khayyam* ("The moving finger writes; and having writ, / Moves on"). Maureen Dowd, impersonating the president in one of her columns, brings up the volume of *Leaves of Grass* that the commander in chief had given the intern. "We'll always have Whitman," Dowd has him saying. *Song of Myself* may not unseat *Casablanca* as the model for heartbreak romance. But you never know. It's gaining. As Ben in *Felicity* exclaims, "Whitman rocks."

It has reached the point that a hard-nosed journalist can with a straight face declare—as Jim Adams does in *Esquire* (April 1999)—that poetry is the "next great nation-sweeping pop-cultural revolution" that "will follow the manly phenomena of cigars and steaks and martinis and leased luxury cars."

What accounts for the boom in poetry? The "leaves of grass-roots" populism goes back to Maya Angelou's inaugural ode in 1993 and the emergence, around the same time, of poetry slams and a vital "downtown" poetry scene. The university symposia continue, but these days there will also be festivals of cowboy balladeers, slammers, rappers, singing poets, railroad and hobo poets, stand-up improvisatory poets, and others—not to mention the free-versifiers, cutting-edge experimentalists, workshop veterans, and even traditional rhymesters who read their work in crowded smoky bars and chic cafés, some of which have the feel of speakeasies. New York residents have long grown used to waitpersons in fashionable restaurants who are actors in disguise. Now they may be poets as well. A friend and I were brunching recently at a Greenwich Village macrobiotic joint. When the French toast with warm fruit and soy links arrived, the waitress, overhearing our conversation, burst out, "Do you love poetry, too?" She went on to tell us that she had always loved poetry but that "it used to be a private thing. Now it feels more like a movement. Less scholastic and more visceral. More a part of my life." A few blocks away, at a Bleecker Street café, the guitarist in the rock band on his break approached the table where five poetry

MFA candidates and their professor were discussing poetry. The guitarist said he'd just read a book by Rimbaud—he couldn't recall the title, because "it was in a different language, like French"—and asked if he could join the workshop.

The aim of *The Best American Poetry* remains the greatest diversity consistent with the highest quality, with each year's edition serving as either a complement to or a corrective of any and all previous editions. The guest editor of this year's volume has had as lively a public career as any of his predecessors. Always outspoken, Robert Bly was a founder, in 1966, of American Writers Against the Vietnam War. He also fought against literary provincialism. He had discovered international modernism during a sojourn in Norway in the late 1950s. Upon his return to the United States he championed important European and South American poets (Neruda, Vallejo, Tranströmer, Machado), then all but unknown. Bly introduced a generation of poets to the possibilities of Surrealism—what he called "leaping poetry"—and the value of storytelling and myth in a laconic American idiom. His prose poems—"The Hockey Poem," for instance—gave that form a new legitimacy and currency. His charismatic readings were events. Bly might wear a primitive mask or accompany himself on a lyrelike instrument or otherwise violate decorum to strategic effect. No one present will soon forget the three lectures he delivered at Bennington College in January 1996. He would read us the poem he had written upon waking that morning, would lecture on the "reptilian" consciousness concealed in the layers of the human mind, and would coach us on "the bodily implications of the seven holy vowels."

With *Morning Poems* (1997), which struck me as his best volume in many years, Bly turned a corner. These "little adventures / In morning longing" address classic poetic subjects (childhood, the seasons, death, and heaven) in a way that capitalizes fully on the pun in the book's title. These are morning poems, full of the delight and mystery of waking in a new day, and they also do their share of mourning, elegizing the deceased and capturing "the moment of sorrow before creation." As I worked with Bly on *The Best American Poetry 1999*, I was struck by the range of his attentiveness—more than fifty magazines are represented here—and by his sustained commitment to a vision of poetry that he has done much to define. He has never lost the intense passion of allegiance to his favorite poets and to an "explosive" style, as he has termed it, in which "the power of the image comes forward as a form of thought."

The year this book commemorates was one of critical controversy. Of the several that spring to mind I would dwell for a moment on the case of Araki Yasusada: the poems purportedly written by a Japanese postal worker in Hiroshima who lost much of his family in the atomic blast of August 6, 1945. Putative translations of some of the poems, and of prose taken from the poet's posthumously unearthed notebooks, appeared to great acclaim in *American Poetry Review* three years ago and were later revealed to be a hoax, the handiwork of a poet named Kent Johnson, a professor at Highland Community College in Freeport, Illinois. *Doubled Flowering: From the Notebooks of Araki Yasusada*, containing the poems and some of the critical debate surrounding them (Roof Books, 1998), has extended this flamboyant, provocative, and incontrovertibly brilliant hoax.

It was not difficult to grasp why Johnson's complex creation incited tremendous passion. The hoaxer had, after all, masqueraded as a survivor of Hiroshima. Some thought this was in questionable taste or even, in the words of one offended magazine editor, a "criminal" act, a fabrication and a counterfeit exploitative of the victims of the first atomic bomb. Others were outraged by what they discerned as either racism or "white man's rage" in the writer's appropriation or imitation of Asian motifs. To his defenders the Yasusada poems and the whole elaborate apparatus of documents and inventions put into practice a clutch of crucial postmodernist notions and advanced critical theories. The hoax builds on Fernando Pessoa's example of inventing heteronyms and their poems; it put the "death of the author" hypothesis to an unexpected use in this constructed voice from beyond the grave. Was it a morally indefensible gesture or a daring avant-garde act in a jaded age that had given up on avant-garde ideals? Much depends on whether the value of the poems is textual and not dependent on information about the author or his method of work. One possible lesson of the hoax was stated by British writer Herbert Read in reference to Australia's Ern Malley poetry hoax in 1944. In the realm of ethics the ends rarely justify the means, Read observed. In the realm of art they always do.

This anthology series itself ignited controversy in 1998. In making the selections for *The Best of the Best American Poetry 1988–1997*, which was published last year, Harold Bloom chose none from the volume edited by Adrienne Rich in 1996. *Boston Review*, which a year earlier had given wide coverage to the Yasusada hoax, devoted a major portion of one issue to Bloom's essay and a major portion of the next issue to the responses it provoked from Marjorie Perloff, Rita Dove, Mark Doty, Thylias Moss, David Mura, J. D. McClatchy, Kevin Young, Donald Revell, Reginald Shepherd, Suzanne Gardinier, Ann Lauterbach, Carol Muske, and Sven Birkerts. I was sometimes asked to participate in or moderate debates centering on this battle of the books. Were these debates—hot-tempered and shrill as some were—a good thing, all in all? Was this controversy one more thing that you could defend on the grounds that it stimulated interest in poetry? I suppose I took some satisfaction in knowing that *The Best American Poetry* had served as the site for a clash of armies. Still, I couldn't help reflecting that this battlefield, like all others, was created with trees and grass and birds in mind and not dead soldiers.

2000

"Now I know how poems feel"

At the Poetry International Festival in Rotterdam in June 1999, a symposium of poets, critics, and editors convened to discuss the state of the art in our various nations. Orhan Koçak of Turkey summed up one familiar complaint: "hypertrophy of supply, atrophy of demand." Several delegates mentioned the decline of good, disinterested, practical criticism. "The best critics are the poets themselves," Poland's Adriana Szymanska said, but Jonas Ellerström, the Swedish publisher, countered that most poet-critics preach to the converted, and the group debated whether critics should or should not be poets themselves. Have poetry readings made as great an impact elsewhere as in North America? Yes, as became clear when Gus Ferguson (South Africa), coining a sort of retroactive neologism along the lines of "snail mail," spoke of "page poetry" to distinguish it from the recited kind. Ferguson warned about the "therapy culture" invading poetry. Al Creighton (Guyana) sounded a more enthusiastic note, dwelling on performance poetry, the influence of reggae music, the use of Creole rhythms and speech, and the "integration of the popular and the literary" in Caribbean verse. Most of the participants agreed that public interest in poetry has grown considerably over the last decade. Christoph Buchwald (Germany) pointed to the popularity of poetry anthologies, Alex Susanna (Spain) to the success of poetry festivals, Marc Reugebrink (Holland) to civic-minded initiatives that put lines of verse on buildings and trucks, Joachim Sartorius (Germany) to poets whose rapport with audiences disproves the charge that poetry is hopelessly elitist and exclusionary.

After three such three-hour sessions, the group crystallized an issue full of paradox that agitated all. The United States was not alone in witnessing a resurgence of poetry. Yet so many manifestations of the poetry boom deserved no laurels on their merits. What did we make of the extraordinary flowering of bad poetry so evident in so many places? In short, is bad poetry bad or good for poetry? Does it devalue the art, lower expectations, diminish the public's capacity to embrace the real thing when it comes along? Or is it a sign that poetry is thriving though not necessarily in ways calculated to win the approval of academies? Michael Schmidt, the poet who heads Britain's Carcanet Press, declared unequivocally that bad poetry is bad for poetry, because it cannot but "coarsen taste and sensibility." Jack Shoemaker, the respected publisher of Counterpoint Press in Washington, D.C., quoted Ezra Pound's dictum that every bad poem you read requires a remedy of six good ones to undo the damage. As Jack's American colleague at the conference, I found it easy to understand and sympathize with this point of view. Who would defend sloppy, sentimental, foolish, demagogic, hackneyed, or self-ingratiating verse? We who love poetry dislike it when it fails to meet our expectations. Inevitably, most poems will disappoint readers spoiled by "To His Coy Mistress," "Tintern Abbey," or "Crossing Brooklyn Ferry."

The series editor of *The Best American Poetry* can hardly wish to speak up for mediocre verse or worse. Still, I can't help thinking that the rapid proliferation of poems in unexpected quarters (bus and subway placards, highway billboards, TV sitcoms and commercials) and unusual forms (competitive slams) from unconventional bards (rock-and-roll troubadours, rap artists) argues for the vitality of poetry today. Doesn't poetry belong as much in bars and breweries as in classrooms and libraries? And if the bad poems declaimed at such venues outnumber the good, is that not true of all venues? Rather than feel threatened, mightn't we borrow or steal what is useful and new and adapt it as we will, discarding what we judge to be meretricious?

The hip-hop performance poems of the slam (dunk) generation have influenced not only rap singers but also mainstream poets. At a reading at the KGB Bar in New York's East Village in November 1999, Craig Arnold demonstrated a surprising continuity between the formal requirements of traditional well-wrought verse and the slam poet's performance techniques. Arnold read "Hot," a rigorously formal poem, in couplets, from the 1998 edition of this anthology. He had memorized the poem, as an actor would memorize a soliloquy, and he performed it gesturally, as if the bar were an impromptu theater. It was exhilarating, a different pleasure, not necessarily superior to the pleasure of reading the poem on the page but a pleasure assuredly all the same.

Of course, there are distinctions to be made. We constantly (and by "we" I mean not only the editors of *The Best American Poetry* but readers everywhere) sort out the good from the bad, the best from the better, though this is quite a complicated process as our opinions change all the time. We also separate poems from other forms of writing that look like poems. Both poems and song lyrics are in verse, but poems are written to be read and songs are written to be sung or played, and there is little to be gained in obscuring this fundamental difference. I admire the lyrics of, say, Johnny Mercer or Lorenz Hart as much as anyone but feel no need to claim them for the dominion of poetry.[1] At the same time, I don't complain when *Rolling Stone* examines rock-and-roll lyrics as one would examine poems, for to do so implicitly pays a compliment to poetry as the criterion art, the art by which others ask to be tested. I am less happy with the stubborn notion that poetry is pitiable, a "money-losing proposition," a "perennial stepchild of publishing," and I dislike the sneer of condescension with which the purist treats any poet or poetry impresario who becomes popular or successfully popularizes others. Sometimes I suspect that the critic who deplores the *best* in the title of this series on the grounds that it is putatively elitist secretly resents the fact that the books are popular, have an audience, and have successfully brought poetry to the people instead of keeping it locked up in a museum case.

Poetry's invasion of space formerly verse-free continues apace. When the star of MTV's *Daria* signs up to read for residents of the Better Days Retirement House, she chooses Allen Ginsberg's "Howl," which is a little like reading aloud the opening of Camus's *The Stranger* to one's mother in a hospital bed ("Mother died today," that book begins). Ginsberg's famous battle cry for the Beats echoed in the mind of novelist Gary Krist, who contributed an op-ed column to the *New York Times* on the best minds of his generation, "who hollow-eyed and caffeine-charged sat up surfing the number-choked screens,

---

1. Nothing resembling consensus exists on this point. Eleanor Wilner chooses Hart's lyric for the immortal Rodgers and Hart standard "The Lady Is a Tramp" as her "poetic first-love," while hard-nosed critic Christopher Ricks conducts seminars on Bob Dylan, bringing Keats, Hopkins, and Eliot to bear on the subject.

whispering the bone-cold litany of Amazon, Cisco, AOL." Who says business and poetry are incompatible? Not Wallace Stevens, who opined that "Money is a form of poetry," demurring however from suggesting that the inverse was true. John Barr, the head of an investment banking firm specializing in public utilities, published *Grace*, an epic poem in loose hexameters, with Story Line Press in 1999. In "Street Life," Andrew Serwer's daily online column, the *Fortune* magazine writer reported that the CEO and founder of e-academy.com had written a poem entitled "Metaphysics, Microsoft, and Me" in the waiting room outside Bill Gates's office. The anagrams of "AOL Time Warner, Inc.," which an unidentified Serwer correspondent contributed after the merger of the two firms, had an avant-garde edge: "I'm a clarinet owner. / Now air-mail center. / Rectilinear woman. / New alarm in erotic. / Win oriental cream."

Margaret Edson's *Wit*, which makes generous use of John Donne's "Holy Sonnets," won the 1999 Pulitzer Prize in drama. The play, about a Donne scholar's losing battle with cancer, makes metaphysical analogies and cunning conceits. "Now I know how poems feel," says the play's heroine regarding her initial days in the hospital, when she is tested, analyzed, critiqued. Eight chemotherapy sessions are like eight "strophes." The protagonist of David Hirson's *Wrong Mountain*, which deserved a better fate than its mixed reviews and short run on Broadway, is a poet consumed from within by the worms of bitterness, resentment, and envy. He suffers from a condition that many of his real-life counterparts know all too well; he has gone, as John Lahr wrote in *The New Yorker*, "from inspiration to publication without circulation." The poets Hirson quotes include W. H. Auden and John Ashbery. Auden's poetry also figures in Tom Bogdan's dance piece, *Tell Me the Truth about Love*, while Tom Stoppard's new play, *The Invention of Love*, focuses on the life, love, and verse of A. E. Housman.

In this presidential election year, David McCullough, Harry Truman's biographer, told columnist Maureen Dowd that the electorate would do well to quiz candidates for the Oval Office on their favorite poem and on the best speech they have ever heard. In January, when Bill Parcells retired as head coach of the New York Jets, he recited a somewhat obscure poem entitled "The Guy in the Glass" by Dale Wimbrow (1934): "You may fool the whole world down the pathway of life / And get pats on the back as you pass, / But your final reward will be heartaches and tears / If you've cheated the man in the glass." The *New York Post* printed the poem in full. During the terrific Super Bowl game between the Rams and Titans on the last Sunday in that month, a stylish black-and-white commercial for Monster.com, the online employment

service, showed a variety of people and children reciting the opening and clos-
ing lines of Robert Frost's "The Road Not Taken." A few months later, a TV
commercial for AIG, the insurance behemoth, quoted a meaty chunk of "The
Love Song of J. Alfred Prufrock" to warn against the pitfalls of risk-averse
behavior.

Poetry has become newsworthy. When Random House and the University
of Pittsburgh Press fought over the rights to Billy Collins's poems, the *New
York Times* covered the controversy on its front page (below the fold). When two
publishers vie for a poet's work, I suppose it does merit front-page treatment.
On the other hand, a spate of lifestyle articles demonstrated either that "all
bad poetry springs from genuine feeling" (Oscar Wilde) or that value judg-
ments are sometimes beside the point. On the same day in February 2000
the *Times* printed verse from a twice-monthly retirees' writing workshop in
Galveston, Texas, while *USA Today* broke the story of the three Seattle poets
("a grad student, a new mother, and a modern dancer who works as a barista,
or espresso bartender") who collaborate on spontaneous poems as a novelty act
at coffee bars. *The New Republic* weighed in that week with the story of a high
school basketball legend whose life went to pieces. The article concludes with
the player's rap poem ("Father, you put me here / Please show me some sign /
Shed some light on this life, especially mine / Confused and scared since the
age of nine / You got that white chalk now draw me a white line"). Certainly an
element of self-parody enters into some of the promotional activities involving
poetry and its uses as therapy, entertainment, and self-expression. The British
proved they could be as silly as we when Andrew Motion, who succeeded Ted
Hughes as England's poet laureate, agreed to write a poem for a Herefordshire
lavatory wall. The project has a name: "Poems on the Throne." Motion said he
hoped people would resist "the urge to make puns on my name." At the Poetry
Olympics held at the Brooklyn Brewery in November 1999, the NYU team
received extra points for saying "who cares" when asked to identify Britain's
current poet laureate.

Speaking of indignities, poor Robert Lowell. I have long felt that the correc-
tions column in a newspaper is an underrated pleasure. The June 1999 issue of
Harper's called attention to a classic of the genre, which, with the logic of a pun,
had to do with the documented popularity of poetry writing at correctional fa-
cilities. Editor Ron Offen of the always lively magazine *Free Lunch* announced
his "sad duty to report that a poem in our special section of prisoner poetry
in our last issue" had been plagiarized from a section of Robert Lowell's "My
Last Afternoon with Uncle Devereux Winslow" in *Life Studies*. The kicker: "To

add insult to injury, I asked the plagiarist for revisions of Lowell's lines on two separate occasions."[2]

The Best American Poetry may disturb the universe of purists or pessimists, for it is testament to the belief that good poetry may be distinguished from bad or merely "competent" verse—and that poetry of intelligence and ambition, sophistication and passion, wit and pathos, can be published to the profit of all. Each year a different guest editor, herself or himself a distinguished poet, makes the selections, thus ensuring that there will be a certain amount of desirable discontinuity from year to year. Rita Dove, the guest editor of this volume, was a natural choice. Born in Akron, Ohio, in 1952, the daughter of a research chemist, she came to the fore in 1987, the year she won the Pulitzer Prize for her book *Thomas and Beulah*. At the time, she was only the second African American poet to be thus honored. Beginning in 1993 she served for two years as U.S. poet laureate, preceding Robert Hass and Robert Pinsky at that post. All three have been activists, determined to raise the national consciousness of poetry, and it was Rita Dove who virtually redefined the office to this end. She has written verse drama (*The Darker Face of the Earth*, an adaptation of *Oedipus Rex* set on a cotton plantation in the South) that has been performed in the United States as well as in England. Her own poems set store by their clarity; she refuses to make a fetish of difficulty. And at the same time that Dove has committed herself to bring poetry to the people, she has also, in assembling this anthology, invoked high standards of excellence in evaluating the many hundreds of poems that begged for our attention. More than forty magazines yielded poems for this volume; more than twice as many were considered and admired.

The greatest diversity consistent with the highest quality remains the goal of this series. In *The Best American Poetry 2000* we have rhymed verse as well as prose poems, poems consisting of both prose and verse, a villanelle, a double sestina, a truncated pantoum, poems that do the work of apology, elegy, salutation, and homage, narrative poems, a variation on an abecedarium. The first poem in the book (arranged, as always, in alphabetical order) begins with a tragic scene, a rape and murder; the last poem ends with the daffodils shooting

---

2. The editor of *Free Lunch* has plenty of company. It is has come to our attention that Jacqueline Dash's poem, "Me Again," chosen for *The Best American Poetry 1996* from *In Time*, a journal of poems from a women's prison, was apparently copied almost verbatim from Pablo Neruda's "Me Again," admirably translated by Ben Belitt, in Neruda's *Five Decades, 1925–1970* (Grove Press, 1974). We regret the error and enthusiastically direct our readers to the true source.

out of the earth in spring and the snow covering all in winter. Between the two, the poets address subjects ranging from jazz to botany, the American family in the eyes of an au pair girl from France, the English literary canon, Mary Todd Lincoln, Henry Clay, the painter Pissarro, postfeminism, semiotics, semantics, fathers and mothers, the Vietnam War, love, work, and death. We mark the arrival of the new millennium with a special feature, "The Best American Poetry of the Twentieth Century," for which the current and previous guest editors of this series were asked to nominate their favorite American poems.

Against expectation ours has turned out to be a period favorable to the poetic imagination. The proliferation of webzines and websites receptive to poetry suggests the compatibility of the ancient art of verse with leading-edge technology. (According to Lycos, poetry was that search engine's eighth most popular "search term" in 1999 behind Pokémon and *Star Wars* but ahead of tattoos, golf, Jennifer Lopez, pregnancy, guns, and Las Vegas.) Poems can be posted for the public to read within hours of their composition, and the knowledge of this possibility may spur the writer to write more poems, or different ones. Like poetry readings and slams, then, the Internet can be construed as a threat to "page poetry." Yet I would not so quickly write off the pleasures of the tangible book, hardcover or paperbound, which you can take with you anywhere, which you can annotate as you peruse, and which shall in time occupy its destined place on the shelf where you keep a record of your history as a reader.

——— 2001 ———

"Everybody else was analog and Nietzsche was digital"

A curious thing has happened. While American poetry continues to flourish, this has occurred in an inverse relationship to the prestige of high culture as traditionally understood and measured. High culture has taken a beating. At regular intervals journalists announce the demise of the "public intellectual." Stories circulate about dysfunctional English departments (Duke, Columbia). Outrageous hoaxes bamboozle the faculty's talking heads, whose peculiar patois and preference for theory over practice provoke savage indignation in some corners and satirical merriment in others. A respected professor at a major university told me that the only thing unifying the warring factions in the English department there is "a common hatred of literature." In the twenty-fifth anniversary issue of *Parnassus: Poetry in Review*, the journal's editor, Herbert Leibowitz, laments the dwindling of "the audience for belletristic criticism—as opposed to the jargon-riddled academic variety." Leibowitz regards poetry criticism as an art, an art in crisis because of bad academic habits on the one side and the timidity of poets on the other ("the reluctance of poets to write honestly about their peers"). He surely has a point and is in an excellent position to know. Yet what is equally noteworthy is that the virus afflicting poetry criticism has left poetry itself uncontaminated.

In the last decade the audience for poetry has grown; enthusiasts keep turning up in unexpected quarters, and the media are paying attention and magnifying the effect. Poetry readings, fairs, and festivals have proliferated. National Poetry Month has raised April sales (without lowering those of other months). Initiatives ranging from "Poetry in Motion" posters in buses and subways to Robert Pinsky's "Favorite Poem Project" have helped bridge the gap between poetry and the ordinary citizen. The radio voice of Garrison Keillor reads a Shakespeare sonnet in drive time, and on the *NewsHour* with Jim Lehrer that evening a retired Air Force officer tearfully recites Yusef Komunyakaa's poem about the Vietnam Memorial, "Facing It." Are these things causes or effects of the poetry boom? Probably both, as are Bill Moyers's PBS documentaries, *The Language of Life* in 1995 and *Fooling with Words* four years later. Moyers's efforts have met with highbrow derision, but that is true of many efforts to popularize a cultural phenomenon with a reputation for difficulty. One critic has called Moyers the "Bob Costas of the American poetry world," the "ultimate fan," which may be one of those left-handed insults that conveys something of a compliment despite its contemptuous intent. Quarrel with Moyers's taste and judgment all you want; there is no denying the value of his TV programs in building an audience for the poets lucky enough to get air time.

More popular than ever, creative writing programs have helped make up for the neglect of literature elsewhere on campus. It is an argument for the health and vitality of contemporary poetry that so many talented young people devote two graduate years to its study despite knowing that "there's nothing in it" (as Ezra Pound's Mr. Nixon warns in "Hugh Selwyn Mauberley"). It is, of course, easy to mock the locutions of the universal workshop, though I find not only humor but also a sort of charm in them. One day in a workshop last February, somebody said, "I had issues with the pronouns in the other lines, too," and off went that little mental explosion that tells me a poem, in the case at hand a villanelle, was on the way. I called it "Issues":

> I had issues with the pronouns in the other lines, too.
> It started to kick in for me with the part about the war.
> Did what I say make sense to you?
>
> I wondered whether what "you" said was true,
> Which may have been what "you" were aiming for.
> I had issues with the pronouns in the other lines, too,

And not just the pronouns but the branding ("Mountain Dew").
I like the imagery especially "in the forest there's a door."
Did what I say make sense to you?

But I wish the poem didn't dodge the repercussions of "Jew,"
And I winced at "hoodlums and whores."
I had issues with the pronouns in the other lines, too,

But in the other lines what comes through is you,
What I hear is your voice, a kind of quiet roar.
Did what I say make sense to you?

Don't get me wrong, I like the second-person point of view,
But it raises issues. Like what. Like gender.
I had issues with the pronouns in the other lines, too.
Did what I say make sense to you?

As one who teaches workshops I recognize their structural defects. I some-
times wonder how certain great poems would fare in a workshop. I can well
imagine that after the class got through with Wallace Stevens's "Of Mere
Being" the amazing last line of that poem ("The bird's fire-fangled feathers
dangle down") would not survive intact. Nevertheless I'm convinced that the
study of poetry, fiction, and serious literature depends more and more on cre-
ative writing programs on all levels. This may seem a supreme irony to anyone
who remembers the combination of condescension and skepticism that En-
glish department regulars directed at their creative writing colleagues twen-
ty-five years ago. Creative writing is sometimes denigrated on the grounds
that few workshop-trained poets will go on to write poems as great as those of
Wallace Stevens, who studied law, not poetry or creative writing. But few poets,
workshop-trained or not, will write great poems. Our mission is to nurture tal-
ent and keep the love of poetry at its liveliest, most receptive, and most creative
state, and if the student publishes few poems but becomes an avid reader we
will have done a job that others have relinquished.

A good deal of creativity has gone into the teaching of creative writing.
Low-residency MFA programs, such as the ones at Bennington in Vermont and
Warren Wilson in North Carolina, which convene for short periods twice a year
and do the rest of their work by correspondence between student and faculty,
enable grown-ups with families, spouses, jobs to give sustained attention to

their writing. Given demographic trends, it is easy to predict the growth of such programs as well as the spread of summer writing conferences lasting anywhere from a weekend to several weeks in picturesque locales. Already the ambitious initiate of whatever age can take instruction at Bread Loaf, Sewanee, Squaw Valley, Saratoga Springs, Provincetown, the Napa Valley, and numerous other desirable sites, including the European cities of Prague, St. Petersburg, Dublin, and Paris. I can hear the retort of the scandalized idealist who associates the creative writing workshop with the decline of civilization: "In the baby boom generation, no one will retire. Instead they will write poetry." Well, maybe, and all of us must sometimes secretly fear that everyone wants to write the stuff and no one wants to read it. At such moments we would do well to recall that Seamus Heaney's verse translation of *Beowulf*, not your conventional potboiler, sold two hundred thousand copies in hardcover and occupied a slot on the *New York Times* best-seller list for ten weeks last year. Readers do exist, more than you might have thought. The trick remains how to reach them.

On the "everyone wants to write the stuff" front, New York Mets' reliever Turk Wendell, he of the animal-claw necklace, writes it ("Life Is Like a Baseball"). Monica Lewinsky moved to New York and came out in favor of "The Love Song of J. Alfred Prufrock," which she imitated (loosely) in a Valentine's Day poem commissioned by a British magazine. Paul McCartney is writing a book of poems. Julia Roberts has written poems for years and particularly loves Neruda. Ashley Judd, who memorizes a poem for each birthday, chose Wordsworth's "Daffodils" last year and is leaning this year toward Rudyard Kipling's "If." Kim Cattrall, who plays Samantha in the HBO hit *Sex and the City*, likes reciting Rupert Brooke while her boyfriend plays the string bass. Helen Hunt says she is "obsessed with Rilke." Her favorite "is an untitled one in a collection that Robert Bly translated," which she proceeds to paraphrase: "I want to unfold because where I am closed I am false; I want to be with those who know secret things or else alone." David Duchovny, who studied with Harold Bloom at Yale, has never made a secret of his admiration of John Ashbery's "Self-Portrait in a Convex Mirror." Asked by a *Movieline* reporter to analyze the poem, the star of *The X-Files* gladly obliged: "It's about a man who's painting his self-portrait, but he's looking into a mirrored ball, and the closer he gets to it, the further away his image seems to be going." Duchovny then drew a parallel between the poem's posture and his own style as an actor: "I'm trying to protect what I advertise. That's my stance on any kind of self-expression."

I have a cultivated interest in the unusual ways people use poetry in their public or professional lives. Last year did not disappoint. Dona Nieto, a California performance artist who calls herself La Tigresa, bared her breasts and declaimed "goddess-based, nude Buddhist poetry" at timber sites north of San Francisco to protest the logging of ancient redwoods. Anonymous cyber-scribes adapted familiar lines by Longfellow, Poe, Whitman, Ogden Nash, Joyce Kilmer, Alfred Noyes, and Clement Moore to satirize the post-election stalemate in Florida. Salman Rushdie in the *Guardian* versified the electoral results in the manner of Dr. Seuss. (Aided by "the great Legal Grinches, / and Grinches of Spin," the Grinch exhorts his cohorts to "Grinch / This election!") On TV, a contestant on *Who Wants To Be a Millionaire?* won $2,000 for shrewdly relying on the audience to know that the number of lines in a couplet is two. In one episode of the TV drama *Bull*, a ruthless tycoon quotes Yeats ("But one man loved the pilgrim soul in you, / And loved the sorrows of your changing face"), while in a different scene a bearded financial shark tosses off an allusion to Edna St. Vincent Millay ("My candle burns at both ends") to ridicule a Smith College alumna during a game of "humiliate the host." In HBO's hit series *The Sopranos*, Anthony Jr. listens as his older sister, Meadow, a Columbia freshman, knowingly explains the symbolism of the snow in Frost's "Stopping by Woods on a Snowy Evening." "That's fucked up," her brother replies. If you get a chance to see Melissa Palmer's movie *Wildflowers*, you'll note that the guest editor of this year's *The Best American Poetry* plays a poet named Robert who gets to recite his poems and court the character played by Daryl Hannah.

After the Los Angeles Lakers won the NBA championship in June 2000, Shaquille O'Neal quoted Shakespeare's "Some are born great, some achieve greatness, and some have greatness thrust upon them" at a victory celebration. While the Lakers' center left it unstated how these lines applied to the situation at hand, none could deny their grandeur. A few months earlier coach Phil Jackson had made a gift to O'Neal of Nietzsche's selected writings. "He was ahead of his time," O'Neal said. "Everybody else was analog and Nietzsche was digital." As the stock market swooned, Charles Millard, the former head of Internet investment banking at Prudential Securities, turned to Keats to explain the inevitable discrepancy between actual and anticipated profits. "Heard melodies are sweet, but those unheard / Are sweeter," Millard quoted, adding: "That reality is now hitting people right in the face." When a jail sentence smacked Dana C. Giacchetto, formerly Leonardo di Caprio's financial advisor, he took up poetry. Sample line: "At the nexus where art meets justice, a chemistry dancing like angels sweating with peace, yet, halfway asleep." Now there's a man who could benefit from a poetry writing workshop.

The Best American Poetry is committed to the notion that excellence in poetry is not incompatible with the pursuit of a general audience. Robert Hass, who succeeded Rita Dove as U.S. poet laureate and now succeeds her as the guest editor of this anthology, has dedicated himself to this project with the zeal that has characterized his efforts over the years to promote literature and literacy on the widest level. As poet laureate Hass, a distinguished critic as well as poet, wrote a weekly column ("The Poet's Choice") for the *Washington Post* recommending poets and poems in language direct and unaffected, adjectives not usually associated with critical writing; he would print the poem in full and comment briefly on it, careful not to let the commentary eclipse the verse. (When, after 212 weeks without a break, Hass gave up the column in January 2000, it was, fittingly, Dove who took it over.) Back when I asked him if he would undertake the editing of this anthology, Hass described himself as the "Raskolnikov of deadlines." After working with him on *The Best American Poetry 2001*, I am able to attest to the justness of this epithet—and to say that working with him was worth stretching any number of deadlines.

In the year 2000, as the IPO market crashed and one dot-com after another went under, some of us cherished all the more such "old economy" staples as books and magazines. Yet for poetry, which resists being turned into a commodity, the Internet remains a particularly friendly and potentially transformative space, offering a revolutionary means and method of publication and distribution. You can't help but admire the energy and enterprise informing electronic magazines and literary websites such as *Slate, Salon,* the *Cortland Review, Poetry Daily, Nerve, Pif, Can We Have Our Ball Back?* (its title evidently a nod to the Beatles' movie *A Hard Day's Night*), and most improbably two different zines named after Arthur Rimbaud's poem, "Le Bateau ivre" ("The Drunken Boat"). Both are brand-new. The one edited by Ravi Shankar (not the sitar player but a recent graduate of Columbia's MFA program) is called *Drunken Boat* (at www.drunkenboat.com) in contrast to the one edited by Rebecca Seiferle, a contributor to *The Best American Poetry 2000,* which is *The Drunken Boat* (at www.thedrunkenboat.com). It was in general an excellent year for Rimbaud, whose "Une Saison en enfer" ("A Season in Hell") is quoted by Marcia Gay Harden playing Lee Krasner in Ed Harris's movie *Pollock.*

This is the fifteenth volume in *The Best American Poetry* series. I have had many occasions to celebrate the accomplishments or recognitions of the fifteen guest editors to date. But until this year I have not had to mourn the passing of one of them. A. R. Ammons died on February 25, 2001, a week after his seventy-fifth birthday. "We're gliding: we," he wrote in the concluding lines of *Sphere: The Form of a Motion,*

are gliding: ask the astronomer, if you don't believe it: but
motion as a summary of time and space is gliding us: for a while
we may ride such forces: then, we must get off: but now this

beats any amusement park by the shore: our Ferris wheel, what a
wheel: our roller coaster, what mathematics of stoop and climb: sew
my name on my cap: we're clear: we're ourselves: we're sailing.

The day now marks a boundary

The year 2001, like the year 1984 before it, arrived with heavy baggage. Both had existed (and do exist) outside of time as visions of tomorrow. Readers of George Orwell's *1984* may forever associate that eponymous year with the dystopian universe of Big Brother, the Thought Police, Newspeak, Hate Week, and Doublethink. Stanley Kubrick's 1968 movie *2001: A Space Odyssey* made the millennial turn seem synonymous with the sci-fi future, antiseptic but threatening, where spaceships dance to the *Blue Danube* and astronauts lose at chess to a sinister computer with a mind of his own. But where the actual 1984 came and went, a year vastly less memorable than Orwell's totalitarian prophecy ("a boot stamping on a human face—forever"), the year 2001 transcended the advance aura that Kubrick's amazing juxtapositions had produced.

The destruction of the World Trade Center and the massacre of the innocents was not only a catastrophic event in American history. It was also a revolutionary event in American consciousness. The day now marks a boundary: what was written, said, done, created before September 11 is seen as vitally different in kind and status from what since. It's as if history has returned to ground zero. The chalkboard has been wiped clean. But with the fresh start comes a new responsibility. Variants on Theodor Adorno's famous rhetorical question—How can there be poetry after Auschwitz?—were asked often against the backdrop of the blaze and rubble of downtown Manhattan. The spontaneous answer given by many was: How can there be not?

In their shock and grief, people everywhere looked instinctively to poetry. One poem more than any other was cited, recited, copied, e-mailed after the terrorist attacks on New York and Washington. W. H. Auden's "September 1, 1939" circulated electronically like one of the messages that "the Just / Exchange" in the form of "ironic points of light" (to borrow phrases from the poem's final stanza). Auden, a recent arrival in New York, wrote this ninety-nine-line poem on the day Germany invaded Poland and World War II commenced. The poem begins in "one of the dives / On Fifty-second Street" in Manhattan. Much of it seemed freshly apposite now: the "blind" skyscrapers in their verticality proclaiming the might of "Collective Man"; the commuters, addicted to their "habit-forming pain," occupying solitary stools in bars. The first stanza ends with lines that resonated eerily in the noxious air:

> The unmentionable odour of death
> Offends the September night.

Friends and strangers in chat rooms quoted this complex, difficult, ambiguous poem. So did sobersided CEOs. Newspapers coast to coast, from the *San Francisco Chronicle* to the *Baltimore Sun* and the *Boston Globe*, reprinted the entire poem on their editorial pages. It was e-mailed to me at least five or six times, and I enjoyed the benefit of a correspondence with the poet and Williams College professor Lawrence Raab about the poem's rich but vexing penultimate stanza, which poets and critics have argued about for years:

> All I have is a voice
> To undo the folded lie,
> The romantic lie in the brain
> Of the sensual man-in-the-street
> And the lie of Authority
> Whose buildings grope the sky:
> There is no such thing as the State
> And no one exists alone;
> Hunger allows no choice
> To the citizen or the police;
> We must love one another or die.

Was one example of the "folded lie" a newspaper? Did the colon after "sky" imply that the lines that follow are types of lies? The most vexing question had to do with the stirring last line. Was it mendacious to the precise extent of its rhetorical effectiveness? In what sense can love prevent or save us from death? Of what use was such a declaration—or was it a piety—in the face of Nazi military aggression? (As Maggie Nelson wrote in a different context, "you can't hug / a Nazi and hope / he'll change.") Auden, who took self-criticism seriously, so despised the stanza's final line (for some the poem's best) that he changed it to the unsatisfactory "We must love one another and die," and later decided to disown the poem altogether. "It may be a good poem, but I shouldn't have written it," he maddeningly said.

The wild popularity of "September 1, 1939" was that rare thing, a phenomenon that had erupted on its own without orchestration or hype. The poem's apparent ubiquitousness was analyzed almost as much as the poem itself. "It is the poem for our present pain," Eric McHenry wrote in *Slate*, in part because it seems "weirdly prescient" and in part because of its mood of doubt. Sven Birkerts in the *New York Observer* called it Auden's "most sustaining" poem, an example of poetry as "the reverse of the terrorist act." I would add that Auden's poems—not only the one in question but also such others as the elegies for Yeats and Freud, "Caliban to the Audience" and "In Praise of Limestone"—attract readers who value the poetry of civilized discourse and believe in the power (and the limits) of human reason. For Dana Gioia in *The Dark Horse*, the immediate resort to "September 1, 1939" helped make the case for poetry's civic, public, and ceremonial uses. It reinforced, in his view, the priority of "expressive power" over "stylistic novelty" as a poetic virtue. On the other hand, Daniel Swift, reporting on the American scene for the London *Times Literary Supplement*, was not alone in recoiling from the "trace of something almost nasty in this poem," either a whiff of self-congratulation (Swift) or evidence of "incurable dishonesty" (Auden). Unsurprisingly there was as little agreement on the cultural meaning of the phenomenon as on Auden's unorthodox use of colons and unusual adjectives ("clever hopes," "the conservative dark") within the poem itself, thus demonstrating that poetry as an essence precedes and supersedes the contestation of meanings and interpretations to which it gives rise.

"September 1, 1939" was not the only poem to hit the bulletin boards. On *Slate* Robert Pinsky recommended Marianne Moore's "What Are Years?" as well as poems by Edwin Arlington Robinson, Czesław Miłosz, and Carlos Drummond de Andrade. Alicia Ostriker on the MobyLives website picked the same sublime Moore poem plus works by Yehuda Amichai, Stephen Dunn, and Hayden Carruth. The hunger for poetry and the need for elegy resulted in impromptu or hastily arranged public readings with overflow audiences. On an October evening, more than a thousand people crowded into the Great Hall of Cooper Union in New York to listen to poems "in a time of crisis." Newspapers ran numerous articles on poetry's power to heal and console. Anthologies comprising "responses" to September 11 or poems from "post-9/11 New York" were planned. For the poets themselves, all this attention was not an unmixed blessing: the pressure to write poetry equal to an occasion can sometimes lead to an outpouring of mediocre verse. A bad poem is no less bad for the nobility of the sentiments expressed. "You can't approach something like this frontally in a poem—at least I can't," Billy Collins told a reporter. "It will knock you over. It is like walking into a big wave. You will fall on your bathing suit." Collins clarified his position in *USA Today.* "It's not that poets should feel a responsibility to write about this calamity," he wrote. "All poetry stands in opposition to it. Pick a poem, any poem, from an anthology and you will see that it is speaking for life and therefore against the taking of it. A poem about mushrooms or about a walk with the dog is a more eloquent response to September 11 than a poem that announces that wholesale murder is a bad thing."

No stranger to this anthology series—his work was chosen by guest editors Charles Simic, Louise Glück, James Tate, John Hollander, Robert Bly, Rita Dove, and Robert Hass—Collins was tapped in June to succeed Stanley Kunitz as the nation's poet laureate. "We should notice that there is no prose laureate," Collins said at the news conference, "although they will probably be lobbying for equal treatment." The new laureate's populist appeal is beyond dispute. You can coerce people to do many things, but buying books of poetry isn't one of them, and people buy Collins's books in quantity. He has real readers, readers who aren't themselves poets, who obey the pleasure principle when it comes to buying a book. But the *New York Times* in a front-page story anointed him as "the most popular poet in America" and he has since become a magnet for envy. In an application of what I've come to call the Resentment Index, I realized that Collins had truly made it when I began hearing his work disparaged regularly. The fall 2001 issue of the *Melic Review* contained no fewer than four poems satirizing the poet's geniality and embrace of the quotidian. (One dastardly fellow's parody would, however, "direct you to that lampshade / made of human skin and tell you / to concentrate on the warm glow // and forget the camps." Even bad taste should have its bounds.) Collins's poetry was too easy for *The New Republic*'s Adam Kirsch, who complained: "Nothing in his work suggests that he even acknowledges that there is a place for difficulty in poetry. His amused indifference resembles wisdom only as death resembles life." Of course, nothing in Collins's work denies a place for difficulty in poetry, or implies even remotely that he aims to dictate what other poets do, but that's not the point. The inflated simile ("as death resembles life") suggests the vehemence of the critical antagonism that a poet of humor and warmth, ease of manner, and above all a large audience can expect. Well, critics will be critics, though the public at any rate clearly counts neither Auden's difficulty nor Collins's accessibility as strikes against them.

Adoring fans weighed in elsewhere. The magazine *Whetstone* published an unconventional marriage proposal in the form of Lisa Beyer's poem "Billy Collins's Wife," the title indicating what she, author or speaker, would yearn to be if there were a vacancy. ("For this to be so / Billy Collins's wife / must die a death / both quick and painless, / but especially quick, / so I will still be 32 / and possessing whatever / loveliness I ever possessed, / for what else can I offer such a man?") As the war against the Taliban and al-Qaeda heated up, the novelist Ira Levin suggested that our poet laureate ("what's he there for?") be asked to propose code names superior to the widely deplored monikers Operation Infinite Justice and Operation Enduring Freedom. Collins soon disclosed "Poetry 180," his own sensible idea for how best to use his office. He crafted a list of 180 poems, one for each school day, in an initiative to get poetry read aloud daily in high schools.

It was poetry as usual for much of 2001, "usual" in this case signifying its opposite, and "poetry" here referring to anything that claims to be such. There were reminders that April, National Poetry Month, begins with a day that honors the fool. In Alaska, the arts council launched a poetry initiative that prompted the Borealis Brewery to print poems on beer bottles. A more dubious second result was that 250,000 Alaskans, or 40 percent of the state's population, opened their telephone, water, and sewer bills in April and found a poem stuffed inside as filler. (It was Tom Sexton's "Beluga," about the white whales that swim Cook Inlet off Anchorage each June.) Later in the year, Oprah Winfrey demonstrated that her awesome marketing muscle applies as well to poetry as to fiction. When she praised the poems of Mattie Stepanek, an eleven-year-old boy who suffers from muscular dystrophy, she did so rhapsodically, with a tear in her eye. "If ever I had a book to recommend, it's Mattie's. If ever you were going to buy a book, I recommend it; this is the one, my friends." (Mattie had previously stolen the show at the Jerry Lewis Labor Day telethon.) *Journey Through Heartsongs* promptly sold 170,000 copies, and a second Stepanek book soon joined it on the best-seller list. An anthology of Jacqueline Kennedy Onassis's *Best-Loved Poems*, also a best seller, included several of Jackie's youthful efforts in verse, which did nothing to diminish her iconic status.

On June 11, Timothy McVeigh, facing execution for his part in the Oklahoma City bombing of 1995, chose to make no personal statement but instead referred the media to W. E. Henley's "Invictus," a nineteenth-century warhorse that schoolchildren used to have to memorize. "My head is bloody, but unbowed," wrote Henley, who suffered from tuberculosis and had to have a leg amputated. The poem concludes: "I am the master of my fate; / I am the captain of my soul." I went on a local New York TV newscast to infer that McVeigh remained unrepentant. In the green room before going on the air I could see the monitor and how I was billed. No name; it just said "execution poem expert." Meanwhile a *New York Times* reporter asked poets and critics which poem they would choose to help them "embrace the moment" if they "knew the hour of their death in advance." The seventeenth-century poet George Herbert won. Molly Peacock, Robert Pinsky, and Helen Vendler all picked a Herbert poem, though Dana Gioia held out for Tennyson's "In Memoriam" and Richard Howard for Wallace Stevens's "Sunday Morning."

Since its inception as an annual anthology in 1988, *The Best American Poetry* has acted on the notion that the best way to honor excellence in poetry is to enlist a poet of distinguished stature to do the choosing each year. By this means each volume in the series necessarily differs from its predecessor, and the books taken together chronicle the taste of some of our leading poets. Robert Creeley, this year's editor, is esteemed among fellow poets across the board irrespective of affiliation and orientation. Donald Hall, who made the selections for *The Best American Poetry 1989*, once said that the poet of his generation he admires most is Creeley: "I love his marching ear and the delicacy of his nuances." Like others I first fell under Creeley's spell when I read Donald M. Allen's *New American Poetry* in the 1960s. His poems had an easy intimacy; they advanced their propositions tersely and without pomp ("If you never do anything for anyone else / you are spared the tragedy of human relation- // ships"). Creeley is universally admired for his skill at line breaks. Trying to explain his magic, I wrote: "it / doesn't matter / what he says / what matters is / the way the lines / break at just / the right moment / each time / uncanny." Few editors in my experience have been as decisive and confident as Creeley. It was, as I could have predicted, a pleasure to work with him.

———

Clever former English majors continue their subversive campaign to insinuate poetry into popular culture, sometimes to brilliant or hilarious effect. In the movie *The Anniversary Party*, Kevin Kline, playing an actor, quotes the conclusion of Matthew Arnold's "Dover Beach" ("Ah, love, let us be true to one another . . .") as a toast to the reconciling Hollywood couple whose anniversary it is. It is solemn, deadpan, and completely inappropriate—quite as if the movie had taken to heart Anthony Hecht's parody of Arnold ("The Dover Bitch") and realized how odd it must feel to be "addressed / As sort of a mournful cosmic last resort." Poetry is a great prophetic warning of "ignorant armies" on contested beachheads, but it is also the lampooning of that impulse. And it is passion, or an adolescent's intense longing for it: the plot of the French thriller *With a Friend Like Harry* hinges on a poem the hero wrote for his lycée literary magazine, which his curious "friend" still knows by heart though many years have elapsed.

Poetry, the art of articulation, renders us inarticulate when it comes to defining it. Purists would discourage us from considering poetry as an essence, or as anything apart from individual texts, but there remains the obdurate attachment to poetry as not only an art but a quality in itself that a person or a work of art may have. "I'm not just a suit," said Gerald Levin when he retired as CEO of AOL Time Warner last December. "I want the poetry back in my life." Similarly, Woody Allen, accounting for his preference in movie westerns, said, "*Shane* achieves a certain poetry that *High Noon* doesn't." It is tempting to conclude that poetry remains the touchstone art, a supreme signifier, emblematic of soulful artistry, the adventurous imagination, and the creative spirit.

"How many people have to die before you can become president?"

On being named the official state poet of Vermont in 1961, Robert Frost acknowledged the honor in epigrammatic verse. "Breathes there a bard who isn't moved, / When he finds his verse is understood," he wrote, declaring himself happy to have won the approval of his old "neighborhood." Twenty-five years later, the position that had dowdily been called Poetry Consultant to the Library of Congress—a position that Frost had held when Dwight Eisenhower was president—received a major upgrade in title. It was to be the same nondescript job (give a reading, give a speech, answer the mail) but henceforth the person would be called U.S. Poet Laureate. The change of name proved prophetic, for the post soon acquired a high prestige. Joseph Brodsky kicked off his tenure in 1992 with a memorable speech proposing that poetry books be sold at checkout counters and provided in hotel rooms beside the Bibles and phone directories. Robert Pinsky, who served three one-year terms as laureate, became a familiar face reading poems on the PBS evening news, and he remains a cultural celebrity. (In 2002, he turned up in Jane Leavy's acclaimed biography of Dodger southpaw Sandy Koufax and in an episode of *The Simpsons*, where he gives a reading at a campus coffee shop surrounded by frat boys who have the name of Japanese haiku poet Bashō—mentioned in the opening lines of Pinsky's poem "Impossible to Tell"—painted on their bare chests.) Billy Collins, the current poet laureate, addressed a special joint session of Congress in Lower Manhattan a day before the first anniversary of September 11, 2001. "The Names," the fifty-four-line elegy he read, appeared in its entirety in the *New York Times*. When Collins, whose books are best sellers, paid a recent visit to a grade school, one awestruck pupil inquired about the presidential line of succession: "How many people have to die before you can become president?"

It now seems that most of the states, many cities, and even a number of boroughs have or want to have their own official laureates. The appointments have proliferated. Though with Whitman and Mark Twain as our mainstays we may remain a little leery of titles, ranks, dukes, and airs, we also seem to revel in some of these things, and we put a value on the ceremonial and public uses of poetry that come with the territory. Not all the appointees rise to the occasion with the laconic wit and grace of Robert Frost, but neither had anyone done harm or caused a furor until last year. Within a month of being named the poet laureate of New Jersey, Amiri Baraka took part in the wildly popular Geraldine R. Dodge Poetry Festival in Stanhope, New Jersey. The observances surrounding the first year anniversary of September 11 were still fresh in people's minds when Baraka—the former LeRoi Jones—read "Somebody Blew Up America," a poem he had written about that atrocious day. These lines made listeners gasp: "Who knew the World Trade Center was gonna get bombed / Who told 4,000 Israeli workers at the twin towers / To stay at home that day / Why did Sharon stay away?" An avid Internet user, Baraka had given credence to a paranoid conspiracy theory that had spread with the speed of electronic spam. In actuality, seven Israelis died in the attacks, two on a hijacked plane and the rest in the Twin Towers, in addition to the many American Jews that perished on September 11. But Baraka had not subjected his poem to a fact-checking test. In interviews he thumbed his nose in doggerel and puns: "It's not a bad thing to be attacked by your enemies. It shows, obviously, that you don't need an enema yet."

As only the second poet laureate in New Jersey history, Baraka benefited from a quirk in the legislation that created the position but failed to specify how a laureate may be discharged or removed. Since Governor James McGreevey couldn't fire him and since he wouldn't resign, the New Jersey state legislature moved to abolish the post of poet laureate altogether. Never did a bill pass through committee so swiftly. Did this demonstrate that poetry is the first casualty of any controversy involving it? Or did it show up Baraka as an aging ego-tripper, who would opt to see the laureateship abolished—and other poets thereby punished—sooner than withdraw his anti-Semitic smear? The satirical newspaper *The Onion* refused to lose its sense of humor. A headline in the October 17–23, 2002, issue declared "Nantucket Poet Laureate Refuses to Apologize for Controversial Limerick." That the headline referred the reader to page 3C, where there was no story, seemed part of the point. Satirical wit involves not the letting loose of calumny but the telling of truths that liars deny, euphemisms hide, and platitudes obscure. In a subsequent issue *The Onion* displayed the kind of fearless humor that makes for a badly needed corrective to sentimentality and "correctness" (always a version of sentimentality) in the reception of poetry. The story of a wheelchair-bound author of best-selling inspirational verse ran under the heartless headline "Nation Afraid to Admit 9-Year-Old Disabled Poet Really Bad."

The widespread notice of an incendiary or scandalous poem—and more than one such surfaced last year—made for intense conversation. Liam Rector, in his column in *American Poetry Review*, asked whether we should regard poems as "works of fiction protected from accountable, verifiable reality by their imaginative basis" or as "works of nonfiction, which abide by an infinitely different set of expectations, rules, and accountability"? Good question. And there are others that poets are debating. What are the author's responsibilities? When does poetic speech become public speech that is subject to a truth-telling standard? Just how does one write about a world historical event on the order of 9/11? While there is no set answer to any of these questions, there are honorable ways to respond to the last of them. Several were chosen for *The Best American Poetry 2003*. A number of other poems in this volume bravely address issues of urgent immediacy. It could be that the inflection of this urgency, whether the subject matter be frighteningly near (terrorism in ghastly deed and threat) or merely eternal (the effect of death on the living, the image of a man running), is what distinguishes this year's edition of the anthology. The press of reality affects poets in diverse ways, and for some, the urge to write about events of great moment amounts to a moral imperative. This impulse is as understandable as it is difficult to resist and, when done with intelligence and skill, admirable. It seems to me, however, that something should also be said for the opposite impulse: the reluctance to speak hastily, the refusal to address a subject, any subject, that the writer himself or herself does not wish to address, or feel able to address. Isn't this a dimension of poetic license? The poets' freedom in regard to subject matter includes the freedom of reticence, whether it originates in the belief that the subordination of poetry to politics proves injurious to the former while leaving the latter unscathed, or whether it follows from the conviction that "the deepest feeling always shows itself in silence" (Marianne Moore). Declining an editor's summons for newly minted verse a few weeks after September 11, Richard Wilbur sent this terse response: "The only thing I can say right now is this. There is no excuse for the cold inhumanity of 11 September, and there is no excuse for those Americans, whether of the left or the religious right, who say that we had it corning to us."

Many poets have rediscovered, with exhilaration, a sense of political purpose in the past year. During the feverish days in February 2003 when the United States prepared its military for war with Iraq, thousands of protesting poets registered their indignation in verse. The emergence of poets and artists "trying to recapture their place as catalysts for public debate and dissent" became itself a part of the media story, though by no means as hotly controversial as the phenomenon of "celebrity activists" such as Martin Sheen or Janeane Garofalo. When Laura Bush invited hundreds of American poets to the White House for a symposium on Whitman, Dickinson, and Langston Hughes, a protest initiated by Sam Hamill, the poet and publisher of Copper Canyon Press, made the First Lady think twice, and the event was canceled. (Here was proof, one scribe sourly noted, that "the most effective poetry reading is the one that never happens.") The antiwar poem, a genre moribund since the last helicopter lifted off a Saigon rooftop in 1975, gained a new currency. Thousands of protest poems were produced, published, or posted. Whether the work had any merit seemed to be beside the point, and that is an oddity of the phenomenon. Self-styled poems of conscience make the peculiar demand that we suspend our faculty of critical discrimination. In February 2003 a seven-line poem entitled "The Bombs" by the British dramatist Harold Pinter—who has written superb plays and screenplays—was printed on page one of London's *Independent*. Here is the poem complete: "There are no more words to be said / All we have left are the bombs / Which burst out of our head / All that is left are the bombs / Which suck out the last of our blood / All we have left are the bombs / Which polish the skulls of the dead." Tired language, mixed metaphors, incoherent imagery: whatever it may have done to rally or reflect public opinion in Britain, this is a really terrible piece of writing. It is a melancholy truth that—as Harvey Shapiro's fine new anthology, *Poets of World War II*, reminds us—both the best war poems and the best antiwar poems generally come from the ranks of the soldiers who do the fighting and the reporters who cover them. That said, it is noteworthy and bears repetition that at a time of intense crisis and color-coded alerts, so many of us turn instinctively to poetry not only for inspiration and consolation but also as a form of action and for a sense of community.

Poets and poetry couldn't stay out of the news last year. A poet was nominated and confirmed as the new chairman of the National Endowment for the Arts: the choice of Dana Gioia garnered rare acclaim on all fronts at a divisive time. "This is a moment of marvelous possibility," Gioia told a New Hampshire gathering of state poets shortly after assuming his new post. "You poets laureate may be working on little or no budget, with few or no resources. What you have at your disposal may be merely symbolic. But we poets are masters of using symbols." Gioia launched a major Shakespeare initiative that will subsidize productions of the Bard's works nationwide. The Pentagon chipped in some extra cash to extend the tour to include military bases. Gioia also disclosed plans for a Shakespeare recitation contest, which he hopes will lead to a national competition encouraging the memorization of great poems. The career of a serious poet is evidently not inconsistent with the administrative and strategic demands of running an important government agency or, for that matter, a treasured cultural foundation. Edward Hirsch, whose poem "The Desire Manuscripts" was selected by Yusef Komunyakaa for this year's anthology, took over the presidency of the Guggenheim Foundation in January 2003. At a poetry forum at the New School in New York City, Hirsch was asked to name a formative experience in his becoming a poet. Like others asked this question, Hirsch replied by naming an unsung heroine, in his case Professor Carol Parsons at Grinnell College, who "taught me, in my freshman year, that poetry is an art of making, and not just of self-expression."

"I am all for poets invading all walks of American life," Billy Collins declared, and the invasion shows no signs of letting up. The world of high stakes poker is the latest field to be conquered. James McManus, whose work appeared in the 1991 (Strand) and 1994 (Ammons) volumes in this series, made more than a quarter million dollars playing championship poker a few years ago. McManus commented on "poker lit" and added significantly to it with his new book *Positively Fifth Street*. It speaks to the enhanced celebrity of the poet in American society that you can collect "poet cards" featuring portraits of Donald Hall, Carolyn Kizer, Adrienne Rich, and worthy others (Mille Grazie Press, Santa Barbara, California) or that Tebot Bach, a nonprofit organization in Huntington, California, is producing a Southern California poets swimsuit calendar with Carol Muske-Dukes, David St. John, Charles Harper Webb, and Suzanne Lummis among the pinups: "You've admired their words, now marvel at the sheer beauty of their bodies!"

Christmas came early to *Poetry* magazine with the November 2002 announcement that Ruth Lilly, the heiress of the Lilly pharmaceutical fortune, had left more than $100 million—by some estimates close to $150 million—to the Chicago-based monthly that Harriet Monroe founded in 1912. It was the single biggest bequest ever given to a poetry organization. As a young woman many years ago, Lilly had submitted her poems to the magazine, but the editors had never accepted any, a fact that spurred wags to quip that rejecting her was the best thing *Poetry* ever did—well, maybe second best after publishing "The Love Song of J. Alfred Prufrock" back in 1915. Proving that poetry—the work itself rather than all the stuff around it—is the news that stays new, T. S. Eliot's great poem continues to cast its spell on English majors and creative people across the arts. A television series (*Push, Nevada*) featuring an IRS agent named Prufrock wowed the critics last year, while director Michael Petroni's new movie with Guy Pearce and Helena Bonham Carter derives not only its title (*Till Human Voices Wake Us*) but its imagery (water) and action (a drowning) from the conclusion of "Prufrock," which the movie quotes reverently. Another allusion to Eliot's poem occurs in a recent episode of *Law and Order*. "I have measured out my life with coffee spoons," a perjurous defense attorney says. "For once in my life I dared to eat the peach," he adds, peach in this context serving as shorthand for a sexual tryst with a homicidal femme fatale. Not to be outdone in the homage-to-Eliot sweepstakes, HBO's hit series *Six Feet Under* gives us an amorous couple in bed sharing poetry. The man says the original title of the poem is "He Do the Police in Different Voices," and the woman says she likes that title more than the one the poet settled on: "The Waste Land."

In an age that looks at ostentatious controversy as the next best thing after celebrity, some poets avoid controversy, some court it, and some have it thrust upon them. The newly appointed poet laureate of Canada created a stir when he denounced slam poetry as "crude" and "revolting." The poet laureate of California resigned after admitting he had falsified his resume. Justice J. Michael Eakin of the Pennsylvania Supreme Court, nicknamed the "poetic justice of Pennsylvania," was rebuked for writing a dissenting opinion in seven quatrains and a footnote. The case hinged on whether a lie about the value of an engagement ring invalidated a prenuptial agreement. ("He has also," the *New York Times*'s Adam Liptak, reported, "ruled in rhyme in cases involving animals and car repair companies.") Nothing will stop a book columnist from building a piece on the demonstrably false premise that only poets read poetry and therefore the poets might as well make themselves useful in other ways. At the same time, *poetry* remains the journalist's honorific of choice when the subject is rock 'n' roll, political oratory, the grace of Kobe Bryant driving to the basket, or almost anything other than poetry itself. "Like every muscle car before it, SUVs are big, dangerous and superfluous, but they're also poetry made of metal," writes the *Wall Street Journal*'s David Brooks.

Václav Havel stepped down as president of the Czech Republic, but the tradition of the poet as international diplomat continues. Dominique de Villepin, the French foreign minister who fenced with Colin Powell at the U. N. Security Council last February, is working on a poetry manuscript. In at least one respect, he is like his American counterparts. Asked to recite a poem, he obliges by reading three. In what almost sounds like a paraphrase of an early poem by the late Kenneth Koch ("You Were Wearing"), the young fashion designer Behnaz Sarafpour tells of wanting her fall line to reflect the poetry she is reading: there is an Emily Dickinson suit ("about hope"), a Herman Melville long blue dress ("about creation of art"), and a couple of Lord Byron dresses with poems embroidered on the hems. A perhaps more unexpected lover of verse is William J. Lennox Jr., the superintendent in charge of the military academy at West Point, a three-star general who earned a doctorate in English from Princeton with a dissertation on American war poets. Speaking to a reporter, the general made a point of stressing the educative importance of a poem of bitter disillusionment, such as Wilfred Owen's "Dulce et Decorum Est," written from the Western Front in World War I. "Most cadets romanticize war," he said. "They need these images from war to help them understand. Confronting this romanticism is what education is about."

Yusef Komunyakaa, who has made unforgettable poetry out of his experiences in Vietnam, has brought to the editing of this volume—the seventeenth in the *Best American Poetry* series—an acute sensitivity to the moral temper of the times and a strong attraction to works of seriousness and ambition. He has written that he chose to write poetry "because of the conciseness, the precision, the imagery, and the music in the lines," qualities that he prizes in the works of others. "I like the idea that the meaning of my poetry is not always on the surface and that people may return to the work," he says. "Sometimes I may not like a poem in the first reading, but, when I go back and read it again, there is a growth that has happened within me, and I become a participant rather than just a reader." We hope the poems gathered here reward multiple readings and hasten a similar transformation of the reader into a sort of participant by proxy. Nor are the subjects limited to "World History," "Jihad," and "After Your Death," to cite three titles. There are poems on blues and jazz (a Komunyakaa enthusiasm I share), poems of wit and invention, a prose poem honoring Max Jacob and a verse poem "After Horace." There are poems in unusual forms, poems on themes ranging from film noir and the conventions of the murder mystery to bread, asparagus, and the restaurant business, as well as poems that take big, important concepts—"Beauty," "Success," "The Music of Time," "A History of Color"—and render them in compelling terms and true. Many names familiar to followers of contemporary poetry are here, but it is the newcomers that may most excite the book's editors and readers. In *The Best American Poetry 2003* two poets are represented with their first published poems: George Higgins (born 1956) and Heather Moss (born 1973). One reason this pleases me especially is that it shows there is a democracy at work even during the very nonegalitarian processes of exercising judgments and making critical discriminations. The oldest poet in this year's edition is Ruth Stone (born 1915, and still going strong, coming off a year when she won the National Book Award). The youngest is Anna Ziegler (born 1979, and thus nine years old when this series commenced). Poems were selected from more than forty magazines; many more were consulted and read with pleasure. Every year of working on this series has renewed my appreciation of the work that magazine editors do, usually without much fanfare but with extraordinary generosity of spirit.

In 2003 occurred the centenary of an event that happened almost invisibly at the Statue of Liberty: the presentation of a bronze plaque with Emma Lazarus's immortal words on it to the War Department post commander on Bedloe's Island in May 1903. Lazarus had written her sonnet "The New Colossus" for a fund-raising auction in 1883. It was not recited, nor was Lazarus present, at the ceremony dedicating the Bartholdi statue in New York harbor. Largely forgotten, the poem went unmentioned in the obituaries when Lazarus died a year later, in 1887. At the time people thought of the woman with the torch in her hand as a monument to fraternal Franco-American relations going back to George Washington and the Marquis de Lafayette. The statue honored liberty, the glow of enlightenment, but the full significance of the site and the statue was not realized until Emma Lazarus's lines were engraved in the public memory, and that did not happen overnight, for poetry can take a long time to achieve its full effect. The plaque hung obscurely on an interior wall of the statue's pedestal from 1903 until a popular effort in the 1930s succeeded in making that great symbol synonymous with the "Mother of Exiles," a welcoming refuge for "the wretched refuse" of Europe. The statue in the harbor was there, a lovely sight, but it remained for a poet to articulate its true significance: "Give me your tired, your poor, / Your huddled masses yearning to breathe free." For many of us who fondly recall climbing the stairs of the statue with a beloved parent or with a busload of grade school chums, the famous peroration is so familiar that we may be blinded from noticing its literary excellence. But "The New Colossus" is not as familiar as it once was, and it deserves close study, perhaps in conjunction with another great sonnet occasioned by statuary, Shelley's "Ozymandias." At a moment of global anxiety it is good to consider this vital part of the American Dream as Emma Lazarus expressed it in a poem that made something happen—something as nearly sublime as the promise of liberty and a fair shake to people who had known only despotism and terror and danger and despair.

canons do not remain fixed for long

"Anthologies are, ideally, an essential species of criticism," wrote Randall Jarrell in *Poetry and the Age*. "Nothing expresses and exposes your taste so completely—nothing is your taste so nearly—as that vague final treasury of the *really* best poems that grows in your head all your life." Every reader is perennially compiling, enlarging, and revising such an anthology, which can never be "final" or definitive any more than a published anthology can be or should be exhaustive or complete. Anthologies are selective; they project an editor's taste, but they are also exercises in criticism. Their job is not only to reflect accurately what is out there but also to pick and choose among the possibilities. Whether they set out to reinforce the prevailing taste or to modify it, they sometimes end up doing a bit of both. Anthologies can educate, can recruit new readers, can even create the conditions by which the new poetry may be savored and in time perhaps even understood, it being the usual case that enjoyment precedes understanding. All anthologies perform an evaluative function. Even where the claim is less absolute than in the title of *The Best American Poetry*, anthologies praise their contents. Donald Allen's *New American Poetry, 1945–1960*, the most influential anthology of the 1960s, which introduced a generation of readers to the Beats and Black Mountain, the New York School and the San Francisco Renaissance, may seem to have a neutral, descriptive title. But does anyone doubt that *new* here means *best*? Anthologies single out works worthy of perpetuation and as such they always constitute a prediction, an assertion, and a gamble.

Anthologies have played an even larger part in the education of modern poets than critics have noticed. Take the numerous poetry editions prepared by the long-lived Louis Untermeyer (1885–1977), who attained eminence despite dropping out of high school and working full-time in his father's jewelry business until he was thirty-eight. Untermeyer was a prolific poet and a skillful parodist, but his real talent went into his carefully annotated poetry compilations. Both John Ashbery and A. R. Ammons, guest editors of the 1988 and 1994 editions of *The Best American Poetry*, have spoken of the powerful effect that Untermeyer's anthologies had on them when they were young men. In grade school, Ashbery won a current events contest sponsored by *Time* magazine and received Untermeyer's *Modern American and British Poetry* as a prize. The volume taught him that verse need not rhyme, that the pleasures of Robert Frost and Elinor Wylie were easily had but that the more "baffling" pleasures of Auden and Dylan Thomas ultimately held more charm. It was an Untermeyer anthology, perhaps the same one, that the late A. R. Ammons discovered as a nineteen-year-old sailor on a U.S. Navy destroyer escort in 1945. Reading it felt like a rite of initiation: "I began to imitate those poems then, and I wrote from then on." A generation later, Untermeyer's anthologies were still in circulation. They had a great effect on me in my teens. To his *Concise Treasury of Great Poems* I owe my first acquaintance with Milton, Keats, Yeats, Frost, Eliot. I remember prizing the editor's running comments. He had an eye for the quirky biographical detail. From Untermeyer I learned, for example, that William Cullen Bryant's father, a country doctor in Cummington, Massachusetts, "attempted to reduce his son's abnormally large head by soaking it every morning in a spring of cold water" and that Bryant died in New York City at age eighty-four upon climbing a flight of stairs shortly after dedicating a statue to Mazzini in Central Park.

There are pitfalls in every anthologist's path. Some are more avoidable than others. The editor who includes his or her own work runs a grave risk. In a 1939 revision of an anthology originally compiled in 1922, Untermeyer put in five of his poems and wrote about himself in the third person: "In 1928 he achieved a lifelong desire by acquiring a farm, a trout-stream, and half a mountain of sugar-maples in the Adirondacks, where he lives when he is not traveling and lecturing. He loves to talk and listens with difficulty." About Untermeyer, e. e. cummings wrote scornfully: "mr u will not be missed / who as an anthologist / sold the many on the few / not excluding mr u." (This was a sort of proleptic obituary: Untermeyer outlived cummings by fifteen years.) Similar complaints were voiced against Oscar Williams, the inveterate anthologist whose books introduced the young Ashbery to the new (and in some cases now undeservedly forgotten) poetry of the 1940s. In a generally favorable review, Randall Jarrell pointed out that an Oscar Williams production contained nine of Oscar Williams's poems and five by Thomas Hardy. "It takes a lot of courage to like your own poetry almost twice as well as Hardy's," Jarrell commented.

Some problems are inherent in the structure of any anthology. On what basis were these poems chosen, and not others? What claim can be made for these works? With what practical effect? The first question is the hardest to answer. The recognition of a great or even a very good poem precedes any articulation of reasons for the choice. A true lover of poetry will know it and savor it when the right thing comes along—though sometimes he or she may need the tug that anthologies and critical essays are supposed to provide. My own criteria as a reader begin with an insistent pleasure principle. "Pleasure is by no means an infallible critical guide, but it is the least fallible," W. H. Auden observed. There is fierce competition for the reader's attention, and where impatience may once have expressed itself only after pages, today you can lose your reader in your opening line. A poem must capture the reader before it can do anything else, and to do that it must give pleasure.

An anthology aspiring to represent the best work in the field requires faith and trust: the editor's faith that a serious general audience for poetry does exist; the reader's trust in the editor's judgment. From the start, the governing assumption of *The Best American Poetry* has been that poetry worthy of reading and reading again is being written in such quantity and of such variety that it would be possible for an annual volume showcasing it to live up to the series name. The challenge is to select that work and to present it so attractively that it will connect with readers who have the curiosity and the goodwill but lack the time and the access to the plethora of print and electronic magazines in which the new poetry is appearing.

There are anthologies that organize themselves by region, genre, gender, movement, theme. Some of these beg the question of quality. Enough for a poem to be written about zucchini to warrant its inclusion in a volume of vegetable poems. But with anthologies that do not thus delimit themselves—anthologies that would speak to an American audience generously conceived—we expect that criteria of excellence have been invoked if not necessarily explained and defended. Helen Vendler has written cogently against "historically representative anthologies" in which the aim is the comprehensive coverage of a given era. She noted that the first two volumes of a Library of America anthology devoted to twentieth-century American poetry added up to eighteen hundred pages: "So many feeble poets; so many non-moving poems; so many withered dictions; so many sterile experiments. And so much pretentiousness; so much well-meaning polemic; so much prose masquerading as poetry; so many dubious poetics." An unsympathetic person might say the same about many a poetry anthology, even one fourteen hundred pages shorter. But while I disagree with Vendler's assessment of the two volumes under review, I believe that a contemporary anthology invites ridicule in precisely these harsh terms if it professes to be value-free in the aesthetic sense, or if it subordinates poetry to sociology, ethics, or politics.

As people groan ritually at puns, even the cleverest ones, some guest editors of *The Best American Poetry* have balked at the word *Best* in the title. This may reflect a culture-wide distrust of hierarchy and anything smacking of elitism. Still, it is noteworthy that editors of similarly titled anthologies of essays and short stories seem to feel little of the compunction that the poets bring to the table. Open a book of the year's best stories or essays and you will not encounter an expression of misgivings about the enterprise. Whatever else it intimates, the poets' self-consciousness about the word "best" is an acknowledgment that there is nothing scientific about the process of selection, that reading and judging are subjective and partial, and that some terms are best used with invisible quote marks around them. Nevertheless, there is something to be said for taking a stand, making a claim. Year after year *The Best American Poetry* recognizes that competition often accompanies the creation of art, which is made by persons of complexity and ambition who compete not just with peers but with ancestors as well. To be chosen by an admired poet for inclusion in a book that has "best" in its title must feel like an honor to all but the most jaded, and it means something because the ratio of poems considered to poems chosen is so extraordinarily one-sided. Thousands of poems are read multiple times in order to arrive in the end at a choice seventy-five. "No poet or novelist wishes he were the only one who ever lived," Auden has written, "but most of them wish they were the only one alive, and quite a number fondly believe their wish has been granted." There's a lot of truth to that. But *The Best American Poetry* also shows that poets who may have little in common, who come from different regions or movements and espouse clashing ideas or traditions, can coexist to each other's benefit in a single book.

In a relativist universe, where to be nonjudgmental is sometimes held up as a great virtue, there may appear to be something quixotic about an enterprise labeling itself "the best." The use of the word may be written off as an example of American hyperbole. But it seems to me that this anthology series is also an attempt to redefine "best" and render it credible by conceiving of each year's edition as initially a clean slate and ultimately an overhaul of the previous year's book. Each year a distinguished poet of national reputation does the selecting. The idea is not to fix a canon but to suggest possible orderings: to acknowledge that canons do not remain fixed for long, and to act on the notion by shifting perspective annually in surveying new poetry in print or electronic circulation. Each volume in the series records the encounters of one poet with the contents of many magazines in one twelve-month stretch. Place the volumes side by side on a shelf, and they also chronicle the taste and judgment of some of our leading poets.

Neal Bowers feels that there is something in the atmosphere of universities that jeopardizes our ability to separate good from bad, best from second-rate, and that the dependence of poets on academic institutions is therefore at the root of this problem as well as others. "To say that something is good or bad, beautiful or ugly, worthwhile or a waste of time is to 'privilege' one thing over another," he writes in the summer 2003 issue of *Sewanee Review.* "Anyone who makes such distinctions had best keep his views to himself else he risk being tarred as a monocultural, nondiverse reactionary." Bowers, a recently retired university poet, was continuing a critique of the creative writing profession that he began a year earlier in the July 2002 issue of *Poetry.* "Students emerge from graduate writing programs with an understanding of poetry as something manufactured for the exclusive inspection of their peers," he laments. Bowers likes employing metaphors drawn from economics. There has been, he charges, an assault on standards with the result that "the undifferentiated supply [of poems] far outstrips demand." The university has a monopoly on poetry: "With a rate of success unmatched even by Wal-Mart, the university has driven almost all independent operations into ruin, controlling the production and distribution of poetry and regulating its worth."

The voicing of objections to the institution of the creative writing workshop is not exactly a groundbreaking event, but Bowers's essays are so obviously heartfelt that they seem worthy of consideration. Though there may be elements of caricature in his description of how writing programs work, he would do us a service nonetheless if his essays provoked students and teachers in MFA programs to mount a defense of what they do. When Bowers argues that writing programs mark "the transformation of poetry from a passion to a professional undertaking," he makes me want to challenge the dichotomy. Why can't poetry be both a passion and a serious professional undertaking? Aren't our best teachers those who inspire and sustain the young poet's passion for the art—and do so in a professional manner? Bowers attacks the notion that the only career path available to an MFA student is as a teacher in an MFA program. "Because poetry matters in and of itself and not as an aspect of employment, [people] can make time to write, whatever job they do to earn an income," he says. I agree. *Go forth into the world* is good advice. But Bowers's plea for "poetry professors" to rise up as one and renounce the "concept and common practices of the poetry workshop" is as absurd as it is unlikely to happen. To ditch the workshop is to ditch the writing programs' raison d'être as well as their most popular and effective structural innovation. Bowers reasons that instructors can reinvent themselves as old-fashioned literature professors. "Because their English-department colleagues have abandoned literature in favor of literary theory, poet-professors could seize the opportunity to restore the reading and discussion of literature." But writing programs do require their students to study the literature of the past; they can perhaps do it better, or more rigorously, but they do it, they keep literature alive as a subject of study and as an indispensable concomitant of the creative imagination. A bad workshop is going to be as painful and wasteful as any failed pedagogical endeavor. A good workshop can change your life.

Poets have recently given us new versions of Dante, *Beowulf, Sir Gawain and the Green Knight*, Aeschylus's *Oresteia*, Sophocles's *Philoctetes*. And poets, whether they come from the ranks of writing programs or not, will contrive new ways to perpetuate the many traditions, movements, schools, and personalities that are conjoined in modern poetry. It is important that poetry have a base in the university. It is even better to find poetry in shops, cafés, bars, and clubs; spilling into the street; entering people's lives. This anthology series is predicated on the profoundly democratic notion that there are readers out there, in some cases far from museums and libraries, who are desperate for poetry to be in their lives.

———————

Lyn Hejinian and I met at a poetry conference in Copenhagen in August 2001. Our Danish hosts had hoped that she and I would come to blows on a panel at which it was thought that she would represent the Language School and I the New York School in a debate. Instead we began a dialogue that lasted months, took different forms on different continents, and gave us both, I think, much pleasure. I knew in what great esteem she is held by the many young writers who consider her autobiographical sequence, *My Life*, to be a modern masterpiece. "I saw a juxtaposition / It happened to be between an acrobat and a sense of obligation / Pure poetry," she wrote in "Nights," a group of "night thoughts intended as an homage to Scheherazade," which Robert Hass picked for the 2001 edition of this anthology. I felt that this respected and admired writer with her eye for poetry, pure and otherwise, would make an excellent choice to serve as guest editor of this year's *The Best American Poetry*, and I am glad I enlisted her. The Berkeley-based Hejinian threw herself into the task, reading as generously as she could while remaining true to her aesthetic convictions and her commitment to poetry of a high experimental bent. One reason the volume is exciting is its strong accent on youth. But we also rejoice in the fact that a book containing a poem written by a high school senior (Marc Jaffee, now an undergraduate at Vassar) also contains a poem by Carl Rakosi, the Objectivist poet who celebrated his hundredth birthday in 2003. Above all, there is satisfaction in knowing that the contents of this book represent a coherent vision of what one important poet considers to be American poetry at its most vital, daring, and aggressively new.

In 2003 Louise Glück became the nation's twelfth poet laureate, succeeding Billy Collins in the post. Glück, who edited the 1993 volume in this series, has made few pronouncements in her new official capacity. She has given us a new poem instead: the beautiful *October*, published as a chapbook by Sarabande. It is a quiet and intimate poem and it has nothing political in it, yet it seems to have a public dimension, speaking to all who can identify themselves with that time of year when the light begins to fail and yellow leaves or none or few still cling to branches. At the end of the poem we reach *the* ultimate condition of lyric poetry: the lonely self contemplating the naked universe.

> From within the earth's
> bitter disgrace, coldness and barrenness
>
> my friend the moon rises:
> she is beautiful tonight, but when is she not beautiful?

The publication of such a poem—or of seventy-five of them, gleaned from a year's intense reading—creates the place where the private consciousness of the creative mind intersects with its most generous impulses toward community.

the creative writing workshop
[and] the fall of civilization

There are many reasons for the surge in prestige and popularity that American poetry has enjoyed, but surely some credit has to go to the initiatives of poets and other interested parties. Some of these projects involve a media event or program; just about all of them end in an anthology. Catherine Bowman had the idea of covering poetry for NPR's *All Things Considered*, and the book of poems culled from her radio reports, *Word of Mouth* (Vintage, 2003), makes a lively case for the art. The "Favorite Poem Project" launched by Robert Pinsky when he was U.S. poet laureate—in which ordinary citizens recite favorite poems for an archive and sometimes for a live TV audience—has generated two anthologies, most recently *An Invitation to Poetry* (edited by Pinsky, Maggie Dietz, and Rosemarie Ellis; W. W. Norton, 2004). Billy Collins, when he was poet laureate, campaigned to get the high school teachers of America to read a poem aloud each school day, and selected an academic year's worth for *Poetry 180* (Random House, 2003) and an equal amount for *180 More* (Random House, 2005). The success of the *Poetry Daily* website led Diane Boller, Don Selby, and Chryss Yost to organize *Poetry Daily* on the model of a calendar (Sourcebooks, 2003). The calendar is also a driving principle for Garrison Keillor, whose *Good Poems* (Penguin, 2003) collects work he has read on his *Writer's Almanac* show, which airs on public radio five (in some areas seven) days a week.

The last several years have given us, in addition, high-quality anthologies organized around themes (*Isn't It Romantic*, eds. Aimee Kelley and Brett Fletcher Lauer; Verse Press, 2004); genres (*Blues Poems*, ed. Kevin Young; Everyman's Library, 2003), and historical periods (*Poets of the Civil War*, ed. J. D. McClatchy; Library of America, 2005). The number and variety of these (and yet other) anthologies make a double point about the poetry-reading public: it is larger than critics grant though smaller than many of us would like it to be; it reflects a period of eclectic taste rather than one dominated by an orthodoxy, as American poetry fifty years ago seemed dominated by the T. S. Eliot-inflected New Criticism.

As a rule, poetry anthologies receive even less critical attention than individual collections, but Keillor's *Good Poems* had a curious fate. Two reviews of the book appeared in the April 2004 issue of *Poetry*, the venerable Chicago-based magazine that inherited more than $100 million from pharmaceutical heiress Ruth Lilly in 2002. Both reviews were written by respected poets. NEA Chairman Dana Gioia wrote a courtly piece, employing a familiar book-reviewing strategy: begin with advance doubts (anticipation of "good poems, but probably not good enough"), acknowledge relief (pleasure in Keillor's "high spirits and determination to have fun, even when talking about poetry"), and progress to appreciation of the finished product. Gioia complimented the anthologist on "the intelligent inclusion of neglected writers" and praised Keillor for his *Writer's Almanac* show. Keillor "has probably done more to expand the audience of American poetry over the past ten years than all the learned journals of New England," Gioia wrote. He "has engaged a mass audience without either pretension or condescension."

When you turned the page to August Kleinzahler's critique of Keillor's anthology, your eyebrows had to go up. It was less a review than an attack on the Minnesota-based creator of public radio's long-running *Prairie Home Companion*, a weekly variety show with skits, songs, a monologue from the host, and occasionally poems from a visiting poet. Kleinzahler called the *Companion* "comfort food for the philistines, a contemporary, bittersweet equivalent to the *Lawrence Welk Show* of years past." That was gentle compared with his treatment of the "execrable" *Writer's Almanac*. Keillor has "appalling" taste, Kleinzahler wrote. Any good poems in *Good Poems* probably got there because a staffer slipped them in; a "superannuated former MFA from the Iowa Workshop would be my guess." (Though to my knowledge, there is no such thing as a "former MFA"—the degree is something you have for life and is not shed upon graduation—Kleinzahler's point was clear enough.) Keillor should be "burned," or perhaps merely locked up "in a Quonset hut" until he renounces his daily radio poem. In brief, Kleinzahler avoids the sound of Keillor's "treacly baritone" voice just as he avoids "sneezing, choking, rheumy-eyed passengers" on the streetcars of San Francisco.

When he gets around to talking about *Good Poems*, Kleinzahler articulates the anti-populist argument that underscores his contempt for Keillor. In every age, Kleinzahler says, there are "very, very few" poets whose work "will matter down the road." The effort to spread the word and enlarge the audience for poetry—an effort that Keillor enthusiastically participates in—is a bad thing, because reading poetry often results in writing poetry, and most poetry is bad, and bad poetry is bad for you and bad for the art. Kleinzahler is vehement to the point of hyperbole: "Poetry not only isn't *good* for you, *bad* poetry has been shown to cause lymphomas." Keillor's brand of "boosterism" may sell books and spur more poets to write, but it amounts to a form of "merchandising" that is itself "the problem, not the solution."

The anti-populist argument has its attractions. Many of us love poetry as a high art and regard our commitment to it as a vocation. And high art has its hierarchies, its idea of greatness or genius as something that few possess. As a poet you are continually inventing yourself by eliminating some models and electing others, defining your idea of what constitutes "good" and "bad." And if your aesthetic commitment is extreme, or your revolt against a prevalent style is desperate, you may come to regard bad poetry as almost a moral offense. This is one reason we need criticism: it can help us to understand those crucial terms, "good" and "bad," whose meaning seems almost always in flux.

But anti-populist arguments tend by their nature to be defeatist and somewhat self-fulfilling. The dubious assumption is that if, against great odds, a poet or a poem wins some public acceptance, the work must be bad to the precise degree that it has become popular, and not merely bad but contagious. Yet Gresham's Law—the economic doctrine that says that bad money shall drive out good—does not really apply here. No one hated bad poetry more genuinely and with greater feeling than Kenneth Koch. But as a teacher of children and nursing home residents, and as the author of a genial "Art of Poetry," he suspended the natural arrogance of the avant-garde artist. Poems, he says, are "esthetecologically harmless and psychodegradable / And never would they choke the spirits of the world. For a poem only affects us / And 'exists,' really, if it is worth it, and there can't be too many of those." It may turn out that the enlargement of poetry's community of readers depends on a toleration not of bad poems but of other people's ideas of what constitutes a good poem. Moreover, if few poets in any given era will achieve the fame of a Keats or Whitman, it does not follow that the appreciation of poetry—great, good, and otherwise—is an activity for only a chosen few. Nor does it follow that the several originals among us are, in Kleinzahler's words, "drowning in the waste products spewing from graduate writing programs." Kleinzahler feels that the great talent of the nineteenth century went into the novel and that poetry's competition today is even stiffer and more diverse. He names "movies, television, MTV, advertising, rock 'n' roll, and the Internet." I don't buy it. The amazing thing is that despite all discouragement, significant numbers of brilliant young people today are drawn to poetry. Many are willing to make pecuniary sacrifices in support of their literary habit; more each year enroll in the degree-granting writing programs at which Kleinzahler sneers. Consider the growth of low-residency programs, in which faculty and students convene for ten days twice a year and do the rest of the work by correspondence. In 1994 when the Bennington Writing Seminars began, it was the fourth such program in the country; today there are more than two dozen. Sure, there are those who associate the rise of the creative writing workshop with the fall of civilization, but it remains a pedagogic structure of unusual popularity, and a talented instructor will know how to use its conventions to promote literary knowledge, judgment, and skill. As for Kleinzahler's contention that "American poetry is now an international joke," I think rather the opposite is true. But then he offers no evidence to support his position, while the evidence I could present to support mine—books published, copies sold, translations made, international conferences devoted to American poetry—Kleinzahler might dismiss out of hand.

The surplus contempt in Kleinzahler's piece—the anger so out of proportion with what had nominally occasioned it, and in such sharp contrast to the mild-mannered article that preceded it—generated a lasting wonder. It was as if one of the two reviews of *Good Poems* was in favor of civilization and the other in favor of its discontents; as if one spoke with the adjudicating voice of the ego, while the other let loose with the rebellious rant of the id. That the two pieces when juxtaposed failed to produce any ground for good-faith discussion seemed perfectly in accordance with the corrosive level of political discourse in 2004. "We campaign in poetry but govern in prose," former New York governor Mario Cuomo has said. But there was no poetry in last year's campaign rhetoric. I noted also that *Good Poems*, the modest and inoffensive title Keillor had chosen for his anthology, had not proved any more resistant to hostile comment than an anthology whose title dares to make greater claims for its contents.

The idea of running two reviews of the same book is one innovation that

Christian Wiman has made since becoming editor of *Poetry*. There remains a problem with the criticism of poetry in America—too little of it is valuable—and Wiman is trying to do something about that. He is trying to create dialogue and exchange, and though not all attempts succeed, sometimes the failure is so spectacular that we're still talking about it months later. He seems to be discouraging easy pats on the back and encouraging people to go public with their peeves. And he prints letters arguing with the critics. All this has made *Poetry* a livelier, more compelling magazine than it had been. But it is also worrisome that the back of the magazine—the part devoted to criticism—has grown steadily. More voices, more pages, do not equal greater clarification. It is sometimes said with heavy tones of lamentation that in this day and age everyone's a poet. The criticism in *Poetry* implies that on the contrary everyone's a critic. And criticism is too often the sound of a gripe and the taste of sour grapes expressed with all the sensitivity and thoughtfulness of a midnight blogger.

Wiman spruced up the October 2004 issue by asking a band of poets to register their antagonisms and talk about them. In his editorial note Wiman says in passing that only the rare student will have the requisite "acuity and temerity" to challenge professors and anthologies by suggesting that "'Tintern Abbey' would be better without its last fifty lines." As Wiman notes, every editor has the right to be wrong, especially when the goal is to stimulate debate. But as one who cannot read "Tintern Abbey" aloud without tears at the end, and is all too familiar with college students' aversion to Wordsworth (though their own first-person-singular work may owe more to Wordsworth than to any of the other Romantic poets), I must rise to the defense of the poem as Wordsworth designed it. The last stanza, the poem's second climax, culminates in Wordsworth's moving prayer for his sister, Dorothy, as lovely a tribute in verse as ever brother penned for sister. But it is the passage just before the prayer itself—a single serpentine sentence spun out across sixteen lines of Miltonic blank verse—that is astonishing. It is like an equation in which either "nature" or "the mind," or the latter as a reflection of the former, triumphantly opposes evil and woe. The poet speaks

> Knowing that Nature never did betray
> The heart that loved her; 'tis her privilege
> Through all the years of this our life, to lead
> From joy to joy: for she can so inform
> The mind that is within us, so impress
> With quietness and beauty, and so feed

With lofty thoughts, that neither evil tongues,
Rash judgments, nor the sneers of selfish men,
Nor greetings where no kindness is, nor all
The dreary intercourse of daily life,
Shall e'er prevail against us, or disturb
Our cheerful faith, that all which we behold
Is full of blessings.

The passage is like a bridge across an abyss, with the reader progressing from joy across the chasm of low spite to a place of safety and blessing. It is a passage that you might quote for its smart use of line breaks. It expresses the "cheerful faith" that is the heart and soul of Romanticism—the conviction that the mind is superior to what it beholds and that imagination can redeem bitter experience. There then follows the "Therefore"—the prayer for Dorothy—that completes and unifies the poem, just as the address to the infant son completes and unifies Coleridge's "Frost at Midnight," the model for "Tintern Abbey." The "conversation poem" that Coleridge initiated and Wordsworth perfected has a form, and "Tintern Abbey" needs its last forty-nine lines to fulfill the demands of that form. Lop off the last stanza and you risk grave peril to the whole; as with the butchering of a cherry tree's branch, it could cause the death of the tree.

Defender that I am of "good poems" and advocate of great ones such as "Tintern Abbey" and "Frost at Midnight," I know it is up to readers present and readers future to decide whether *The Best American Poetry 2005* lives up to its name. Like its predecessors in a series now eighteen volumes strong, it reflects the best efforts of a guest editor, himself a distinguished poet, who went through the periodicals of 2004 looking for seventy-five poems that merit and reward our attention. Paul Muldoon, who made the selections, brings a unique transatlantic perspective to the task. Born in Belfast, an eminent figure in contemporary Irish and British poetry, Muldoon has lived in the United States since 1987 and is an American citizen. He holds a titled professorship at Princeton University, and when he began reading for this anthology, he had just completed a five-year stint as the Oxford Professor of Poetry, which is pretty much the highest academic appointment you can get in the United Kingdom. He had also recently won the 2003 Pulitzer Prize for *Moy Sand and Gravel*. I have admired his poetry since discovering *Why Brownlee Left* (1980) and *Quoof* (1983) when I worked on a *Newsweek* piece in 1986 about the extravagance of literary talent to have emerged in Northern Ireland, site of the "troubles." Muldoon's handling of a form like the sestina—"The Last Time

I Saw Chris" in *The Best American Poetry 2004*, for example—or an ad hoc form like the errata slip ("For 'ludic' read 'lucid'"), his expert use of rhyme and off-rhyme, make his work exemplary. He is crafty, skillful, able to reconcile rival traditions, and I believe his take on American poetry will prove valuable for many years to come. Like Paul, I am proud of this year's book, and delighted to have had this chance to collaborate with him.

The late Thom Gunn observed that it may make sense to have movements and sects, with or without manifestos, when there is a "monolithic central tradition," as was true when Eliot and the New Critics ruled the roost. But when there is no central tradition, as now, the "divide and conquer" mentality—with poets "separating ourselves into armed camps"—seems less defensible. No volume in this series has been the exclusive province of a sect. While each editor will naturally represent most amply the poems he or she feels most in sympathy with, all have worked to transcend a narrow bias and labored to bring to the fore talents unlike their own. Lyn Hejinian, guest editor of *The Best American Poetry 2004*, when asked about the omission of certain redoubtable poets known to be her friends, said pointedly that she did not want to represent somebody with less than that person's best work.

Though poems may do no harm, the life of the poet is still felt to be full of perils. In April 2004, an article in the *Journal of Death Studies* reflecting a professor's study of 1,987 dead writers from different countries and different centuries revealed that poets tend to die younger than do other writers. Poets on average die at sixty-two, playwrights at sixty-three, novelists at sixty-six, and nonfiction writers at sixty-eight. This study in comparative lifespans came as news to CNN and the *New York Times*, which ran stories speculating on the psyche of poets. James Kaufman of the Learning Research Institute at California State University at San Bernardino, whose study caused the fuss, suggested that the poets' higher death rates might correspond to their higher rates of mental illness. Franz Wright, who learned earlier in the same month that he had won the 2004 Pulitzer Prize in poetry, was asked to comment on Professor Kaufman's study. "Since in the U.S., the worse you write the better your chances of survival, it stands to reason that poets would be the youngest to die," he said gloomily. Meanwhile, the backlash against National Poetry Month continues, as witness a brief item that ran in the satirical newspaper the *Onion* in late April 2005: "This month marks the 10th National Poetry Month, a campaign created in 1996 to raise public awareness of the growing problem of poetry. 'We must stop this scourge before more lives are exposed to poetry,' said Dr. John Nieman of the American Poetry Prevention Society at a Monday fundraising luncheon. 'It doesn't just affect women. Young people, particularly morose high-school and college students, are very susceptible to this terrible affliction. It is imperative that we eradicate poetry now, before more rainy afternoons are lost to it.' Nieman said some early signs of poetry infection include increased self-absorption and tea consumption."

Nevertheless, despite the glum news, more people are writing poetry, and going public with it. Rosie O'Donnell's blog features what she calls "the unedited rantings of a fat 43 year old menopausal ex-talk show host," mostly in verse. From a typically lively March 2005 entry: "marriot marquee / lois walks me in thru the kitchen— / I felt like elvis presley—a head of state / a great fake important me." Who says poetry and Wall Street are incompatible? *Business Week* began a profile of Robert Smith, the fund manager of T. Rowe Price's Growth Stock mutual fund, with eight lines from Smith's "Up on Deck," which he says is a metaphor for risk-taking in the stock market. (The poem's risk-averse speaker "never saw how close the wreck / And never cheered the winds first still / As I might have up on deck.") Calvin Trillin gathered some of the politically charged doggerel he has written for *The Nation* and the book became a surprise best seller. "A lot of people in America hear the words 'rhyme' and 'poetry' and think it might as well be Canadian," Trillin quipped. He has no plans to give up what he calls his "deadline poetry." In "A Poem of Republican Populism" from *The Nation* of October 11, 2004, the Republican Party is the collective speaker. Here's the poem's conclusion: "Yes, though we always represent / The folks who sit in corporate boxes, / The gratifying paradox is— / And this we love; it's just the neatest— / The other party's called elitist."

News reports circulated that Saddam Hussein writes poetry in his air-conditioned cell in a U.S. military prison. One poem concerned George Bush, though the leak did not specify whether it was number forty-one or forty-three. In the *New York Times* "men's fashion" supplement of September 19, 2004, Michael Bastian, the "man behind Bergdorf Goodman Men," held up Frank O'Hara as a fashion template. "We wanted to capture that whole tweedy, rumpled city-gun feeling, like a character in Cheever or Salinger, or like the poet Frank O'Hara," said Bastian, sporting a $995 Cantarelli tweed jacket and $390 Marc Jacobs chinos. Poetry is glamorous! For a reality check, we had the movie *We Don't Live Here Anymore.* Peter Krause ("Hank") plays a blocked writer, who looks sad despite getting word that *The New Yorker* has accepted one of his poems. Laura Dern ("Terri") tries to cheer him up. "You're getting published," she says. "It doesn't get much better than that." He replies sharply, "It's a poem, Terri. It's really nothing important."

One other celebrity almost made news as a closet poet last year. In March 2004, a senior editor at *Us Weekly* asked me to read and comment on a poem that Jennifer Lopez had written. The poem had three stanzas. The phrase "I am lovely" appears in two of the stanzas; in the first, the line reads, "I am lonely." Wanting to praise something in the poem prior to suggesting revisions or making criticisms, I singled out the progress from "lonely" to "lovely"—only to learn that the variation was the product of a typo in an editor's e-mail. In the end, the story didn't run, because more pressing news bumped it: Tom Cruise and Penelope Cruz had broken up. It remains a pleasure to welcome J.Lo to the poets' club, which is as democratic among the living as it is elitist when canons are fixed and all entrants are posthumous.

Accessibility—as a term and, implicitly, as a value

B ack in 1992, when he made his first appearance in *The Best American Poetry*, Billy Collins was a little-known, hardworking poet who had won a National Poetry Series contest judged by Edward Hirsch. He had supported himself for many years by teaching English and was, like many other poets, looking for a publisher. Charles Simic chose "Nostalgia" from *The Georgia Review* for *The Best American Poetry 1992* and for the following year's *Best*, Louise Glück selected "Tuesday, June 4th, 1991" from *Poetry*. Others, too, recognized Collins's talent. The University of Pittsburgh Press began to publish his books in its estimable series directed by Ed Ochester. Radio host Garrison Keillor gave Collins perhaps the biggest boost of all by asking him to read his poems on the air. He did, and the audience loved what it heard. Collins grew popular. At the same time, it was understood that he was no less serious for having the common touch. Asked to explain his poetic lineage, he liked citing Coleridge's "conversation" poems, such as "This Lime-Tree Bower My Prison." And for all their genial whimsy, many of Collins's efforts have a decidedly literary flavor, with such subjects as "Tintern Abbey," Emily Dickinson, *The Norton Anthology of English Literature*, poetry readings, writing workshops, "Keats's handwriting," and Auden's "Musée des Beaux Arts." John Updike put it exactly when he described Collins's poems as "limpid, gently and consistently startling, more serious than they seem." In 2000, two publishers quarreled publicly over the rights to publish Collins's books, and the *New York Times* reported the story on page one. The unlikely success story reached its apogee a year after September 11, 2001, when Billy Collins read "The Names," a poem he had written for the somber occasion, to a rare joint session of Congress.

By then Collins had become a phenomenon. While remaining a member in good standing of the poetry guild, an entity with a purely notional existence whose members would theoretically starve for their art, he had regular contact with honest-to-goodness book-buying readers who were not themselves practicing poets. They numbered in the tens of thousands and made best-sellers of his books. He won a Guggenheim Fellowship and a grant from the National Endowment for the Arts. His poems were published in respected journals such as *The Atlantic* and *Poetry* and were chosen by the diverse quartet of John Hollander, Robert Bly, Rita Dove, and Robert Hass for four consecutive volumes of *The Best American Poetry*. In June 2001, Collins succeeded Stanley Kunitz as poet laureate of the United States, and I remember hearing people gripe about the appointment. Collins was regularly dismissed as an "easy" or "anecdotal" poet. It was then that I knew he had made it big. Harold Bloom has propounded the theory that poets fight Oedipal battles with ancestors of their choice, so that Wallace Stevens had to overcome Keats's influence as Wordsworth had earlier overcome Milton's. It sometimes seems to me that a different Freudian paradigm—sibling rivalry—may explain the behavior of contemporary poets, for the backbiting in our community is ferocious, and nothing signifies success better than ritual bad-mouthing by rivals or wannabes.

The story as I've sketched it broadly here illustrates more than one useful lesson. Probably the most important is that poetry has the potential to reach masses of people who read for pleasure, still and always the best reason for reading. Radio is a great resource for spreading the word, and attention from programs such as Keillor's *Writer's Almanac*, Terry Gross's *Fresh Air*, and the interview shows of Leonard Lopate in New York City and Michael Silverblatt in Los Angeles is among the best things that can happen to a book or an author. Another lesson is that some poets share a resistance to popularity—other people's popularity, above all—though they might bristle if you called them elitist. It's a problem that afflicts us all to some extent. We say we want real readers, who buy our books not as an act of charity but as a free choice, yet should one in our party escape the poetry ghetto, we tremble with ambivalence, as if having real readers means a sure loss in purity. Inevitably the discussion turns to a question that seems substantive. What accounts for an individual poet's popular appeal? Does popularity result from (or result in) a loss of artistic integrity? What makes the lucky one's star shine so bright that it can be seen to sparkle even in the muddy skies of the metropolis, where industrial wastes have all but abolished the sighting of a heavenly body?

To the second of these questions, the answer is a simple no. Collins's readers came to him; he did not alter his style or his seriousness to curry anyone's favor. (It is, in fact, entirely possible that the poet setting out to be the most popular on the block stands the least chance of achieving that goal.) The answer to the other questions begins with the surface of Collins's poems, which is amiable, likable, relaxed. Even critics of Collins would concede that his poems have a high quotient of charm. He is, to ring a variant on a theme from Wordsworth, unusually fluent in the language of an adult speaking to other adults in the vernacular. Moreover, he insists on the primacy of the ordinary, as when he expresses contentment in "an ordinary night at the kitchen table, / at ease in a box of floral wallpaper, / white cabinets full of glass, / the telephone silent, / a pen tilted back in my hand." I would wager that Collins's ability to find and express contentment in the ordinary has contributed in a major way to his popular appeal. Wit and humor, traits of his verse, don't hurt. Above all, his poems make themselves available to the mythical general reader that book publishers crave. You don't need to have been an English major to get a Collins poem such as "Osso Buco" or "Nightclub." Such poems insist on a poetic pleasure principle. They are, to use a charged word, *accessible.* "Billy Collins's poetry is widely accessible," said Librarian of Congress James Billington in June 2001. "He writes in an original way about all manner of ordinary things and situations with both humor and a surprising contemplative twist." Collins himself has reservations about *accessible,* a word that he says suggests ramps for "poetically handicapped people." He prefers *hospitable.* But there's no dodging *accessible,* and in the introduction to his anthology *180 More,* Collins granted that the quality denoted by the word was what he looked for in a poem. An "accessible" poem, he wrote, is one that is "easy to enter," in the sense that an apartment or a house may be welcoming. "Some poems talk to us; others want us to witness an act of literary experimentation," he wrote, declaring his preference for the former and arguing that pleasure in poetry—its paramount purpose, according to Wordsworth—demands clarity.

The opposition between clarity and difficulty, or between communication and experimentation, is happily not absolute. Nor can we take it for granted that any of these terms has a fixed meaning that all can agree on. Accessibility —as a term and, implicitly, as a value—has been attacked recently by Helen Vendler in *The New Republic.* "'Accessibility' needs to be dropped from the

American vocabulary of aesthetic judgment if we are not to appear fools in the eyes of the world," Vendler wrote in the context of defending John Ashbery, "with his resolve against statement bearing the burden of a poem." Yet it is of course conceivable, it is even perhaps inevitable, that a poem by John Ashbery should be among the seventy-five poems chosen by Billy Collins for *The Best American Poetry 2006*. And so it has happened. Abstract discussion is one thing, poetic creativity and intuition is another, and it takes the former a long time to catch up with the latter. Let the debates continue. The poets themselves will make their choices, but they will do so on the basis of poems loved rather than positions held, rebuffed, or discarded.

There may be a structural antagonism between poets and critics, but at its best, criticism can make better writers of us, link poetry to its readership, and help build a community. The work of explanation, evaluation, and elucidation is there to be done. Unfortunately, much contemporary criticism is singularly shrill, sometimes gratuitously belligerent, even spiteful. I wonder where the rage comes from. Is it to overcompensate for the widespread if erroneous perception of poets as a band of favor-trading blurbists forever patting one another on the back? Or is the explanation simply that it is and always has been easier to issue summary judgments than to grapple with new art? I wonder, too, whether young poets flocking to MFA programs or working on their first manuscripts know what they're in for. It sometimes seems to me that the fledgling poet is in the position of the secret agent in Somerset Maugham's *Ashenden*, who gets his marching orders from a superior known only by his initial. "There's just one thing I think you ought to know before you take on this job," R. says. "And don't forget it. If you do well you'll get no thanks and if you get into trouble you'll get no help."

Perhaps when we review the reviewers, we should put a higher value on moments of mirth, such as Thom Geier of *Entertainment Weekly* provided last year. Geier opined inventively that John Ashbery's "oeuvre is not unlike Paris Hilton's" but "much, much smarter." There is so much to admire in this formulation—the word "oeuvre" bumping against that fussy "not unlike," and the double "much"—that one feels like a killjoy pointing out the comic outrageousness of the comparison. In the same magazine Billy Collins was characterized as simultaneously the Oprah of poetry, "the best buggy-whip maker of the 21st century," poetry's answer to Jerry Seinfeld ("hilariously funny"), a "modern-day Robert Frost," and "like Rodney Dangerfield," a figure who "doesn't get much respect in some serious literary circles," in part because his work is, yes, "accessible." Well, whatever else he is, Billy Collins is a natural choice to edit this year's *The Best American Poetry*, and he has crafted an anthology that demonstrates the vitality of American poetry and showcases poems of wit, charm, humor, eloquence, ingenuity, and comic invention.

Every year I screen hundreds of newspaper articles touching on poetry, and there are always one or two items that linger longer in the memory. Two last year stood above the rest. One was in the obituaries for Jerry Orbach, an actor as skillful playing a cop on *Law and Order* as singing a chorus in *Carousel*. It turned out that Orbach wrote hundreds of short poems to his wife. Some were read at his funeral. In contrast to this loving memory was the terse funereal report filed by Carlotta Gall in the *New York Times* on November 8, 2005: "Afghan Poet Dies after Beating by Husband." Nadia Anjuman, twenty-five, who had just published a book of poems—*Gule Dudi*, or "Dark Flower"—and had a second one ready for publication, had an argument with her husband. He beat her up, gave her a black eye, and knocked her unconscious; she died in the hospital. Five days later, Christina Lamb's article in the *Sunday Times* of London fleshed out the story. Nadia Anjuman was a woman of great courage as well as talent. In the city of Herat in western Afghanistan, she had joined a group that called itself the "Sewing Circles of Herat." Under this cover the women met, at the Golden Needle Sewing School, not to make clothes but to study literature and poetry in defiance of the Taliban's edicts forbidding women from studying. (The Taliban also forbade women to laugh out loud.) The women of the "Sewing Circles" risked grave penalties, imprisonment or worse, if caught. Nadia Anjuman survived these underground heroics but not, apparently, the wrath of a family that regarded as shameful the publication of a woman's poems about love and beauty. Brutally murdered, she left behind a six-month-old child and poems that continue to be read. "My wings are closed and I cannot fly," she laments in one ghazal, which concludes, "I am an Afghan woman, and must wail."

Was this tragic sequence of events a parable about the continuing plight of Afghani women four years after the defeat of the Taliban? An allegory in which the wielders of the pen suffer devastating losses before triumphing over the wielders of the sword? It may have been neither of these or other things that spring to mind. Yet I couldn't help translating the story into one in which poetry, emblem of free expression that it is, may be threatened with violent reprisal ending in death. Poetry, even the poetry of humor and delight, is an agent of the imagination pressing back, in Wallace Stevens's phrase, against the pressure of reality.

Undoubtedly the most parodied of all poems

A parody, even a merciless one, is not necessarily an act of disrespect. Far from it. Poets parody other poets for the same reason they write poems in imitation (or opposition): as a way of engaging with a distinctive manner or voice. A really worthy parody is implicitly an act of homage. Some great poets invite parody: Wordsworth's "Resolution and Independence" prompted Lewis Carroll to pen "The White Knight's Song" in *Through the Looking Glass.* In a wonderful poem, J. K. Stephen alludes to the sestet of a famous Wordsworth sonnet ("The world is too much with us") to dramatize the wide discrepancy between Wordsworth at his best and worst. "At certain times / Forth from the heart of thy melodious rhymes, / The form and pressure of high thoughts will burst," Stephen writes. "At other times—good Lord! I'd rather be / Quite unacquainted with the ABC / Than write such hopeless rubbish as thy worst!"

Among the moderns, T. S. Eliot reliably triggers off the parodist. Wendy Cope brilliantly reduced "The Waste Land" to five limericks ("The Thames runs, bones rattle, rats creep; / Tiresias fancies a peep— / A typist is laid, / A record is played— / Wei la la. After this it gets deep") while Eliot's late sententious manner stands behind Henry Reed's "Chard Whitlow" with its throat-clearing assertions ("As we get older we do not get any younger"). In

113

a recent (2006) episode of *The Simpsons* on television, Lisa Simpson assembles a poem out of torn-up fragments, and attributes it to Moe the bartender. The title: "Howling at a Concrete Moon." The inspiration:"The Waste Land." The cigar-chewing editor of *American Poetry Perspectives* barks into the phone, "Genius. Pay him nothing and put him on the cover."

Undoubtedly the most parodied of all poems is Matthew Arnold's "Dover Beach," which has long served graduation speakers and Polonius-wannabes as a touchstone. Arnold turned forty-five in 1867, the year the poem first appeared in print. Here it is:

Dover Beach

The sea is calm to-night.
The tide is full, the moon lies fair
Upon the straits;—on the French coast the light
Gleams and is gone; the cliffs of England stand,
Glimmering and vast, out in the tranquil bay.
Come to the window, sweet is the night-air!

Only, from the long line of spray
Where the sea meets the moon-blanch'd land,
Listen! you hear the grating roar
Of pebbles which the waves draw back, and fling,
At their return, up the high strand,
Begin, and cease, and then again begin,
With tremulous cadence slow, and bring
The eternal note of sadness in.

Sophocles long ago
Heard it on the Aegean, and it brought
Into his mind the turbid ebb and flow
Of human misery; we
Find also in the sound a thought,
Hearing it by this distant northern sea.

The Sea of Faith
Was once, too, at the full, and round earth's shore
Lay like the folds of a bright girdle furl'd.
But now I only hear

Its melancholy, long, withdrawing roar,
Retreating, to the breath
Of the night-wind, down the vast edges drear
And naked shingles of the world.

Ah, love, let us be true
To one another! for the world, which seems
To lie before us like a land of dreams,
So various, so beautiful, so new,
Hath really neither joy, nor love, nor light,
Nor certitude, nor peace, nor help for pain;
And we are here as on a darkling plain
Swept with confused alarms of struggle and flight,
Where ignorant armies clash by night.

The greatness of this poem lies in the way it transforms the painting of a scene into a vision of "eternal sadness" and imminent danger. Moonlight and the English Channel contemplated from atop the white cliffs of Dover by a man and woman in love would seem a moment for high romance, and a reaffirmation of vows as a prelude to sensual pleasure. But "Dover Beach," while remaining a love poem, is not about the couple so much as it is about a crisis in faith and a foreboding of dreadful things to come. It communicates the anxiety of an age in which scientific hypotheses, such as Darwin's theory of evolution, combined with philosophical skepticism to throw into doubt the comforting belief in an all-knowing and presumably benevolent deity. The magnificent closing peroration, as spoken by the poet to his beloved, has the quality of a prophecy darkly fulfilled. Genocidal violence, perpetrated by "ignorant armies," marked the last century, and it is undeniable that we today face a continuing crisis in faith and confidence. Seldom have our chief institutions of church and state seemed as vulnerable as they do today with, on the one side, a citizenry that seems alienated to the extent that it is educated and, on the other side, enemies as implacable and intolerant as they are medieval and reactionary.

Though traditional in its means, "Dover Beach" is, in its spirit and its burden of sense, a brutally modern poem, and among the first to be thus designated. "Arnold showed an awareness of the emotional conditions of modern life which far exceeds that of any other poet of his time," Lionel Trilling observed. "He spoke with great explicitness and directness of the alienation, isolation, and excess of consciousness leading to doubt which are, as so much of later literature testifies, the lot of modern man." And Trilling goes on to note that in "Dover Beach" in particular the diction is perfect and the verse moves "in a delicate crescendo of lyricism" to the "great grim simile" that lends the poem's conclusion its desperation and its pathos.

While perfect for the right occasion, a recitation of the poem is, because of its solemnity, absurd in most circumstances, as when, in the 2001 movie *The Anniversary Party*, the Kevin Kline character recites the closing lines from memory in lieu of an expected lighthearted toast, and the faces of the other characters change from pleasure to confusion and alarm. Inspired responses to "Dover Beach" spring to mind. In "The Dover Bitch," Anthony Hecht presents the situation of Arnold's poem from the woman's point of view. She rather resents being treated "as a sort of mournful cosmic last resort," brought all the way from London for a honeymoon and receiving a sermon instead of an embrace. Tom Clark lampoons "Dover Beach" more farcically. His poem begins as Arnold's does, but where in the third line of the original "the French coast" gleams in the distance, in Clark's poem light syrup drips on "the French toast," and the poem continues in the spirit of "crashing ignorance." A third example is John Brehm's "Sea of Faith," which Robert Bly selected for the 1999 edition of *The Best American Poetry*. Here a college student wonders whether the body of water named in the poem's title exists in geographical fact. The student's ignorance seems to confirm Arnold's gloomy vision, but it also spurs the instructor to a more generous response. After all, who has not felt the unspoken wish for an allegorical sea in which one can swim and reemerge "able to believe in everything, faithful / and unafraid to ask even the simplest of questions, / happy to have them simply answered"?

Poets like to parody "Dover Beach" because the poem takes itself so very seriously and because Arnold's wording sticks in the mind. But not everyone agrees on what lesson we should draw from this case. The poet Edward Dorn, author of *Gunslinger* and other estimable works, called "Dover Beach" the "greatest single poem ever written in the English language." What amazed Dorn was that it should be Arnold who wrote it. According to Dorn, Arnold "wrote volume after volume of lousy, awful poetry." The anomaly "proves that you should never give up," Dorn added. If Arnold with his "pedestrian mind" could write "Dover Beach," then "anybody could do it."

I have dwelled on "Dover Beach" as an object of irreverence not only because the parodic impulse, which informs so many contemporary poems (including some in this volume), is misunderstood and sometimes unfairly derogated, but also because of a superb counterexample that came to my attention this year. In his novel *Saturday* (2005), Ian McEwan makes earnest use of "Dover Beach" as a rich, unironic emblem of the values of Western Civilization. It is not the only such emblem in the book. There are Bach's *Goldberg Variations* and Samuel Barber's *Adagio for Strings*, to which the book's neurosurgeon hero listens when operating, and there is the surgeon's knife, the antithesis of the thug's switchblade. But a reading aloud of "Dover Beach" in the most extreme of circumstances marks the turning point in the plot of this novel whose subject is terror and terrorism.

Set in London on a day of massive antiwar demonstrations, *Saturday* centers on a car accident that pits Henry, the surgeon, against Baxter, a local crime boss. Henry gets the better of Baxter in the confrontation, and in retaliation the gangster and a henchman mount an assault on the surgeon and his family in their posh London home. Baxter systematically humiliates Henry's grown daughter, an aspiring poet, forcing her to strip off all her clothing in front of her horrified parents, brother, and grandfather. But the young woman's just-published first book of poems, lying on the coffee table, catches Baxter's eye, and he commands her to read from it. She opens the book but recites "Dover Beach" from memory instead—with startling consequences. The transformation of the gangster is abrupt and total. In a flash he goes "from lord of terror to amazed admirer," a state in which it becomes possible for the family to overpower him. Thus does poetry, in effect, disarm the brute and lead to the family's salvation.

With the restoration of safety and order, McEwan allows himself a little joke at the expense of both Matthew Arnold and his own protagonist. The surgeon tells his daughter of her choice of poem, "I didn't think it was one of your best." The joke, a good one, reminds us of the poem's complicated cultural status: revered, iconic, but also mildly desecrated, like a public statue exposed to pigeons and graffiti artists. But McEwan has already made his more significant point. Just as the instructor in John Brehm's poem can find himself yearning for an escape to an allegorical Sea of Faith, so I believe we all secretly think of poetry, this art that we love unreasonably, as somehow antidotal to malice and vice, cruelty and wrath. We know it isn't so, and yet we persist in writing poems that shoulder the burden of conscience. In *The Best American Poetry 2007* you will find poems in a variety of tonal registers—by such poets as Denise Duhamel, Robert Hass, Frederick Seidel, Brian Turner, and Joe Wenderoth—that address subjects ranging from "Bush's War" to the "language police," from the decapitation of an American citizen in Iraq to the overthrow of the shah of Iran.

For such a poem to gain entry into this volume, it had to meet exceptionally high criteria. Heather McHugh, the editor of *The Best American Poetry 2007*, sets store, she told an interviewer, by wordplay, puns, rhymes, the hidden life of words, "the *is* in the wish, the *or* in the word. No word-fun should be left undone." McHugh has spoken with cutting eloquence against glib and simplistic poems by well-meaning citizens: "So much contemporary American poetry is deadly serious, reeking of the NPR virtues: back-to-the-earth soup eaten fresh from the woodstove, all its spices listed, then some admirable thoughts to put to paper when we get home. Hey, Romanticism isn't dead—it's simply being turned to public pap. Against that tedium, a little unholiness comes as a big relief—the skeptic skeleton, the romping rump." But it should also be noted that McHugh herself, for all the wit and wordplay in her poems, has written a poem that I would not hesitate to characterize as powerful, earnest, and political: "What He Said" (1994), which culminates in a definition of poetry as what the heretical philosopher Giordano Bruno, when burned at the stake, "thought, but did not say," with an iron mask placed on his face, as the flames consumed him.

In his poem "My Heart," Frank O'Hara wrote, "I'm not going to cry all the time / nor shall I laugh all the time, / I don't prefer one 'strain' to another." By temperament and inclination I favor both kinds of poems—the kind that celebrates and the kind that criticizes; the kind that affirms a vow and the kind that makes merry; the poem of high seriousness that would save the world and the poem of high hilarity that would mock the pretensions of saviors. I believe, with Wordsworth, that the poet's first obligation is always to give pleasure, and I would argue, too, that a poem exhibiting the comic spirit can be every bit as serious as a poem devoid of laughter. The poems McHugh gathers in this volume are unafraid to confront the world in its contradictory guises and moods. The unlikely cast of characters includes authentic geniuses from far-flung places: Catullus, Leonardo, Voltaire, Kant, the lyricist Lorenz Hart. There are sonnets and prose poems, a set of haiku and a country-western song, a double abecedarian and a lover's quarrel with a famous Frost poem. And there are poems that take a mischievous delight in the English language as an organic thing, a living system, full of puns that reveal truths just as jokes and errors served Freud: as ways the mind inadvertently discloses itself. Some of these poems are very funny, and need no further justification. "The human race has one really effective weapon, and that is laughter," Mark Twain remarked.

There is a dangerous if common misconception that a political poem, or *any* poem that aspires to move the hearts and minds of men and women, must be reducible to a paraphrase the length of a slogan, be it that "war is hell" or that "hypocrisy is rampant" or that "it is folly to launch a major invasion without a postwar strategy in place." For such sentiments, an editorial or a letter to the editor would serve as the proper vehicle. We want something more complicated and more lasting from poetry. An anecdote from the biography of Oscar Hammerstein II, who succeeded Lorenz Hart as Richard Rodgers's lyricist, may help here. When Stephen Sondheim, then in high school, appealed for advice to Hammerstein, his mentor, the latter criticized a song the young man had written: "This doesn't say anything." Sondheim recalls answering defensively, "What does 'Oh, What a Beautiful Mornin'' say?" With a firmness Sondheim would not forget, Hammerstein responded, "Oh, it says a lot."

The parodist in each of us will continue to enjoy a secret laugh at "Dover Beach." But we also know that people who live in newspapers die for want of what there is in Arnold's poem and in great poetry in general. Real poetry sustains us. György Faludy, the Hungarian poet and Resistance hero, died on September 1, 2006, sixty-seven years to the day after the Nazis invaded Poland. Faludy attacked Hitler in a poem but managed to escape to the United States and served in the American army during World War II. He wasn't nearly so fortunate when he returned to Hungary following the war. For three years, from 1950 to 1953, the Soviets imprisoned Faludy in Recsk, Hungary's Stalinist concentration camp. He endured terrible hardships, but even without a pen he wrote, using the bristle of a broom to inscribe his verses in blood on toilet paper. He had to write. Poetry was keeping him alive. He recited his poems and made fellow prisoners memorize them. The imagination created hope, and the heart committed its lines to memory. When Faludy called his prose book about the years in the camp "My Happy Days in Hell," it was with obvious irony, but it also hinted at his faith. He had listened to the melancholy, long withdrawing roar of the sea, survived the shock, and outlived the Soviet occupation just as his beloved Danube River had done.

Who says that hot poems can't get
you into trouble in 2008?

In a wonderful essay in *The Dyer's Hand* (1962)—an essay written far in advance of the ubiquitous writing workshop—W. H. Auden prescribed the curriculum of his "daydream College for Bards." Matriculated students in the "daydream college" must learn at least one ancient and two modern languages. They have to memorize thousands of lines of verse. Forbidden from reading criticism, they must exercise their critical faculties by writing parodies. They need to take courses in prosody, rhetoric, and comparative philology. Most unconventionally, they are required to study three subjects from a varied group, including "archaeology, mythology, liturgics, cooking," and they are expected also to take up gardening or to adopt a four-legged pet.

While the proposed banning of literary criticism from the college library may go too far, I think Auden is right about a lot of things. The value of knowing a poem by heart lies not in the public recitation but in the inward recollection of the lines when one is in a vacant or a pensive mood; there is simply no better way to possess a poem than to memorize it. A good parody is an act of practical criticism, as instructive and more amusing than most. Among the most efficacious exercises are those that involve writing in set forms and handling various metrical and stanzaic patterns. I agree, too, on the value of such nonliterary activities as cooking and gardening, which in their creative processes and structures bear more than a passing resemblance to the act of writing. Given the sheer number of graduate writing programs in the country today—urban or pastoral, low or high residency, fancy or no frills, traditional or innovative—it's a wonder, in a way, that none has given Auden's curriculum a try.

Auden begins "The Poet & the City" with the observation that a great many young people of limited talent, "when asked what they want to do in life," answer neither sensibly ("I want to be a lawyer, an innkeeper, a farmer") nor romantically ("I want to be an explorer, a racing motorist, a missionary, President of the United States"), Instead they want to become writers, "creative" writers. The phenomenon had long astonished and vexed the author. In "The Prolific and the Devourer," written in 1939, the year Auden first took up residence in America, he asserts that the secret meaning of "I want to write" is "I don't want to work." Art as a form of play, he adds, "is the least dependent on the goodwill of others and looks the easiest." For the shirkers, Auden's message is that you must work very hard not only at becoming a poet but also at earning a living. He goes on to recommend learning a craft or taking up a trade that does not "involve the manipulation of words," a very Audenesque piece of advice that his own industrious practice as an essayist and anthologist belies. Perhaps, to paraphrase Oscar Wilde, the only thing to do with good advice is pass it on and assume that it doesn't apply to you. Richard Howard, the guest editor of the 1995 volume in this series, recollects the time that "Wystan [Auden's first name] scolded me for translating books from the French. He thought manual labor was a much more suitable idea." On another occasion, Auden voiced his opinion that "poets should dress like businessmen," while he wore, in James Schuyler's words, "an incredible peach / -colored nylon shirt."

Such inconsistencies are amusing but do not affect the central point, and we may thank Auden for raising the whole question of what job options there are for, in his phrase, "the average poet." Many young writers today can see their lives unfold in a seamless transition from one side of the classroom to the other without an intervening period of living in the place that professors sometimes call the "quote-unquote real world." The importance of going out into the world and encountering its complexity and range of possibility is surely one thing we might stress in our latter-day College for Bards.

The proliferation of graduate, degree-granting writing programs in the thirty-five years since Auden's death may not have surprised one so suspicious of the vanity of young writers. Yet even a critic of the workshop structure, centering as it does on the student rather than on canonical texts, might welcome the news that MFA programs continue to flourish—if only because writing requires reading and because we may owe to these programs the perpetuation of the art that we practice and the "influences" we honor and sometimes contend with like uncles and aunts and grandparents. The Association of Writing Programs (AWP) held its annual conference in New York City in 2008, and the sold-out event, attracting more participants and book exhibits than any in the organization's history, was nothing if not a sign of a profession in vigorous health. In undergraduate education, too, creative writing has become a vital force. The Association of Departments of English (ADE), a branch of the Modern Languages Association (MLA), periodically takes up a recurrent problem: the decline in the percentage of undergraduates majoring in English.[1] In response to the predicament, a number of English departments have expanded their offerings in creative writing. This has proved a shrewd maneuver. The success of the gambit attests not just to the lure of self-expression but also to the assertion of the pleasure principle in matters of art and literature. Who would not choose the pleasure of making narratives and lyrics if the alternative is to "problematize a text"?

We who teach writing know how pure and strong the literary impulse remains among our students. We are impressed with their ambition and their commitment. But we know also that reading and writing exist in a symbiotic relationship, and many of us wonder how it came about that even some of our most talented and energetic young writers got through college with having read so little. When I wrote *Signs of the Times: Deconstruction and the Fall of Paul de Man* (1991), the joke in currency was that if you crossed a mafioso and a deconstructionist, what you got was someone who makes you "an offer that you can't understand." The beauty of the joke was that it did three things at once: it confirmed the iconic status of *The Godfather*; it made the point that jargon and abstruse terminology result in incomprehensible prose; and it attributed a mob mentality to a clique that was reputedly skillful, even ruthless, at the academic game of chutes and tenure ladders. I worried then that the hegemony

---

1. See, for example, "The Undergraduate English Major," the report of the 2001–2002 ADE Ad Hoc Committee on the English Major, which was formed to study "the recent decline in the number of English majors and recommend ways in which departments can address the decline and its possible underlying causes." The committee affirms that "curricular changes inside English departments are not, as some would claim, a primary factor responsible for the flight of students from English—a flight that can seem an educational disaster" but isn't if you take the long view. *ADE Bulletin*, no. 134–35 (spring–fall 2003): 68–91.

of critical theory may serve to rationalize and would probably accelerate the neglect of authors and the decay of practical criticism. It gives the maker of that prediction little satisfaction to see it come true.

Something larger than the ideological and political conflicts between and within academic departments is at stake here. In the real culture war, the war for the survival of the literary culture, the dummies seem to be winning. There are days when even an unflagging champion of the written word may fear that his or her best efforts may turn out to have the same effect as a prayer to the patron saint of lost causes. The force against literacy in the old-fashioned sense of reading books, understanding traditions, and recollecting history is, in the old-fashioned sense, awesome. In 2004 the National Endowment for the Arts issued its grim report *Reading at Risk*, and a year ago the NEA followed up with *To Read or Not to Read*. The reports make the case that "reading skills" correlate directly to individual achievement and career success, not to mention the health of the culture and the education of the citizenry. And by all standards, we are failing. The percentage of the U.S. population that reads books went down from an estimated 61 percent in 1992 to under 57 percent ten years later. That's a slow but steady rate of decline. There's little surprise and less comfort in learning that the rate of decline is faster when it comes to works of fiction and poetry. Between 1982 and 2002, the percentage of the population that had read a "creative" book in the previous twelve months went down from 56.9 to 46.7. "More alarming [than the decline in newspaper circulation and in household spending on books] are indications that Americans are losing not just the will to read but even the ability," Caleb Crain writes in *The New Yorker*. Crain summarizes the view of some sociologists that reading books for pleasure may someday become "an increasingly arcane hobby."[2] If one culprit among many is television, one effect is the "dumbing down" of culture—a trend so powerful it brought a new phrase into currency. People know astoundingly little about, say, American history, and this (they think) is no big deal. Every now and then an author risks being called a "curmudgeon" or a "crank" for airing misgivings about this state of affairs, while indulging the guilty pleasure of circulating anecdotes of epic American ignorance. Patricia Cohen's *New York Times* piece on Susan Jacoby's book *The Age of American Unreason* begins with the "adorable platinum blonde" who thought that Europe was a country. She was a contestant on the FOX game show *Are You Smarter Than a 5th Grader?*—the whole premise of which is that Americans are stupider than

2. Caleb Crain, "The Twilight of the Books," *The New Yorker*, December 24 and 31, 2007, 134–35.

ever and reveling in it. Jacoby herself says she wrote her book because (in Cohen's paraphrase) "anti-intellectualism (the attitude that 'too much learning can be a dangerous thing') and anti-rationalism ('the idea that there is no such things as evidence or fact, just opinion') have fused in a particularly insidious way." Jacoby's immediate trigger was an overheard conversation in which one well-dressed man told another that Pearl Harbor "was when the Vietnamese dropped bombs in a harbor, and it started the Vietnam War."[3]

In the teeth of an epidemic of ignorance, we must decide what and how to teach the young people who come to us convinced that they have a poetic vocation. We should encourage them to read widely—to read everything they can. But we should assuredly not mock anyone for what they do not know or have not yet read. Rather, respond with ardor to their list of unread books: for though rereading is a great art, nothing can beat the first time you live with *Crime and Punishment* or Keats's odes and letters or Genesis or Homer or Dante or Emily Dickinson or Byron's *Don Juan*. It's a list-maker's delight, devising the syllabus for a course on, say, what Keats called the "vale of soul-making"—the making of a poet. We may take as our motto this line from Ben Jonson's ode to the memory of Shakespeare: "For a good poet's made, as well as born." On my syllabus I'd include some of the aforementioned works, as well as Emerson's essays, Gertrude Stein's lectures and *The Autobiography of Alice B. Toklas*, Wordsworth's *Prelude*, and Rilke's *Letters to a Young Poet*. What, gentle reader, would you choose?

Our obligations to our students do not stop at texts and assignments, instruction on the preparation of a manuscript, information about the literary marketplace, methods of dealing with writer's block, models for how to disagree without resort to fisticuffs. By our example we can prove that a conversation or debate about poetry need not reflect the corrosive nature of the national political discourse. There is also the need for students—for all of us, really—to come to terms with the likelihood of rejection and the inevitability of injustice. Someday someone else in the room will win the award or the fellowship or the honor that *you* deserved. But envy is always an error, and to win a prize or an award is not the reason you wrote poetry in the first place. Return to that original impulse. Don't give in to resentment and bitterness, the enemies of poetry. We could probably devote an entire course in the "daydream College" to one aphorism from Auden's prologue to *The Dyer's Hand*: "No poet or novelist wishes he were the only one who ever lived, but most of them wish they

---

3. Patricia Cohen, "Dumb and Dumber: Are Americans Hostile to Knowledge?," *New York Times*, February 14, 2008.

were the only one alive, and quite a number fondly believe their wish has been granted."[4]

When *The Best American Poetry* series was new, I would use this space to explain our rules and procedures. Undoubtedly the most important decision we have to make annually is the identity of the person who will put his or her stamp on a volume in a series that chronicles the taste of our leading practitioners. Honored among his peers, Charles Wright seemed a natural for this editorial job and brought a keen sense of responsibility to it. He worked hard to be ecumenical, balancing the desire to be inclusive with the unrelenting need to favor excellence. Born in Pickwick Dam, Tennessee, Wright discovered his poetic vocation while serving in U.S. Army Intelligence in Italy in the 1950s. After completing four years of active duty, he left the army in 1961 and soon was studying with Donald Justice at the University of Iowa. Since 1983 Wright has taught at the University of Virginia. His poetry has a spiritual, even a religious flavor—"each line is a station of the cross," he has said—though it calls to mind a religion based on doubt more than faith. In a poem in *Scar Tissue* (2006), Wright depicts himself as a song and dance man—but one who has the west wind whistling and Dante's souls dancing in his brain. The urge to pray outlasts the conviction that God will hear the prayer. Yet the capital G in the opening phrase of this arresting passage performs a little miracle of poetic transformation:

> A God-fearing agnostic,
> > I tend to look in the corners of things,
> Those out-of-the-way places,
> The half-dark and half-hidden,
> > the passed-by and over-looked,
> Whenever I want to be sure I can't find something.

As this excerpt from "Confessions of a Song and Dance Man" illustrates, Wright has a distinctive way of breaking his lines in the middle: the second half begins where the first left off, one line space lower on the page. The device in his hands is a potent means of punctuating space, as well suited to his poetic pursuits as A. R. Ammons's colons are to his project of "colonizing" the known universe.

---

4. W. H. Auden, *The Dyer's Hand* (New York: Vintage, 1962; rprt. 1989), 14.

The year 2007 was favorable for guest editors past and present of *The Best American Poetry*. Charles Simic, who edited *The Best American Poetry 1992*, succeeded Donald Hall (*The Best American Poetry 1989*) as U.S. poet laureate. (Counting Simic, seven *The Best American Poetry* guest editors have held the post.) During that same week in August, the Academy of American Poets announced that Simic had won this year's prestigious Wallace Stevens Award. Robert Hass (*The Best American Poetry 2001*) garnered the National Book Award and a Pulitzer for *Time and Materials*. Paul Muldoon (*The Best American Poetry 2005*) became poetry editor of *The New Yorker*. John Ashbery (*The Best American Poetry 1988*) was named poet laureate of MTV. And the 2007 Griffin Prize went to Charles Wright for *Scar Tissue*.

On February 14, 2008, Scribner published *The Best American Erotic Poems: From 1800 to the Present*. On the same day, an assistant principal of a high school in Springfield, Ohio, was suspended (and was eventually obliged to resign) when school officials learned he had posted erotic poems on the net under the pseudonym Antonio Love. This all happened (the local newscast reported) "after a parent complained about the alleged poetry." (The *alleged* there is a final twist of the knife.) Who says that hot poems can't get you into trouble in 2008? Poetry remains a bad influence all these years after Plato banished the poets from his ideal republic.

"that is how I should talk if I could talk poetry"

What is a poet? In his "Defense of Poetry," Shelley writes, "A poet is a nightingale, who sits in darkness and sings to cheer its own solitude with sweet sounds; his auditors are as men entranced by the melody of an unseen musician, who feel that they are moved and softened, yet know not whence or why." The solitude and sweet darkness, the emphasis on the unseen, the nightingale as the image of the poet, the listeners entranced but bewildered: how romantic this formulation is—and how well it fits its author. Matthew Arnold alters the metaphor but retains something of its tone when he calls Shelley "a beautiful and ineffectual angel, beating in the void his luminous wings in vain." Kierkegaard in *Either/Or* goes further than either Shelley or Arnold in accentuating the negative. In a passage I've long admired, Kierkegaard identifies the poet as one whose heart is full of anguish but whose lips transform all sighs and groans into beautiful music. Kierkegaard likens the fate of this "unhappy" individual to the cruel and unusual punishment meted out by the tyrant Phalaris, whose unfortunate victims, "slowly roasted by a gentle fire" in a huge copper bull, let out shrieks that turn into sweet melodies by the time they reach the tyrant's ears. The success of the poet, then, corresponds to the amount of agony endured. Readers clamor for more, for they are aware only of the music and not of the suffering that went into it. The critics, too, stand ready to applaud—if, that is, the poet's work meets the requirements of the immutable "laws of aesthetics." And here Kierkegaard's parable acquires an extra layer of irony, the better to convey his contempt for critics. "Why, to be sure," he writes, "a critic resembles a poet as one pea another, the only difference being that he has no anguish in his heart and no music on his lips." And therefore, Kierkegaard concludes with a flourish, sooner would he be a swineherd understood by the swine than a poet misunderstood by men.

Kierkegaard's argument proceeds by the logic of his similes—the sweet music, the barbaric torture, the prosaic peas in the pod, the swineherd as an honorable profession—and the abrupt tonal shift at the end from sarcasm to defiance. If, as Wallace Stevens asserted, "poetry is almost incredibly one of the effects of analogy," here is a gorgeous example. The passage has the virtue, moreover, of raising questions about the occupational hazards that poets face and about their relation to a world of readers and reviewers.

In one way, at least, Kierkegaard's parable is untrue to the experience of American poets, who rarely have to fend off legions of avid admirers. But the notion that the job of the critic is to find fault with the poetry—that the aims of criticism and of poetry are opposed—is still with us or, rather, has returned after a hiatus. It was once erroneously thought that devastating reviews caused John Keats's untimely death in his twenty-sixth year. Lord Byron in *Don Juan* had Keats and his reviewers in mind when he wrote, "Tis strange the mind, that very fiery particle, / Should let itself be snuff'd out by an article." In reality, however, it was not criticism but consumption that cut short Keats's life.[1] Many of us delight in Oscar Wilde's witty paradoxes that blur the identities of artist and critic.[2] The critical essays of T. S. Eliot and W. H. Auden are continuous with their poems and teach us that criticism is a matter not of enforcing the "laws of aesthetics" or meting out sentences as a judge might pronounce them in court. Rather, the poet as critic engages with works of literature and enriches our understanding and enjoyment of them. Yet today more than a few commentators seem intent on punishing the authors they review. It has grown into a phenomenon. In the March 2009 issue of *Poetry*, the critic Jason Guriel

---

1. Not that the critics were blameless. The anonymous reviewer writing for *Blackwood's Edinburgh Magazine* (August 1818) called Keats's *Endymion* "imperturbable driveling idiocy." Endymion was supposed to be "a Greek shepherd loved by a Grecian goddess," but in Keats's hands, he was "merely a young Cockney rhymester."

2. In *The Critic as Artist*, Wilde radically revises Matthew Arnold on the function of criticism. According to Arnold, the endeavor is "to see the object as in itself it really is." According to Wilde, the aim is "to see the object as in itself it really is not."

defends "negativity" as "the poetry reviewer's natural posture, the default position she assumes before scanning a single line." The title of Guriel's piece sums it up: "Going Negative."

The romantic image of the poet as a vulnerable personage in a hostile universe has not gone out of currency. The poet is doomed to go unrecognized and to pay dearly for his music-making powers. The gift of poetry comes not as an unalloyed blessing but as the incidental virtue of a defect or as compensation for a loss, an injury, an ailment, a deficiency. Edmund Wilson coined the phrase that readily comes to mind for this dynamic of compensatory balance: "the wound and the bow." Before it served Wilson as the title of a collection of his essays (1941), the phrase headed his study of the myth of Philoctetes, which the critic took as paradigmatic of the artist's situation. Aeschylus, Euripides, and Sophocles treated the myth in plays; the *Philoctetes* of Sophocles survives. The hero, who excels even Odysseus at archery, possesses the invincible bow that once belonged to Hercules. Philoctetes joins the Greeks in their assault on Troy but is bitten by a poisonous snake, and the suppurating wound emits so foul an odor that his comrades-in-arms abandon him on the island of Lemnos. There he is stranded for ten miserable years. But when a Trojan prophet is forced to reveal that the Greeks will fail to conquer Troy without the unerring bow of Philoctetes, a platoon is dispatched to reenlist the archer—who is understandably reluctant to return to the fray—and to recover his arms by any means necessary. In Sophocles, Philoctetes is cured at Troy. He goes on to kill Paris, the Trojan prince whose abduction of Helen precipitated the epic conflict, and he becomes one of the heroes of the Greek victory. One lesson, according to Wilson, is that "genius and disease, like strength and mutilation, may be inextricably bound up together." In the most speculative and provocative sentence in the essay, Wilson ventures that "somewhere even in the fortunate Sophocles there had been a sick and raving Philoctetes."

W. H. Auden's early prose poem, "Letter to a Wound" (1931), is a powerful modern statement of the theme: "You are so quiet these days that I get quite nervous, remove the dressing, I am safe, you are still there." Addressing the wound as "you" is not merely a grammatical convenience but the vehicle of a linguistic transformation; the ailment becomes an active, willful muse and companion—albeit one whose traits include "insane jealousy," "bad manners," and a "passion for spoiling things." The letter writer has learned to live with his incurable condition as with a secret partner, an illicit lover. They have even gone through a "honeymoon stage" together. "Thanks to you," Auden writes, "I have come to see a profound significance in relations I never dreamt of considering before, an old lady's affection for a small boy, the Waterhouses and their retriever, the curious bond between Offal and Snig, the partners in the hardware shop in the front." The wound is not named, though we read of a visit to a surgeon, who begins a sentence, "I'm afraid," and need not add a word. The particular virtue of this epistolary prose poem is that "I" and "you," a pair of pronouns, are raised to the level of a universal duality and are therefore greater than any specific duality that seems appropriate—whether "artist" and "wound," or "self" and "soul," or "ego" and "id," or "lover" and "beloved."

It is difficult not to fall under the spell of Wilson's wound and bow or of the corresponding myth in the Hebraic tradition. In the thirty-second chapter of Genesis, Jacob—who twice in the past had got the better of his brother Esau, both times by cunning or deceit—must wrestle with "a man" who will not reveal his name and who must flee the scene at daybreak. The struggle takes place on the eve of his first encounter with Esau after many years, in the deep darkness of the night, and it is physical combat of a kind not associated with Jacob. When he fights the angel to a standstill, he receives a blessing and a new name, Israel (because he has "contended with God and men and has prevailed"). But he has also suffered a wound "in the hollow of his thigh" that causes him to limp thereafter. The story is rich and mysterious in inverse proportion to its length: nine biblical verses. Though each is said to be a source of power, the Hebrew blessing bestowed on Jacob is utterly different from the Greek bow. Yet at bottom we find the familiar dialectic of compensation.

Such myths may console us. The logic of Emerson's essay "Compensation" has saved my spirits on many a dismal afternoon. "The sure years reveal the deep emotional force that underlies all facts," Emerson writes. "The death of a dear friend, wife, brother, lover, which seemed nothing but privation, somewhat later assumes the aspect of a guide or genius; for it commonly operates revolutions in our way of life, terminates an epoch of infancy or of youth which was waiting to be closed, breaks up a wonted occupation, or a household, or style of living, and allows the formation of new ones more friendly to the growth of character." It is to Emerson's essay that I turn when I need to tamp down the impulses of resentment or envy and reconcile myself to realities. There is wisdom here and truth, a counterargument if not exactly a solution to the problem of evil that Gerard Manley Hopkins stated summarily: "Why do sinners' ways prosper? And why must / Disappointment all I endeavor end?"

There is also, however, a danger in the intimate association of genius and illness, especially mental illness, especially at a time when many of us engaged in the discourse of poetry come into contact with ever-increasing numbers of impressionable young people who want to study creative writing. The romantic conception of the poet can lead too easily to self-pity or worse, the glorification of madness and the idealization of the self-inflicted wound. We need to remember that poetry springs from joy as often as from sorrow: the impulse to praise is as strong as the impulse to mourn. Lionel Trilling's essay "Art and Neurosis" is a vital corrective to the tendency to assent too readily to propositions obscuring the differences between genius and madness. Trilling accepts the premise that all of us, including "the fortunate Sophocles," are ill; we are all neurotic. In that case, it is not the primal hurt but the ability to rise above it that distinguishes the artist. Poetry is not a matter of divine madness but the product of labor and conscious mind. "Nothing is so characteristic of the artist as his power of shaping his work, of subjugating his raw material, however aberrant it be from what we call normality," Trilling writes. "What marks the artist is his power to shape the material of pain we all have."

My favorite sentence in Kierkegaard's parable is the one in which poets and critics are considered identical except that the latter lack the very qualities—the anguish in the heart and the music on the lips—that are definitive of the poet. For many years I resisted Kierkegaard's "either/or" logic. I felt that there needn't be a structural enmity between poetry and criticism. Now I wonder.

The characteristic badness of literary criticism in the 1980s was that it was heavily driven by theory and saddled with an unlovely vocabulary. T. S. Eliot, in "The Function of Criticism" (1923), says he "presumes" that "no exponent of criticism" has "ever made the preposterous assumption that criticism is an autotelic activity"—that is, an activity to be undertaken as an end in itself without connection to a work of literature. Eliot did not figure on poststructuralism and the critic's declaration of independence from the text. If you wanted criticism "constantly to be confronted with examples of poetry," as R. P. Blackmur recommends in "A Critic's Job of Work," you were in for a bad time in the 1980s. The academic critics' disregard of contemporary poetry paralleled the rise of creative writing as a field of study and, partly in consequence, the writing of poetry did not suffer, though from time to time you would hear the tired refrain that poetry—like God, the novel as a form, and the author altogether—had died. This shibboleth itself has not perished. *Newsweek* reports that, despite "anecdotal evidence that interest in poetry is on the rise," statistics show a decline. "Is an art form dying?" the magazine asks.[3] Donald Hall wrote the definitive response to these premature death notices, "Death to the Death of

3. Marc Bain, "The End of Verse?," *Newsweek*, March 25, 2009.

Poetry," which served as the introduction to *The Best American Poetry 1989.*
Hall's assertion remains valid: "American poetry survives; it even prevails."

Poetry criticism at its worst today is mean in spirit and spiteful in intent,
as if determined to inflict the wound that will spur the artist to new heights if
it does not cripple him or her. Somewhere along the line, the notion took hold
that poets were reluctant to write honestly about their peers. But in the absence
of critics who are not themselves poets, surely the antidote is not to encourage
the habit of rejection without explanation, denunciation without a reasoned
argument, and a slam of the gavel in high dudgeon as if a poem were a felony.
Hostile criticism, criticism by insult, may have entertainment value, but ani-
mus does not guarantee honesty. As one who knows from firsthand experience
what a book reviewer faces when writing on deadline, I can tell the real thing
when I see it, and the hysterical over-the-top attack is as often as not the prod-
uct of a pose. Every critic knows it is easier (and more fun) to write a ruthless
review rather than a measured one. As a reviewer, you're not human if you don't
give vent to your outrage once or twice—if only to get the impulse out of you.
If you have too good a time writing hostile reviews, you'll injure not only your
sensibility but your soul. Frank O'Hara felt he had no responsibility to respond
to a bad poem. It'll "slip into oblivion without my help," he would say.

William Logan typifies the bilious reviewer of our day. He has attacked,
viciously, a great many American poets; I, too, have been the object of his
scorn. Logan is the critic as O'Hara defined the species: "the assassin of my
orchards." You can rely on him to go for the most wounding gesture. Michael
Palmer writes a "Baudelaire Series" of poems, for example, and Logan com-
ments, "Baudelaire would have eaten Mr. Palmer for breakfast, with salt."
The poems of Australian poet Les Murray seem "badly translated out of Old
Church Slavonic with only a Russian phrase book at hand." Reviewing a book
by Adrienne Rich is a task that Logan feels he could almost undertake in his
sleep. Reading C. K. Williams is "like watching a dog eat its own vomit."

For many years, Logan reserved his barbs for the poets of our time. More
recently he has sneered at Emily Dickinson ("a bloodless recluse") and conde-
scended to Emerson ("a mediocre poet"). And still the *New York Times Book
Review* turned to Logan to review the new edition of Frank O'Hara's *Selected
Poems* last summer. Logan's piece began with the observation that O'Hara's
death at the age of forty in a freak accident was a "good career move." This
is not a particularly original phrase, but in O'Hara's case it is doubly unkind,
giving the false impression that he died by his own hand.

Logan's treatment of Langdon Hammer's Library of America edition of Hart

Crane's poetry and prose—which ran in the *New York Times Book Review* in January 2007—provoked among many readers the feeling that here he had gone too far. The piece dwelled on Crane's "sexual appetites," which "were voracious and involved far too many sailors," and included a flip dismissal of Crane's poem "Chaplinesque" (a "dreadful mess"). The review triggered off a spate of letters that the *Times* duly printed. Rosanna Warren summed up what many felt: "Snide biographical snippets about homosexuality and alcoholism are not literary criticism, nor are poems illuminated by sarcastic bons mots ('a Myth of America conceived by Tiffany and executed by Disney,' 'like being stuck in a mawkish medley from *Show Boat* and *Oklahoma!*'). Crane's revelatory weaknesses as well as his, yes, genius, deserved a more responsible accounting."

Wounded by the outcry, Logan wrote a lengthy defense of himself and his procedures in the October 2008 issue of *Poetry*. More letters to the editor followed: three pages of them in the December 2008 issue, along with a concluding comment by Logan longer than the combined efforts of the correspondents. For one who routinely seeks to give offense, Logan turns out to be thin-skinned. In the end he falls back on the argument that it is fruitless to argue in matters of taste. "The problem with taste is, yours is right and everyone else's is wrong," Logan writes. Bosh. The real problem is that Logan confuses taste with bias. Using the Romantic poets as an example, he writes: "You can't stand that ditherer Coleridge, she can't stand that whiner Keats, I can't stand that dry fussbudget Wordsworth, and we all hate Shelley." Only someone for whom poets are merely names, abstractions that never had a flesh-and-blood existence, could so gleefully reduce these poets to those epithets. But when Logan returns to "Chaplinesque," Hart Crane's "hapless little" poem (and how that unnecessary "little" rankles), he gives the game away.

Here is "Chaplinesque":

> We make our meek adjustments,
> Contented with such random consolations
> As the wind deposits
> In slithered and too ample pockets.
>
> For we can still love the world, who find
> A famished kitten on the step, and know
> Recesses for it from the fury of the street,
> Or warm torn elbow coverts.

We will sidestep, and to the final smirk
Dally the doom of that inevitable thumb
That slowly chafes its puckered index toward us,
Facing the dull squint with what innocence
And what surprise!

And yet these fine collapses are not lies
More than the pirouettes of any pliant cane;
Our obsequies are, in a way, no enterprise.
We can evade you, and all else but the heart:
What blame to us if the heart live on.

The game enforces smirks; but we have seen
The moon in lonely alleys make
A grail of laughter of an empty ash can,
And through all sound of gaiety and quest
Have heard a kitten in the wilderness.

To Logan the poem's concluding lines are self-evidently "embarrassing," an adjective he uses twice without substantiation. In the three separate pieces in which Logan brings up the poem, he lazily repeats the same charges, uses the same modifiers: the penultimate stanza of "Chaplinesque" is "hapless and tone deaf," the ending is "schmaltz," and the poem as a whole is evidence that the poet was "star-struck" by Charlie Chaplin, whose movies inspired Crane.

Everyone is entitled to an opinion, but a professional critic has the responsibility to develop opinions, not just to state them. Rather than make the effort to see how Crane's poem works as a response to Chaplin's film *The Kid*, Logan ridicules the "star-struck" poet, likening Chaplin then to Angelina Jolie now, a comparison of dubious value that manages to insult everyone, including Chaplin, Crane, Angelina Jolie, and the "seventy-seven American poets" who, Logan says in his patented blend of self-regard and snarky wit, have written odes to Jolie because Logan wrote that Crane met Chaplin after writing "Chaplinesque."

I do not claim to comprehend "Chaplinesque" perfectly, but I believe that the lover of poetry will recognize the genius in this poem before any irritable reaching after paraphrase. Crane's repeated use of the homonym for his first name—"We can evade you, and all else but the heart: / What blame to us if the heart live on"—seems to me, for example, well worth pondering in the context of the lines' pronominal ambiguity. The poem's opening stanzas are so rich one wants to say them over and over, to speculate on the idea of the Chaplin persona as an image of the poet, of the "famished kitten" as an image of poetry, or to contemplate the remarkable sequence of "smirk," "thumb," and "squint" in the third stanza. The finger-in-the-eye slapstick comedy routine has never seemed so threatening, even if we can "Dally the doom of that inevitable thumb / That slowly chafes its puckered index toward us." The poem's ending is particularly memorable. You may not make easy sense of that "grail of laughter" created by the moon out of a garbage can in a deserted alley. But this arresting image that fuses the sacred and the profane, sky and slum, will not soon depart from your consciousness. The key phrase here, a "grail of laughter," is a great example of a poetic image that defies logical analysis, for we instinctively grasp it as a figure of the sublime, though we know that a grail cannot be "of" laughter in any conventional sense. The laughter is the "sound of gaiety and quest," and "we" can see the miracle, behold the grail, because we have heard the cry of the alley cat, and we know that poetry is not simply a grand visionary quest but also something very precious and vulnerable, a kitten in the wilderness.

The critic whose take on "Chaplinesque" I'd like to see is Christopher Ricks. Ricks begins his book *T. S. Eliot and Prejudice* with a reading of the most audacious poetic debut of the twentieth century. You might have thought that "The Love Song of J. Alfred Prufrock" would require the critic to digress from a consideration of prejudice, the focal point of Ricks's study of Eliot. Not so. Ricks quotes the uncanny stand-alone couplet that Eliot uses twice: "In the room the women come and go / Talking of Michelangelo." What have scholars said about the lines? The Oxford don Helen Gardner hears "high-pitched feminine voices" that are absurdly inadequate to the "giant art" of Michelangelo. Grover Smith says he has "no doubt" the women are talking "tediously and ignorantly." To Hugh Kenner, the women are "trivial." John Crowe Ransom, discerning "contempt" in Eliot's voice, rephrases the couplet as a rhetorical question about the women: "How could they have had any inkling of that glory which Michelangelo had put into his marbles and his paintings?"

Yet, as Ricks observes, nowhere does Eliot tell us how to react to these women entering and leaving the drawing room. He chooses "talking" to describe what they are doing when he could as easily have said "prattling." He uses no adjective to denigrate the women, though at his disposal he had those I've already given ("trivial," "ignorant," "tedious") and more ("shallow," "affected," "fashionable"). Nor does Eliot praise the "glory" of Michelangelo's "giant art" by way of emphasizing the discrepancy between the women and the object of their conversation. It is a measure of Eliot's subtlety and skill that he disdains such modifiers as would bully a reader into the desired response. But Ricks's larger point is that even redoubtable critics are unaware of "how much their sense of the lines is incited by prejudice."

Ricks's treatment of Eliot illustrates how canny a close reader he is. It may remind us also of the pleasure to be had from such acts of critical acumen. And if, as Wordsworth insisted in the preface to the *Lyrical Ballads*, the giving of pleasure constitutes the poet's first obligation to the reader, may it not be reasonable to expect the critic of poetry to honor this same imperative? Yet what Wordsworth calls the "grand elementary principle of pleasure" is missing from discussions of contemporary poetry. Schadenfreude is a poor substitute. True delight accompanies edification when a lover of poetry shows us how to read a poem on its own terms, paying it the respect of careful attention, leaving aside the prejudices of the anathematist, the ideologue, the apostle of received opinion, or the bully on the block.

It may just be that the most appealing alternative to the negativity of contemporary criticism is the selective inclusiveness of a dedicated editor. For thirty-six years David Wagoner edited *Poetry Northwest*. The value of a supportive editor is incalculable, and Wagoner was among the best. His editorial practice can be seen as an extension of his humane poetics. For more than a half century, he has written about ordinary lives and real landscapes with grace and emotional complexity. A master of the plain style, for whom clarity and directness are cardinal virtues, he is a poet of wisdom and wonder. In their unostentatious way, his poems remind us of what it means to be human. Although we set our sights on the heavens, what we see from the wrong end of the telescope may prove more vital, for it "shows us just how little the gods see / if they look back." Yet like actors in a grand comedy we turn and change, turn and change, "like young heavenly objects / endlessly reembodied" with "wardrobes as various / as the wonders of new stars." I am conflating quotations from two poems in Wagoner's latest collection, *A Map of the Night*, which appeared last year—the year Wagoner spent reading for *The Best American Poetry 2009*. He has selected poems from an unprecedented number of print or electronic journals: fifty-six. The poets explore subjects ranging from love and death to God, Freud, the beauty of the matriarchs in Genesis, the animals with which we share the planet, "the land to the south of our neighbors to the north," the movies, and "The Great American Poem." A number of the poets address crises in the body politic: the damaged Mississippi Gulf Coast ("Liturgy"), the assassination of Daniel Pearl ("Forty"), the massacre at Virginia

Tech ("Ringtone"). We read about the prospect of a change in government ("A Sea-Change") and are confronted with "A Democratic Vista" and the assurance that "Ultimately Justice Directs Them."

The biggest political story of 2008, the campaign and election of Barack Obama as president of the United States, sparked great enthusiasm among American poets. No sooner had the election results come in than the speculation began as to whom the incoming administration would tap to read a poem at the inauguration. Only two previous presidents (Kennedy and Clinton) had incorporated a poem in the inaugural proceedings, but everyone was confident that Obama would renew this tradition and everyone was right. Elizabeth Alexander was entrusted with the task. But even after her name was disclosed, the print and broadcast media continued to run stories on the importance of poetry in the national discourse. Perusal of the poems written by U.S. presidents of the past revealed Lincoln to be our best presidential poet. Anecdotes surfaced on Theodore Roosevelt's admiration of Edwin Arlington Robinson and Franklin Delano Roosevelt's recognition of Archibald MacLeish's talents as a speechwriter, librarian, and adviser at large. The Associated Press reporter Nancy Benac asked a number of poets to write—and, where practicable, recite for the camera—ceremonial poems written with Obama's inauguration in mind. Billy Collins, Yusef Komunyakaa, Alice Walker, Christopher Funkhouser, Amiri Baraka, cowboy poet Ted Newman, Julia Alvarez, Gary Soto, Bob Holman, and I composed poems for the occasion. The results are still accessible via the Internet.

The Internet has multiplied the number of places in which a poem may appear. If it was difficult previously to cover American poetry, even with a company of skillful readers, it is now quite impossible. As David Wagoner notes in his introduction to this year's *The Best American Poetry*, there are more venues for poetry than ever before. Websites, online magazines, and blogs have enabled us to close up the lag between the composition and dissemination of any piece of writing. It remains to be seen how this technological advance will affect the nature of the writing itself, although the odds are that it will abet not only the tendency toward informality but also the impulse to buck it by emphasizing new and unusual forms: the abecedarius (or double abecedarius), the lipogram, the use of "found forms" such as the index of first lines in the back of a book of poems. Poems in such forms as these have turned up in recent and current volumes of *The Best American Poetry*, as have, to be sure, sonnets, sestinas, riddles, prose poems, a villanelle, a cento, a blues poem, a pantoum. The rediscovery of old forms and the fabrication of new ones is one notable tendency in contemporary poetry. A second is the growing appeal of the conversational style that David Kirby calls "ultra talk": a poem that sounds as natural as talk—if we could script our talk. After observing that "every revolution in poetry" is at base "a return to common speech," T. S. Eliot in "The Music of Poetry" (1942) goes on to give the rationale for this sort of "talk poetry": "No poetry, of course, is ever exactly the same speech that the poet talks and hears: but it has to be in such a relation to the speech of his time that the listener or reader can say 'that is how I should talk if I could talk poetry.'"

In 2008, *The Best American Poetry* launched our blog, which seemed at first to be an indulgence, then a convenience, before we understood that it could function as a kind of magazine, the contents of which change daily and feature an ever-changing roster of contributing writers and columnists. We post poems and comments on poems but also news, links, photos, illustrations, and prose on any subject that engages the mind of a poet. There are certain recurring features. We like aphorisms ("There are people who are too intelligent to become authors, but they do not become critics": W. H. Auden) and brainteasers ("Lives in winter, / Dies in summer, / And grows with its root upwards").[4] From time to time we have run contests. Mark Strand judged Gerald Greland the winner of the inaugural ode contest we posted a day or two after Barack Obama's electoral victory. Paul Violi judged Frank Osen the winner of the previous year's competition, in which contestants were asked to decipher an anagram and to write an acrostic poem based on the result. I am still marveling at the notion that, in contrast to the strict limitations of space in a print magazine, we can publish 365 poems in a calendar year. And we can do things like monitor the cultural markers on an acclaimed television show.

The spirit of Frank O'Hara hovered over the second season of the TV series *Mad Men* on AMC in 2008. In the first episode, ad man Don Draper (played by Jon Hamm) finds himself at a Midtown bar not far from where O'Hara loitered during his lunch hours when he worked as a curator at the Museum of Modern Art. On the barstool next to Draper sits a man with horn-rimmed glasses and curly hair reading O'Hara's *Meditations in an Emergency*. It is 1962. John F. Kennedy is president. Marilyn Monroe is still alive. Draper asks the man about the book. "You probably wouldn't like it," he is told. But Don buys it, we see him reading it in his office, and as the episode concludes, he mails the book to person or persons unknown and, in a voice-over, recites the fourth and

---

4. "When a riddler, using the bold weapon of metaphor, forces us to contemplate an icicle *as* a plant, it is an imaginative coup; briefly, and in a small way, our sense of the structure of reality is shaken." Richard Wilbur, "The Persistence of Riddles," *The Catbird's Song: Prose Pieces, 1963–1995* (New York: Harcourt Brace, 1997), 44.

final part of O'Hara's poem "Mayakovsky" in *Meditations in an Emergency*. The unforgettable phrase "the catastrophe of my personality" occurs here. The charm of such ironic self-deprecation, which is part of O'Hara's character armor, extends to the voice-over. The last words in "Mayakovsky" imply a split in the speaker's personality. "It may be the coldest day of / the year, what does he think of / that? I mean, what do I? And if I do, / perhaps I am myself again." The grammatical fact that, in a narrative, the same person can be either "I" or "he" turns into an apt metaphor for Don Draper, who bears someone else's name—he switched identities (we learned in season one) with a fallen comrade in a skirmish during the Korean War.

Meditations in an Emergency returns as the title of the thirteenth and final episode in season two of *Mad Men*. Marilyn Monroe has died. It is October. President Kennedy is addressing the nation on TV. Virtually all the characters in the show are going through an emergency of one kind or another, while the country as a whole faces the grave emergency that was the Cuban Missile Crisis. Unlike radio, which has always been a congenial medium for poems and verse plays, TV and poetry have seemed as irreconcilable as dance and architecture. Not the least of Matthew Weiner's accomplishments is the brilliant way he has used O'Hara's poetry to govern the themes of a dramatic series on TV. *Mad Men* is a big hit, sales of *Meditations in an Emergency* continue to climb, and a new generation of readers has fallen in love with the poems of Frank O'Hara.

———2010———

McChrystal sent copies of "The Second Coming" to his special operators

Over the years I've read novels centering on lawyers, doctors, diplomats, teachers, financiers, even car salesmen and dentists, but not until 2009 did I come across one about the travails of the editor of a poetry anthology. When word of *The Anthologist*, Nicholson Baker's new novel, reached me last September, I couldn't wait to read it. Baker's novels defy convention and reveal an obsessive nature, and I wondered what he would make of American poetry, for surely his novel would reflect a strenuous engagement with the art. The title character here, Paul Chowder by unfortunate name, has put together an anthology of poems he is calling *Only Rhyme*. The phrase describes the notional book's contents and indicates the editor's conception of poetic virtue. Paul has chosen the contents of his anthology but is now, on the eve of a deadline, afflicted with writer's block. He needs to write a foreword but cannot. "How many people read introductions to poetry anthologies, anyway?" he wonders, then volunteers, "I do, but I'm not normal."

Having asked myself that same question and given a similar answer, I can appreciate the speaker's troubling awareness of the many poets who have to be left out of his book—and the relatively few people who will bother to read his introductory essay. The task of writing a prefatory note becomes no less difficult when it is an annual requirement, though Nicholson Baker may have made my job a little easier this time around. Every editor has the impulse to use the introductory space to open the door, welcome the guest, and disappear without further ado. But some things are worth saying, and one such is Baker's defense of anthologies. For a poet facing all the perils that lurk in a poet's path—a poet very like the novel's Paul Chowder—anthologies represent the possibility of a belated second chance. And it is that possibility, however slim, that spurs the poet to stick to a vocation that offers so much resistance and promises so few rewards. The "you" in these sentences refers to the American poet—and perhaps to American poetry itself, an oddity in an age that worships celebrity. "You think: One more poem. You think: There will be some as yet ungathered anthology of American poetry. It will be the anthology that people tote around with them on subways thirty-five, forty years from now." The poet's conception of fame exists within modest limits, but it is persistent: "And you think: Maybe the very poem I write today will somehow pry open a space in that future anthology and maybe it will drop into position and root itself there."

Baker's skeptical distance from the fray makes his take on things particularly compelling. The opinions he puts forth are provocative and entertaining. A proponent of the sit-com as the great American art form, Baker's anthologist believes that "any random episode of *Friends* is probably better, more uplifting for the human spirit, than ninety-nine percent of the poetry or drama or fiction or history ever published." That is quite a statement, even allowing for the complexity of irony. (After all, to be "uplifting for the human spirit" may not be the ideal criterion by which to judge poetry or history.) The speaker establishes his credentials as an American poet with his realism for self-pity's sake. He suspects that poets form a "community" only in the realm of piety: "We all love the busy ferment, and we all know it's nonsense. Getting together for conferences of international poetry. Hah! A joke. Reading our poems. Our little moment. Physical presence. In the same room with. A community. Forget it. It's a joke."

Baker (or his mouthpiece) likes Swinburne, Poe, Millay, Elizabeth Bishop, Louise Bogan, and the contemporary British poets Wendy Cope and James Fenton. He disapproves of free verse, distrusts the "ultra-extreme enjambment" that you find in William Carlos Williams or Charles Olson, and argues that "iambic pentameter" is something of a hoax. As for the unrhymed poems that dominate literary magazines and university workshops, he feels it would be more accurate to call them "plums" and their authors "plummets" or "plummers." How did we get to this state of affairs? In Baker's account, the chief villain is Ezra Pound, "a blustering bigot—a humorless jokester—a talentless pasticheur—a confidence man." Pound advocated modernism in verse with the same bullying arrogance that went into his radio broadcasts on behalf of Mussolini, and that is no accident, because the impulse that led to fascism also gave rise to modern poetry. Modernism as Pound preached it and T. S. Eliot practiced it—in "The Waste Land," "a hodgepodge of flummery and borrowed paste"—was, in short, probably as ruinous for the art of verse as fascism was for Europe. The popularity of translations, especially prose versions of exotic foreign verse rendered from a language that the translator doesn't know, also did its part to hasten the "death of rhyme."

The views articulated in *The Anthologist* are antithetical to contemporary practice in ways that recall Philip Larkin's conviction that Pound ruined poetry, Picasso ruined painting, and Charlie Parker ruined jazz: the dissenting position, pushed to an amusing extreme, and stated with uncompromising intelligence. The narrator can sound a sour note. To teach creative writing to college students is to be "a professional teller of lies," he maintains, gleefully quoting Elizabeth Bishop on the subject: "I think one of the worst things I know about modern education is this 'Creative Writing' business." Nevertheless Baker's opinions are worth pondering, especially when the "difficulty versus accessibility" question becomes the subject of debate. And his advice to the aspiring poet is astute. Don't postpone writing the poem, he says. "Put it down, work on it, finish it. If you don't get on it now, somebody else will do something similar, and when you crack open next year's *Best American Poetry* and see it under somebody else's name you'll hate yourself."

The Anthologist was well received and prominently reviewed in book supplements that rarely notice poetry books, let alone anthologies of them, except with a certain contempt, which was a mild irony but an old story. Some laudatory articles went so far as to declare that "you" will enjoy the work "even if you generally couldn't care less about verse." But then, when poetry or the teaching of poetry is discussed, commentators have a hard time avoiding a note of condescension. Poetry is called a "lost art." It is thought to be something young people go through, a phase; something you have to apologize for, as when a poet at a reading reassures the audience that only three more poems remain on the docket. And yet poetry retains its prestige. The term exists as a sort of benchmark in fields ranging from politics to athletics. Columnists enjoy reminding newly elected officials that "you campaign in poetry but govern in prose"—an axiom that aligns poetry on the side of idealism and eloquence against the bureaucratic details and inconveniences of prosaic administration. In the *Financial Times*, the Czech photographer Miroslav Tichý, who spied on women with his homemade viewfinder, "stealing their likenesses as they giggled, gossiped and dreamed," is described as "a peeping Tom with a poet's eye."

Of Nancy Pelosi, readers of *Time* learned that, to the speaker's credit, when a colleague's mother dies, she "encloses a poem written by her own mother with her condolence." In the same issue of the magazine, a flattering profile of General Stanley McChrystal, commander of U.S. forces in Afghanistan, appeared. During the Iraq war, McChrystal sent copies of "The Second Coming" to his special operators, challenging them to flip the meaning of Yeats's lines: "The best lack all conviction, while the worst / Are full of passionate intensity."

Has there ever been a really good movie about a poet as opposed to the many excellent movies in which poetry is quoted to smart effect? *Bright Star*, Jane Campion's film about the ill-starred romance of John Keats and the barely legal Fanny Brawne, came out in 2009 and showed there is life left in the familiar stereotype of the consumptive poet burning a fever for love. Campion won over Quentin Tarantino. "The movie made me think about taking a writing class," the director of *Pulp Fiction* said. "One of the best things that can happen from a movie about an author is that you actually want to read their work." On television, poetry continues to put in regular appearances on *The PBS NewsHour* with Jim Lehrer and sometimes sneaks into scripted shows. When an advertising copywriter on *Mad Men* loses his job, he doesn't take it well. He "did not go gentle into that good night," an ex-associate observes. The critic Stephen Burt believes that *Project Runway* holds some useful lessons for poetry critics: "*Project Runway* even recalls the famous exercises in 'practical criticism' performed at the University of Cambridge in the 1920s, in which professor I. A. Richards asked his students to make snap judgments about unfamiliar poems." I have commented on the inspired way that quotations from poems turn up in classic Hollywood movies, and if you're lucky enough to catch *It's Always Fair Weather* the next time Robert Osborne shows it on TCM, you'll see a superb 1950s movie musical (music by André Previn, book and lyrics by Betty Comden and Adolph Green) that sums itself up brilliantly in three lines from *As You Like It* that enliven a conversation between Gene Kelly and Cyd Charisse:

> Most friendship is feigning, most loving mere folly.
> Then heigh-ho, the holly!
> This life is most jolly.

Meanwhile, you can't pull the wool over the creative writers responsible for *Law and Order: Criminal Intent*. In a 2009 episode, a celebrated campus bard is murdered by his ex-girlfriend, who is handy with a knife. Has he been pimping out his attractive young assistants to wealthy donors? After learning how rotten the poets are to one another, the major case squad detective says that if her daughter ever says she wants to be a poet, she'd tell her to join the Mafia instead: "Nicer people." As convalescents confined to hospital beds know, you can go wall to wall with reruns of *Law and Order*, and sure enough, the day after this episode aired I saw a rerun of *Law and Order: Criminal Intent*, in which the villain is a nerdy insurance man, an actuary with Asperger's syndrome, whose name is Wallace Stevens. The detectives call him Wally affectionately. I spent the rest of my bedridden day with Stevens's collected poems.

Haaretz, Israel's oldest Hebrew-language daily, turned over its pages entirely to poets and novelists for one day in June 2009. The results were unsurprising in some ways (a lot of first-person point of view) but inventive and unconventional in the coverage of the stock market ("everything okay") and the weather (a sonnet likening summer to an unsharpened pencil). The experiment reminded me of W. S. Di Piero's assertion that the writing of good prose is the acid test of a poet's intelligence. "Some shy from putting prose out there because it's a giveaway," Di Piero has written. "You can't fake it. It reveals quality of mind, for better or worse, in a culture where poems can be faked. Find a faker and ask him or her to write anything more substantial than a jacket blurb, and the jig is up." When we posted Di Piero's remark on *The Best American Poetry* blog, Sally Ashton added an apt simile (a poem can be faked "like an orgasm") and a few inevitable questions ("Who is fooled? Who benefits?"). Speaking of *The Best American Poetry* blog, there are days when it resembles nothing so much as a cross-cultural newspaper written by poets and poetry lovers. Recent visitors to *The Best American Poetry* blog could read Catharine Stimpson's reaction to homicidal violence at the University of Alabama; Lewis Saul's meticulously annotated commentary on thirty films by Akira Kurosawa; Jennifer Michael Hecht's heartfelt plea to poets contemplating the suicide of Rachel Wetzsteon ("don't kill yourself"); Laura Orem's obituaries for Lucille Clifton, Jean Simmons, and J. D. Salinger; Katha Pollitt on Berlin in the fall; Larry Epstein on Bob Dylan; Ken Tucker on new books of poetry; Todd Swift on young British poets; Phoebe Putnam on the covers poets choose for their books; Mitch Sisskind's "poetic tips of the day" (e.g., "Secrecy sustains the world"); Gabrielle Calvocoressi at the sports desk; Terence Winch on Irish American music; Stacey Harwood on *nocino*, the Italian liqueur made from under-ripe green walnuts; and a James Cummins epigram entitled "Anti-Confessional": "What it was like, I don't recall, or care to; / believe me, you should be grateful I spare you."

The Best American Poetry anthology itself, now in its twenty-third year, remains committed to the idea that American poetry is as vital as it is various and that it is possible to capture the spirit of its diversity and a measure of its excellence in an annual survey of our magazines, in print or online. As the selections are made by a different editor each year, each a distinguished practitioner, the series has inevitably become an annotated chronicle of the taste of our leading poets. I persuaded Amy Gerstler to make the selections for the 2010 edition of *The Best American Poetry* because of my delight in her poems and my respect for her judgment, and it was wonderful to work with her. Amy's new book, *Dearest Creature*, came out last year, and augmented her reputation as arguably the most inventive and ambitious poet of her generation. Gerstler can be very funny without forfeiting her right to be taken seriously; she has a quality of sincerity, of truth telling, that can coexist with the most sophisticated of comic sensibilities. Her poems of deep feeling may take on an insouciant disguise: a letter to a cherished niece about the virtues of an encyclopedia, a conversation between a black taffeta and strapless pink dress, a riff consisting entirely of slang phrases from the not too distant past. Yet always at the heart of the poetry is an insight into the human condition and the ability to state it simply and powerfully: "Some of us grow up doing / credible impressions of model citizens / (though sooner or later hairline / cracks appear in our facades). The rest / get dubbed eccentrics, unnerved and undone / by other people's company, for which we / nevertheless pine." David Kirby reviewed *Dearest Creature* in the *New York Times Book Review.* "Gerstler is skilled in every kind of comedy, from slapstick to whimsy," Kirby wrote. "Yet there's a deep seriousness in every one of these poems, like the plaintive 'Midlife Lullaby,' in which the cow who is now the meatloaf in somebody's sandwich speaks of life's passing pleasures as hauntingly as one of those skeletons who tend to pop up in medieval allegories to remind young knights of their mortality." Kirby concluded his review with a ringing endorsement: "In Amy Gerstler I trust."

The world has been slow to react to the case of Saw Wai, the imprisoned Burmese poet who was arrested two years ago for publishing a love poem for Valentine's Day with a secret message critical of Burma's military dictator, Than Shwe. But the story refuses to die, and the anonymously translated poem itself has now been published (in *Pen America*) and reprinted (in *Harper's*, in February 2010). What early journalistic accounts called a "straightforward" or "innocuous" love poem turns out to be something much richer and stranger. Entitled "February 14," Saw Wai's poem, which appeared in the Rangoon magazine the *Love Journal*, was initially said to have been a torch song to the fashion model who rejected the poet but taught him the meaning of love. Nothing of the sort. It exemplifies rather a particular strain of modernist poetry, the leading-edge poems of the 1930s that were aped (and perfected) by the Australian hoax poet Ern Malley. The poem is an acrostic—that is, the first letters of the lines, when read down vertically, spell out a message, and in this case that message is, "General Than Shwe is power crazy." In Burmese, Than means "million" and Shwe means "gold," so when Saw Wai concludes his poem with the injunction "Millions of people / Who know how to love / Please clap your gilded hands / And laugh out loud," he is secretly urging his compatriots to laugh the "power crazy" head of the junta off the stage. It took courage to write these lines. It also took an extraordinary talent for modern poetry considered as a kind of cipher, and the result in its English translation might be read as either a brief for the methods of modernism or a textbook illustration of what Nicholson Baker would have us see as the tempting dangers of the non-rhyming, prose-saturated "plum":

> Arensberg said:[1]
> Only once you have experienced deep pain
> And madness
> And like an adolescent
> Thought the blurred photo of a model
> Great art
> Can you call it heartbreak.
> Millions of people
> Who know how to love
> Please clap your gilded hands
> And laugh out loud.

---

1. Walter Conrad Arensberg, the noted art collector and donor of great paintings to the Philadelphia Museum of Art, wrote *The Cryptography of Shakespeare* (1922), purporting to find, in the Bard's plays, anagrams and acrostics that prove Francis Bacon's authorship. Arensberg wrote symbolist-influenced poetry, but it is conceivable that spurious cryptography is his real contribution to the radical element in modern poetry.

————— *DAVID LEHMAN* —————

in Dickinson's brain, "wider than the sky"

What makes a poem great? What standards do we use for judging poetic excellence? To an extent, these are variants on an even more basic question. What is poetry? Poetry is, after all, not a neutral or merely descriptive term but one that implies value. What qualities in a piece of verse (or prose) raise it to the level of poetry? The questions face the editor of any poetry anthology. But only seldom do we discuss the criteria that we implicitly invoke each time we weigh the comparative merits of two or more pieces of writing. And to no one's surprise, it turns out to be far easier to recognize the genuine article than to articulate what makes it so, let alone to universalize from a particular instance. Thus, so astute a reader as Randall Jarrell will linger lovingly on the felicities of Robert Frost's late poem "Directive" only to conclude sheepishly: "The poem is hard to understand, but easy to love."

The standard definitions of poetry spring to mind, each one seeming a near tautology: "the best words in the best order" (Coleridge), "language charged with meaning to the utmost possible degree" (Pound), "memorable speech" (Auden). Other justly celebrated statements may stimulate debate but have a limited practical application. Is poetry the "spontaneous overflow of powerful feelings" (Wordsworth) or is it precisely "not the expression of personality but an escape from personality" (T. S. Eliot)? The statements contradict each other except in the mind of the reader who enjoys with nearly equal gusto the poetry of the Romantic movement, of Wordsworth and Coleridge, on the one hand, and that of the modernists who reacted so strongly against them (Eliot, Pound), on the other.

Poetry is "what gets lost in translation" (Frost); it "strips the veil of familiarity from the world, and lays bare the naked and sleeping beauty" (Shelley); it "is the universal language which the heart holds with nature and itself" (Hazlitt). Although poems do come along that seem to exemplify such statements, the problem remains unsolved except by individual case. Archibald MacLeish's famous formulation ("a poem should not mean / But be") is conceptually useful in a class of writers but leaves us exactly where we started. Asking herself "what is poetry and if you know what poetry is what is prose," Gertrude Stein makes us understand that poetry is a system of grammar and punctuation. "Poetry is doing nothing but using losing refusing and pleasing and betraying and caressing nouns"—a valuable insight, but try applying it to the task of evaluating poems and see if it gets any easier. Wallace Stevens, a master aphorist, has a score of sentences that begin with the words *poetry is*. Poetry is "a search for the inexplicable," "a means of redemption," "a form of melancholia," "a cure of the mind," "a health," "a response to the daily necessity of getting the world right." It is metaphorically "a pheasant disappearing in the brush," and it is also, in one word, "metaphor" itself. The proliferation of possibilities tells us a great deal about Stevens's habits of mind. But epigrams will not help the seasoned reader discriminate among the dozens of poems crying for attention from the pages or websites of well-edited literary magazines.

The emancipation of verse from the rules of yore complicates matters. It is tough on the scorekeeper if, as Frost said, free verse is like playing tennis without a net. (Some varieties of free verse seem to banish ball as well as net.) But even if we set store by things you can measure—rhyme, meter, coherence, clarity, accuracy of perception, the skillful deployment of imaginative tropes— the search for objective criteria is bound to fail. Reading is a frankly subjective experience, with pleasure the immediate objective, and in the end you read and judge the relative value of a work by instinct. That is, you become aware of the valence of your response, whether it is positive or negative, thumbs-up or -down, before you become aware of why you reacted the way you did. There is in fact no substitute for the experience of poetry, though you can educate your sensibility and become better able to summon up the openness to experience that is the critic's first obligation—that, and the ability to pay attention to the poem and to the impact it has made on you. Walter Pater asked these questions upon reading a poem or looking at a picture: "What effect does it really produce on me? Does it give me pleasure? And if so, what sort or degree of pleasure? How is my nature modified by its presence, and under its influence?"

Whatever else it is, American poetry today is as plentiful as it is diverse. And because very good poems may reflect aesthetically incompatible ideas, an editor's job has an added complication; one must be willing to suspend one's natural critical resistance. Poetry may happen "in the valley of its saying," in Auden's phrase, but discussions of poetry take place on academic battlefields. There are possibly as many different movements or schools, cliques or cabals, as there are states in the union. Conflicts may erupt, just as states may quarrel over their share of the federal budget. (The budget for poetry is small and exists therefore in an inverse ratio to the intensity of the skirmishing among poets.) The good reader is or tries to be indifferent to all this—to everything, in fact, except his or her own experience, when sitting down with, say, the latest issues of *FIELD*, *Antioch Review*, *New England Review*, and *Green Mountains Review*. I can report, having just spent pleasant evenings with these magazines, that there is a wonderful symposium on Richard Wilbur in *FIELD*, that one of Richard Howard's schoolboy memory poems graces *Antioch Review*, that Joanne Dominique Dwyer has a brilliant poem addressed to St. Teresa of Avila in *New England Review*, and that there is compelling work in *Green Mountains Review* from two poets previously unknown to me: Anna Maria Hong and the Canadian poet Robert Bringhurst, whom Stephen Dunn singles out in an interview. Many poems in these and other new journals pass the first and arguably most crucial test a critic asks of them—that they give pleasure, sustain interest, and compel a second reading.

It may be that in specifying these pragmatic criteria, I have strayed from my original question when I meant merely to rephrase it. What do we ask for in poems of high excellence? To answer you need to make a list, and by the time you get to the third or fourth item you realize that no poem can do all the things people expect from poetry, not only because we may be perfectionists when it comes to judging the works of others but also because we want mutually exclusive things. Do we read for moral fortitude, humane knowledge that can help us lead our lives? (Thus, to elucidate the dominant strain in Frost's poetry, W. H. Auden quotes Samuel Johnson: "The only end of writing is to enable the readers better to enjoy life or better to endure it.") Or are we more interested in what the scholar calls transcendence and the reader knows to be escape— whether to Xanadu or Byzantium? (Thus Emily Dickinson: "There is no Frigate like a Book / To take us Lands away / Nor any Coursers like a Page / Of prancing poetry.") Perhaps we respond to feats of ingenuity: complicated verse forms mastered and married to colloquial speech, as in Elizabeth Bishop's sestinas; diabolically clever meaning-making puns in the service of a narrative, as in a sonnet sequence by James Merrill. There is a delight in artifice. In past editions, *The Best American Poetry* has published a poem consisting entirely of palindromes (Lydia Tomkiw: "sad as samara, ruff of fur, a ram; as sad as / Warsaw was raw") and another that exemplifies the zeugma in every line (Charles North: "To break the silence or your newly acquired Ming vase, / or raise my expectations and the flag over the Brooklyn Navy Yard"), in addition to tricky sestinas, villanelles, pantoums, centos, traditional sonnets, ballads, the occasional abecedarius, chant royal, and narrative in terza rima, though these are vastly outnumbered by the many varieties of poems in plain speech, such as you will find exemplified by Robert Hass in the 2011 volume ("When the police do a forced entry for the purpose / Of a welfare check and the deceased person is alone, / The body goes to the medical examiner's morgue") and by Mary Ruefle in a completely different way ("I hated childhood / I hate adulthood / And I love being alive").

Marianne Moore valued the "compactness compacted" that she found in Louise Bogan's poems. But excess has its proponents as well, and there will always be those who want the act of writing to be an act of defiance before it is anything else. Too many poems fail because they try too hard to change the world. But then along comes a work proving that poetry does make something happen. The timely cry of protest may have a longer shelf life than poems with immortal designs on them. Consider the case of Allen Ginsberg's "Howl," tried for obscenity in San Francisco in 1957, lionized nationally more than a half century later with the release of Rob Epstein and Jeffrey Friedman's full-length film homage in 2010. The actor James Franco, who has studied creative writing at Columbia, UCLA, and in the Warren Wilson low-residency MFA program, "captures the Ginsberg we hear in our heads and know in our bones," Ken Tucker writes in his review. The acting borders on impersonation. Franco "looks at the camera with Ginsberg's cockeyed, moist deadpan, or reproduces the Elated Allen Grin—an ear-to-ear face-splitter that can vanish in an instant." Ginsberg's "Kaddish" and "America" may be better poems than "Howl," but the latter has become a battle cry for the ages, an American icon as famous as an Andy Warhol soup can.

In sum, we may like poetic conventions and traditions—and we may like seeing them sent up, too. We want poems of eloquence to recite on grave occasions, and at the same time we have a hankering to parody such utterances. We admire the artistry that conceals itself in the finished work. But we are not immune to the charms of the flamboyant or to what Wallace Stevens calls the "essential gaudiness of poetry." We want something that sounds "at least as alive as the vulgar" (Frank O'Hara) and is in some sense original. All this, and we want the poet to surprise us with lines and phrases that echo in the mind days, even weeks, after we encountered them, because they have insinuated themselves in our consciousness.[1] Everyone has his favorite touchstones. Consider the sequence of ten monosyllables that kicks off Frost's "Directive": "Back out of all this now too much for us." Or the work that the definite article does to separate states of nothingness in the last line of Stevens's "The Snow Man"; "Nothing that is not there and the nothing that is." Think of Emily Dickinson's genitive phrases (a "transport / Of cordiality," "the power to die," "A privilege of Hurricane"), of Hart Crane's jolting juxtapositions ("and love / A burnt match skating in a urinal"), or of the amazing things that W. H. Auden can do with even so commonplace a figure as the "journey of life" in his masterly prose poem "Caliban to the Audience."

In his "Essay on Criticism" (1711), Alexander Pope laid down the law for exponents of the heroic couplet. He prized elegance and pith: "True wit is Nature to advantage dressed: / What oft was thought but ne'er so well expressed." For his odes addressing the Grecian urn, the nightingale, and the condition of melancholy, Keats in 1819 went in pursuit of something different: an agency of imagination "capable of making all disagreeables evaporate"—a force of such intensity, and in so close a relationship with Beauty and Truth, that it can redeem "unpleasantness" and bury "repulsiveness." In the American grain, Walt Whitman and Emily Dickinson belong to the Romantic tradition Keats exemplified but embody two extreme positions. Dickinson says that she knows exactly what poetry is. "If I read a book [and] it makes my whole body so cold no fire can warm me I know *that* is poetry. If I feel physically as if the top of my head were taken off, I know *that* is poetry." Poetry is, then, an intense sensation, not altogether enjoyable, like the "heavenly hurt" in Dickinson's poem that begins "There's a certain Slant of light." Whitman's most memorable criterion is as "hankering, gross, mystical, nude" as the persona of the author of "Song of Myself." Toward the end of his prose preface to the 1855 edition of *Leaves of Grass*, Whitman tells us he makes this demand of a poem, any poem: "Will it help breed one goodshaped and wellhung man, and a woman to be his perfect and independent mate?"

---

1. "It is hard to ask the two questions, 'Is this good, whether I like it or not?' and 'Do I like this?' at the same time: and I often find that the best test is when some phrase, or image, or line out of a new poem, recurs to my mind afterwards unsummoned." T. S. Eliot, "What Is Minor Poetry?" (1944), in *On Poetry and Poets* (New York: Farrar, Straus and Giroux, 1957), 50.

Harold Bloom speaks in awe of the quality of "strangeness" in the canonical works he prizes.[2] I share the conviction that great poems have an uncanny power—uncanny in the loose sense but sometimes also in the Freudian sense that what we repress returns to haunt us. You feel the uncanny at work when you read "Crossing Brooklyn Ferry," and have the illusion, as if by hypnotic suggestion, that Whitman is there in the room with you, his voice in your ear across the divide of a century and a half. The quality of strangeness is perhaps even stronger in "Out of the Cradle Endlessly Rocking," the poem in which Whitman accounts for his calling as a poet. Whitman had been, in Mark Van Doren's characterization, "a lazy, eccentric, uneducated, unsuccessful, little-known newspaper man" when he underwent the transformation, or endured the vision, out of which all his poetry seems to emanate.[3] But when he sits down to write about the experience that initiated him into manhood and made him a bard, Whitman recalls the moment when, as a boy alone on the shore in Long Island, he heard two mockingbirds sing, and then one stopped singing and the other missed his mate and sang elegiac songs to her, and suddenly Whitman understood his purpose in life, "what I am for." The next words are climactic: "And already a thousand singers, a thousand songs, clearer, louder and more sorrowful than yours, / A thousand warbling echoes have started to life within me, never to die." The eight lines that follow constitute a credo and a vow:

> O you singer, solitary, singing by yourself—projecting me;
> O solitary me, listening—nevermore shall I cease perpetuating you;
> Never more shall I escape, never more the reverberations.
> Never more the cries of unsatisfied love be absent from me,
> Never again leave me to be the peaceful child I was before what there, in
>   the night,
> By the sea, under the yellow and sagging moon,
> The messenger there arous'd—the fire, the sweet hell within,
> The unknown want, the destiny of me.

---

2. "'Strangeness' for me is *the* canonical quality, the mark of sublime literature. . . . Strangeness is uncanniness: the estrangement of the homelike or commonplace. This strangeness is likely to manifest itself differently in writers and readers. But in both cases strangeness renders the deep relation between sublimity and influence palpable." Harold Bloom, *The Anatomy of Influence: Literature as a Way of Life* (New Haven: Yale University Press, 2011), 19.

3. "Walt Whitman, Stranger," in Mark Van Doren, *The Private Reader* (New York: Henry Holt, 1942), 85.

And here Whitman makes a move that lifts the poem into a higher realm of strangeness. As if unsatisfied with the epiphany he has achieved, he renews his quest or request. "O if I am to have so much, let me have more!" He begs for a "clew," a "word final, superior to all," that will reveal the full meaning of the parable of the two mockingbirds. And the sea obligingly "Lisp'd to me the low and delicious word death, / And again death, death, death, death." The word *death* appears a total of ten times in the space of five lines, and I submit that the extraordinary force of the passage owes something to the reader's astonishment at the sight of Whitman ecstatic with the discovery that death is the "word of the sweetest song and all songs." This is in another register altogether from Keats's restrained admission, in "Ode to a Nightingale," that "for many a time / I have been half in love with easeful Death," but it confirms the seductive power and uncanny appeal that the death wish has for the poet in a period of doubt and anxiety. Death is either "the mother of beauty" (Wallace Stevens) or a carriage driver of marked civility (Emily Dickinson), a strangely familiar presence in either case, maternal and kind.

The power of the uncanny is pronounced in Dickinson's "There's a certain Slant of light." You feel it from the moment you register the double meaning of "certain" in the first line and the arresting "Heft / Of Cathedral Tunes" two lines later:

> There's a certain Slant of light,
> Winter Afternoons—
> That oppresses, like the Heft
> Of Cathedral Tunes—
>
> Heavenly Hurt, it gives us—
> We can find no scar,
> But internal difference,
> Where the Meanings, are—
>
> None may teach it—Any—
> 'Tis the Seal Despair—
> An imperial affliction
> Sent us of the Air—
>
> When it comes, the Landscape listens—
> Shadows—hold their breath—

When it goes, 'tis like the Distance
On the look of Death—

This cryptic utterance is as much a poem about poetic inspiration as "Out of the Cradle" is. Only in the realm of the uncanny sublime—or in Dickinson's brain, "wider than the sky"—can the trope for illumination, a "Slant of light," so naturally associate itself with "despair." The author, who begins a later poem with the imperative "Tell all the Truth but tell it slant," receives the "certain" gift of heaven on condition that she be wounded in the process. "It is possible to see the greater part of her poetry as an effort to cope with her sense of privation," Richard Wilbur writes, adducing "three major privations: she was deprived of an orthodox and steady religious faith; she was deprived of love; she was deprived of literary recognition."[4] For the hurt there is compensation. The "internal" meaning-making power that Wordsworth, a more orthodox Romantic poet, called the "inward eye" enables her to tell "all the Truth" but slant, in riddling poems of extreme brevity. The "very Lunacy of Light," as she calls it in another poem, offers enchantment: bees become butterflies, butterflies turn into swans, and the imagination turns the "meanest Tunes" in the forest into "Titanic Opera." Nevertheless she feels the gift to be oppressive, a burden. In the key phrases, "Heavenly Hurt" and "imperial affliction," the nouns pull in one direction, the adjectives in the other, but that is only right if inspiration is a form of creative despair. The aftereffect of that slant of light, as described in the poem's last stanza, compounds the reader's amazement. "The listening landscape and breath-holding shadows are among Dickinson's finest figurations," in Bloom's words, "but her ellipsis is finer still."[5] The dash that ends the poem, the dashes that punctuate it throughout, proclaim the radical strangeness of her art, a feeling that is strengthened when we encounter a Dickinson poem in which the poet asserts that "success" is understood best by a fallen soldier among the defeated or when we read her pithy definition of "Heaven" as "what I cannot reach!"

Mark Van Doren, whose Columbia University students included Allen Ginsberg and John Berryman, taught that "the one thing which all new poets possess in common is strangeness." For Van Doren, Robert Frost's strangeness consisted in the "conversational tone" of his blank verse; for Randall Jarrell, the strangeness of Frost's "Directive" is "far under the surface, or else so much

---

4. Richard Wilbur, "Sumptuous Destitution," in *Emily Dickinson: A Collection of Critical Essays*, ed. Judith Farr (New Jersey: Prentice-Hall, 1996), 54.

5. Harold Bloom, *The Western Canon* (New York: Harcourt Brace, 1994), 303.

on the surface . . . that one slides into it unnoticing." Ever mindful of his surname, Frost sometimes depicts himself as a lonely wanderer on a snowy evening, an alien in the universe. The element of the uncanny is present in such dark, wintry poems as "Desert Places" and "Stopping by Woods on a Snowy Evening." But you find it also in the genial "Mending Wall," one of the poems that prove Frost to be not only subtler than innocents who take him at his word but also wiser than sophisticates who think they see through the subterfuge. The latter may argue that Frost's poem is an argument against fences, boundaries, and property lines—that he is gently satirizing the laconic neighbor, who quotes the authority of his father: "Good fences make good neighbors." And certainly the poem's speaker does seem to side with the natural forces that want walls to crumble in winter weather. "Something there is that doesn't love a wall," he says to open the poem, and he likes the line enough to repeat it as the poem draws to a close. There is, he points out, no reason for a fence between his property and his neighbor's—no reason beyond the neighbor's seemingly mindless repetition of a father's saying, a local tradition. But you read the poem again slowly and it dawns on you that the facts do not quite line up in support of this reading. You realize that the Frost persona not only joins his neighbor in rebuilding the wall but also that it is he who initiates the action; that "mending" in the title is a synonym for healing; and that Frost gives the neighbor the last word. Along the way you come across these lines:

> Before I built a wall I'd ask to know
> What I was walling in or walling out,
> And to whom I was like to give offense.

The pun on *fence* in the last word is an exquisite example of Frost's subtlety. Is a *fence* a means to avoid giving *offense?* Analyzed this way, the poem leads not to an aporia of uncertainty but a surfeit of meaning. "And there," in the words of Wallace Stevens, the poet finds himself "more truly and more strange."

———————

One of the hallmarks of *The Best American Poetry* is that each annual volume in a series now numbering twenty-four reflects the sensibility of a different guest editor, himself or herself a distinguished practitioner of the art. No single volume is definitive; each may be viewed not only as an addition but also as a corrective. Kevin Young, who made the selections for *The Best American Poetry 2011*, has established himself as a singularly talented poet and man of letters. *Ardency: A Chronicle of the Amistad Rebels*, his most recent collection, is characteristically larger than the sum of its parts; it is unified in tone, style, subject matter, and ambition. Young comes at you in the form of a minstrel show in one poem, a hymn in another, proverbs and prayers, diary entries and letters, to look at the 1839 slave-ship mutiny with the multiple perspectives the truth calls for. Young has edited several important anthologies. *Giant Steps* in 2000 presented African American poets who had recently come to the fore or were about to do so. Subsequent volumes include anthologies of jazz poems, blues poems, and a selected edition of John Berryman, the white poet who dared to adopt a persona in blackface for his most original work, *The Dream Songs*. Last year brought us *The Art of Losing: Poems of Grief and Healing* (Bloomsbury USA), a collection of poems exemplifying the modern elegy in its various guises and, as Young sees it, six stages of mourning, "from Reckoning to Regret, through Remembrance to Ritual and Recovery" and finally to Redemption. It does not necessarily follow from Mr. Young's previous labors, but there is a strong element of the elegiac in *The Best American Poetry 2011*. There are two poems with "Elegy" in their titles and many more that mourn brother, lover, father, friend. There are poems entitled "Valediction" and "The Funeral Sermon," musings on angels and the afterlife. I hasten to say that there are also poems about banking, coffee, dating, poppies, the disastrous oil spill in the Gulf last year, snow, pears, and the end of a love affair, in forms ranging from an inventory of aphorisms to a crown of sonnets. The alphabetical arrangement of the contents produces serendipitous linkages: the late Rachel Wetzsteon's haiku sequence "Time Pieces" prefigures the haiku stanzas of the poem that follows, Richard Wilbur's "Ecclesiastes II:I."

I favor the idea of being as comprehensive and inclusive as possible when surveying the landscape for an enterprise that confers, in the end, an exclusive distinction. The struggle I have annually is not with unsolvable questions of poetic value, the definition of "America," or the use of a superlative. The struggle I have is simply keeping up with the plethora of poems and poets out there begging for a hearing. Much of the mail I get is gratifying. People write that a volume in the series, or a particular poem, had a decisive effect on them. Contributors say they are happy to be included. They call it an honor. They've been reading *The Best American Poetry* and now their own work is in there. Some of the poems we have featured have become poetry standards. It's nice to think that we played a hand in that or in the stubborn refusal of poetry to lose its power of attraction in a period of information overkill.

Poetry is unkillable. The very word is too useful. When he found out that I write poetry, a software manufacturer congratulated me on practicing "a craft that will never become obsolete"—unlike last year's version of this year's operating system. Whether or not he meant to be ironic, the irony is he is right. The desire to write poetry is a precious thing. It turns into a need on the one hand and a habit or practice on the other. If we were making a list of reasons to stay alive, and it seems we keep needing to do so, poetry would occupy a cherished place on the list. We have the testimony of people from any and every class, category, and income bracket. To the extent that we can bring to the publishing of poetry the same imaginative energy that goes into the writing of a poem, we will have succeeded in doing something important for the art itself, for our poets, and for readers prepared to embrace poetry if only it were presented to them in an appealing way.

the "uncanny" is a category too little invoked

A few years ago my wife and I moved into a New York apartment house with a flower shop on the ground level. As an inveterate anthologist who loves flowers and likes picking up a last-minute rose, I took it as an auspicious sign that the shop is called Anthology. It is a splendid name for a florist: "anthology" derives from the Greek words for "flower" and "collection." The horticultural meaning preceded the literary sense, and editors of poetry books gathered "flowers of verse" long before a French revolutionist published his "flowers of evil." It is good to have a daily reminder of this connection between poems and "glowing violets," "fair musk-rose blooms," and daffodils "with the green world they live in," for the making of an anthology is only incidentally like the art of flower arrangement. In practice it can be a pretty fraught affair. If it is successful, the endeavor will generate discussion and debate, some of it heated, even pugnacious, and more appropriate to a fight club than to a quiet bower, where "the mind, from pleasure less, / Withdraws into its happiness."

"If you want to start an argument, put together an anthology, especially one that claims to be comprehensive," a jazz reviewer notes. "No matter how noble the intent, it invites disaffection. Make the subject area jazz, and you create a minefield of sensitive historical, political, social and musical issues. It's a treacherous endeavor—as is reviewing it."[1] The statement remains true if you substitute "exclusive" for "comprehensive" and "poetry" for "jazz." On the other hand, it's a sure proof that you're doing your job if your anthology quickens argument and dispute. People like anthologies—there's something for everyone. Practitioners like being in them, spectators like knowing who's in and who's out, critics like laying down the law, and malcontents like the occasion to air their grievances. As for the maker of poetry anthologies in particular, there is the gratification of reaching an educated readership for the elusive but vital art form whose death has so often been predicted. Something beyond nobility, something in defiance of disaffection and even treachery, is at work here. Pascal's aphorism has a special application to poetry and its devotees: the heart has its reasons that reason can only guess at.

The Best American Poetry 2012 is the twenty-fifth volume in the series—twenty-sixth if you count Harold Bloom's 1998 distillation, *The Best of the Best American Poetry 1988–1997*. The books have provided a template for similar annuals from other nations. On my desk as I write, I have the 2009 volume of *The Best Canadian Poetry in English* (ed. A. F. Moritz, series ed. Molly Peacock) and *The Best Australian Poems 2011* (ed. John Tranter), each with its compelling new voices. *The Best Irish Poetry 2010* (ed. Matthew Sweeney) joins the famous (Seamus Heaney) and the emerging (Leanne O'Sullivan) in the time-honored fashion. *The Best New Zealand Poems*, which got its start in 2001, explains on its homepage that "We have shamelessly modeled this online project on the successful US paperback anthology, *The Best American Poetry*. Each year we publish twenty-five poems from recent literary magazines and poetry collections, where possible including notes about and by the poet, as well as links to related publishing and literary websites. In this way we hope that readers will be able to follow up fresh discoveries. There are plenty to be made." Last year brought a welcome newcomer, *The Best British Poetry 2011* (ed. Roddy Lumsden). Other than consisting of seventy rather than seventy-five poems, the venture employs the identical structure and even the same typeface and design as *The Best American Poetry*. If there is one assumption common to all these "best of" books, it is that poetry has managed to thrive in the face of all the technological changes that seem, on the surface at least, so hostile to the muse.

Reporters are interested in trends, and you, cornered, may feel the impulse to invent one out of whole cloth just to please an interviewer. But I feel confident in my prediction that more and more arranged marriages will be taking

---

1.   Stuart Isacoff, "Anthology by Committee," *Wall Street Journal*, April 28, 2011.

place between poetry and video—confident enough to call this development a trend. Tom Devaney's online *ONandOnScreen* is devoted to poets pairing their work with a video of their choice. The aim is a dialogue between "moving words and moving images" in the expectation that the "essential strangeness" of each medium will be enhanced. In 2011, *The Best American Poetry* partnered with Motionpoems, a Minneapolis-based poetry and video initiative founded by Todd Boss, himself a poet whose work has appeared in this series, and the animator Angella Kassube. Motionpoems commissioned video artists—commercial and freelance animators, filmmakers, musicians, sound designers, and producers—to make short films of poems chosen from *The Best American Poetry 2011*.[2] Where the poets choose their visual accompaniment in Devaney's project, Motionpoems reverses the order. The animators pick the poems and take it from there. To this observer, the dozen Motionpoems screened in October 2011 vindicated the concept of such "passive collaborations" between poets and visual artists, passive only in the sense that the poet's job is done after writing the poem and the video maker is on his or her own. The idea of basing a video on a poem may one day seem as natural and inevitable as the setting of poems to music used to be.

While I am not sure that it constitutes a trend, exactly, I believe that the "uncanny" is a category too little invoked in discussions of American poetry. The poets of our time are drawn to ghostly demarcations, spectral presences. There are ghosts in the machine, ghosts in the martini, and they turn up regularly—angelic or demonic, benevolent or cruel—in poems. When, in late December, a senior editor at NPR asked me to name three of my favorite poems of 2011 and to record some thoughts about them, I noticed only after assembling the trio that they share this quality of mystery and the uncanny, offering a spooky but also exhilarating glimpse of a spiritual world beyond our own. Mark Strand's "The Mysterious Arrival of an Unusual Letter," a prose poem, owes something of its effect to its brevity; it contains all of ten sentences, most of them short. The poet tells us about arriving home one night after a grueling day at the office. On the table he sees an envelope with his name on it. "The handwriting was my father's, but he had been dead for forty years. As one might, I began to think that maybe, just maybe, he was alive, living a secret life somewhere nearby. How else to explain the envelope? To steady myself, I

---

2. Films based on poems by Erin Belieu, Matthew Dickman, K. A. Hays, Jane Hirshfield, L. S. Klatt, James Langenbach, Bridget Lowe, Eric Pankey, Mark Strand, David Wagoner, Richard Wilbur, and the series editor were shown in two public screenings at Open Book in Minneapolis on October 25, 2011.

sat down, opened it, and pulled out the letter. 'Dear Son,' was the way it began. 'Dear Son' and then nothing." The poem ends there, as eerie as a dream visitation from a deceased parent or lover.

Like Strand's poem, Stephanie Brown's "Notre Dame" was chosen by Mark Doty for *The Best American Poetry 2012*. Though not in prose, Brown's lines approach plain speech, an unadorned directness, eschewing the glamour of rhyme or traditional form. Brown describes staying with her family in an apartment near the great cathedral in Paris. One morning she wakes up and apprehends "two angels hovering" to protect her younger son. Only when the poem ends do we get the full context of this vision or waking dream: "It's sad to walk around the Seine when you are getting divorced while everyone else / Is kissing and filming their honeymoons or new loves. Even / My husband, after we got back together, laughed at that. / Because he, too, had been heartsick on another part of the planet."

My third pick was Paul Violi's "Now I'll Never Be Able to Finish That Poem to Bob" in the Brooklyn-based literary magazine *Hanging Loose*. The poem is jolly and even madcap, featuring "a man in a chicken suit / handing out flyers on Houston Street" among other urban wonders. "It would have been a long poem," the poem concludes, "and it would have made a lot of sense / and shown why I believe Bob Hershon is a wise man." (Hershon edits *Hanging Loose*.) What makes the poem almost heartbreaking is the knowledge that Violi wrote it in the face of his own death. Diagnosed with pancreatic cancer in January 2011, this amazingly inventive poet died on April 2 and yet was able to infuse the writing of this, his last poem, with such high spirits that it almost becomes a cheerful missive to us from that other world from which no traveler has ever returned.

Our poems are haunted, as our lives are, by that unknown territory on the other side of a wall too high to climb and see over. In *The Best American Poetry 2012* the "spirit in the dark" comes to light in poems that consider "The Gods" and "The Afterlife," the stories of Magdalene and the road to Emmaus. The poems wonder where "we go after we die"; they whisper rumors of the other side, about which all we know for certain is that it is "something entirely else." Mark Doty, who chose the poems for this year's volume, has a keen ear for the poetry of the uncanny. In his poems he has explored heaven as an earthly possibility, has delved into the realm of dreams more real than waking life, has encountered the apparition of a deceased poet obliviously enjoying his lunch at "the Eros Diner, corner / of 21st Street." Doty has won acclaim for his poetry (*Fire to Fire: New and Selected Poems* won the National Book Award for Poetry in 2008) and his prose (*Dog Years* was a *New York Times* best seller in

2007) not only in North America but also in the United Kingdom, where he is the sole American ever to receive the T. S. Eliot Prize. He cares deeply about poetry and poets, loves the language, values good writing. He is as sympathetic a reader as I could have wanted, as generous, and as open to new voices. Mark writes about poetry with passion and acumen. Read him on Hart Crane or May Swenson, on William Blake's "Ah! Sunflower" and on Alan Shapiro, in his book *The Art of Description*, and you will see why I felt he was an irresistible choice to edit this volume of *The Best American Poetry*.

To write poetry, to read it, to go to poetry readings, is a way of being in the world, and there will always be those who get suspicious and feel that maybe Plato was right to exclude the poets from his ideal Republic. Poetry, as they see it, is a form of "divine madness" that can lead you astray like a drug. It may be that all criticism has its origin in this rationalist rejection of the poet's way of being in the world. Faced with uncomprehending or dismissive criticism, the young poet might take heart from something T. S. Eliot once wrote: "Upon giving the matter a little attention, we perceive that criticism, far from being a simple and orderly field of beneficent activity, from which impostors can be readily ejected, is no better than a Sunday park of contending and contentious orators, who have not even arrived at the articulation of their differences." To counter the din of contentious oratory, very little of which will help the writer (or reader) in any useful way, I turn instinctively to the rhetorical question that animates Shakespeare's sonnet sixty-five: "How with this rage shall beauty hold a plea, / Whose action is no stronger than a flower?"

The Best of the Best American Poetry, Twenty-Fifth Anniversary Edition

―――2013―――

"Every time I read Pessoa I think"

Forty years ago, two professors working independently—Harvard's Walter Jackson Bate and Yale's Harold Bloom—changed the way we think about literary tradition. In *The Burden of the Past and the English Poet* (1970), Bate challenged the idea that literary influence was a largely benign activity on the model of mentor and sometimes rebellious pupil. In *The Anxiety of Influence* (1973), Bloom went further and propounded a compelling new theory, which quickly caught on. Students today learn that poets labor under the weight of their self-chosen masters—that, for example, the Romantic poets had Milton on the brain or that James Merrill in the United States and James Fenton in Britain illustrate two rival ways of absorbing the masterly influence of the transatlantic W. H. Auden. The encounter with the master is bound to provoke anxiety. What the latecomer does with that anxiety determines his or her chances at originality. Anxiety can certainly prove a source for poetry. When, for a commemorative volume, Bloom selected poems from the first ten years of *The Best American Poetry*, it is telling that he chose two poems that are not about anxiety as much as they appear to spring from it: "Anxiety's Prosody" by A. R. Ammons from the 1989 volume (ed. Donald Hall) and John Ashbery's "The Problem of Anxiety" from that of 1997 (ed. James Tate). Bloom's theory may help us practically in our confrontations with such works and their authors.

His love of poetry, the passion on display when he quotes touchstone passages from his prodigious memory, make an essay of his, whether on Hamlet or the King James Bible, Walter Pater or Walt Whitman, a profound and at times sublime experience.

Yet I contend that the process by which one poet assimilates the influence of another is not always quite so joyless, anxiety-ridden, or bereft of affection, as the theory would seem to imply. The pugilistic metaphors that appealed to Hemingway and Norman Mailer don't quite fit. The competition between and among poets is more like a team sport—you have teammates as well as opponents, you play for a chance at post-season glory (the sportswriters call it "immortality"), but you also play the occasional "exhibition game" (U.S.) or "friendly" (Britain). The best poetry anthologies demonstrate that there is often an element of sport and gamesmanship in the way that a poet can take note of an ancestor, an ally, or a rival. And in consequence, it's as though the poems they write are engaged in a dialogue.

To one who loves poetry and teaches Marvell's "The Garden" in relation to the first three chapters of Genesis, or William Carlos Williams's *Pictures from Brueghel* in relation to poems by W. H. Auden and John Berryman on the same paintings, it seems a self-evident proposition that poems partner with other poems. E. M. Forster's metaphor in *Aspects of the Novel* applies to poems—he imagines a timeless British Museum Reading Room where the books of any and all eras may converse among themselves, sharing secrets and trading intimacies. I love the metaphor but would amend it to say that favorite poems have a way of pairing off, like the characters of certain books—like Don Quixote and Sancho Panza, say, or Holmes and Watson, or Beatrice and Benedick in *Much Ado About Nothing*—that continue to live after the reader has returned them to the shelf.

Looking over the poems published in *The Best American Poetry* over the last twenty-five years, I am struck by the number of such poem pairings. In *The Best American Poetry 2012* (ed. Mark Doty), Jennifer Chang and Angelo Nikolopoulos react to Wordsworth's daffodils just as Billy Collins, back in the 1998 edition (ed. John Hollander), responded to the same poet's "Tintern Abbey." Also in the 2012 volume, Amy Glynn Greacen confronts William Blake on the matter of the sunflower ("and fie, / By the way, on any and all, who'd think to call / You weary of time"), and David Mason addresses the gap between Shelley's life and his ideals—the subject of a poem by Galway Kinnell that Paul Muldoon chose for The *Best American Poetry 2005*. In 1999 (ed. Robert Bly), John Brehm's "Sea of Faith" ponders Matthew Arnold's "Dover Beach"; in 2001 (ed. Robert Hass), Alan Feldman's "Contemporary American Poetry" struggles with Donald Hall's "Kicking the Leaves"; in 2008 (ed. Charles Wright), Ron Padgett's "Method, or Kenneth Koch" pays homage to a mentor; in 2007 (ed. Heather McHugh), Albert Goldbarth's poem takes its title from Robert Frost's "Stopping by Woods on a Snowy Evening," with which it has a lover's quarrel. Of "The Rose Has Teeth," Terrance Hayes's poem in the 2012 volume, its author writes, "My poem found its bones after I read Matthew Zapruder's marvelous poem, 'Never to Return,' in the 2009 edition of *The Best American Poetry*."

Let me linger over another example or two. Julie Sheehan's poem in *The Best American Poetry 2005* confronts the problem of writing a contemporary love poem. How do you avoid the clichés or the embarrassment of either purple patches or pink ones? Sheehan expresses the emotion by turning it on its head. Where the word "love" would ordinarily be found, she substitutes *hate*: "I hate you. Truly I do. / Everything about me hates everything about you." The poem ends with this crescendo:

> My breasts relaxing in their holster from morning till night hate you
> Layers of hate, a parfait.
> Hours after our last row, brandishing the sharp glee of hate,
> I dissect you cell by cell, so that I may hate each one individually and at
>   leisure.
> My lungs, duplicitous twins, expand with the utter validity of my hate,
>   which can never have enough of you,
> Breathlessly, like two idealists in a broken submarine.

Sheehan may have inaugurated a new subgenre. Go to *The Best American Poetry 2009* (ed. David Wagoner) and you will find Martha Silano's riff ("Love") on Sheehan's "Hate Poem." In her note on "Love," Silano acknowledges the debt. She had, in fact, given herself and her students the "assignment" to "write a poem of address" modeled on "Hate Poem."

The desire of poems to link themselves explicitly to others can cross cultural boundaries of time and space. Walt Whitman's poems achieve such an immediacy of effect upon readers that many find themselves adopting his signature characteristics—the use of anaphora, long lines, extended arias, an imperial *I* that insists on its egolessness, and a penchant for making inclusive lists that substitute simultaneity for hierarchy as a governing principle. Among the writers of many nationalities who have given in to the impulse to talk back to Whitman, the Portuguese poet Fernando Pessoa (1888–1935) holds a prominent place. Pessoa, who was born in Lisbon, lived there, and infused a strong flavor of the city and the river Tagus in his poems, adopted heteronyms—like pseudonyms, except that each is outfitted with an identity and life story. One of them writes an ecstatic "Salutation to Walt Whitman": "I salute you, Walt, I salute you my brother in the Universe." In accents that recall "Crossing Brooklyn Ferry," he adds, "And just as you felt everything, so I feel everything, and so here we are clasping hands, / Clasping hands, Walt, hands, with the universe doing a dance in our soul."[1] It is as if the very form of the writing constituted an expression of affection and praise.

Now the lovely unexpected thing about these literary partnerships is that they have a way of doubling back to the source. Pessoa's "Salutation to Walt Whitman" has stimulated not one but two rather different responses from American poets, and both have been anthologized in *The Best American Poetry.* "Salutation to Fernando Pessoa" by Allen Ginsberg was chosen by Richard Howard for the 1995 volume, was reprinted in Harold Bloom's selection, and appears again here. Catching the spirit of extravagant self-celebration undermined by shrewd irony at the expense of the self, Ginsberg conceives his poem as a challenge to Pessoa—or, rather, as a statement of his own superiority. Here is how his poem opens:

> Every time I read Pessoa I think
> I'm better than he is I do the same thing
> more extravagantly—he's only from Portugal,
> I'm American greatest Country in the world
> right now End of XX Century tho Portugal
> had a big empire in the 15th century never mind
> now shrunk to a Corner of Iberian peninsula
> whereas New York take New York for instance
> tho Mexico City's bigger N.Y.'s richer think of Empire State
> Building not long ago world empire's biggest skyscraper—

The writer goes on to observe that Pessoa lived "only till 1936" whereas he is still alive nearly sixty years later. The odd logic is part of the poem's charm, as is our knowledge that Ginsberg's braggadocio is meant half-seriously—it is his means of laying claim to the spirit that animates Whitman and Pessoa alike, which involves a huge assertion of self but also a dissolution of the ordinary barriers between self and other. With cheerful immodesty Ginsberg tells us

---

1. Fernando Pessoa, *Poems of Fernando Pessoa*, trans. Edwin Honig and Susan M. Brown (San Francisco: City Lights Books, 1998).

that at five feet seven and a half inches he is taller than Pessoa and that his "celebrated 'Howl'" has "already [been] translated into 24 languages," a boast Pessoa could not make.

In *The Best American Poetry 2000* (ed. Rita Dove), a second poem provoked by Pessoa's appeared. Lynn Emanuel's "Walt, I Salute You!" directly addresses Whitman, as Pessoa's "Salutation" does. The poem annotates its excitement with a liberal use of exclamation points that signify not only passion but also the equally needed undercutting irony. The union of identity the speaker celebrates is so strong that it blurs ordinary gender differences:

> You have been women! Women with white legs, women with black
>   mustaches,
> waitresses with their hands glued to their rags on the counter,
> waitresses in Dacron who light up the room with their serious wattage.
> Yes! You are magically filling up, like milk in a glass, the white
> nylon uniform, the blocky shoes with their slab of rubber sole!
> Your hair is a platinum helmet. At your breast, a bouquet of rayon violets.

The poem reaches its climax when the barrier between the female self and the male other breaks down completely:

> Walt, I salute you!
> And therefore myself! In our enormous hats! In our huge mustaches!
> We can't hide! We recognize ourselves!

Acts of adulation, these poems—Ginsberg's, Emanuel's, and the Pessoa poem behind them—were quickened into existence by the large-souled poet reaching out to "men and women of a generation, or ever so many generations hence."

Alexis de Tocqueville wrote *Democracy in America* before Whitman materialized as that previously absent being, a poet of the democratic republic. Tocqueville envisaged the problems that an aristocratic art form must endure in a populist culture based on equality. In a democracy, he wrote, "the number of works grows rapidly, while the merit of each diminishes," and some will see in American poetry today a fulfillment of the vision Tocqueville recorded in the fourth decade of the nineteenth century: "Form will usually be neglected and occasionally scorned. Style will frequently seem bizarre, incorrect, exaggerated, or flaccid and almost always seem brazen and vehement. Authors will aim for rapidity of execution rather than perfection of detail. Short texts will be more common than long books, wit more common than erudition, and imagination more common than depth."[2] There is truth to this, and critics of the MFA degree, the writing workshop as a pedagogical model, the proliferation of small presses, and the idea of teaching poetry writing to schoolchildren, will find much in Tocqueville to comfort them, though it is possible to rebut or modify any of the specific charges brought against contemporary poetry. Take, for example, the accusation that our poets neglect form. While free verse and colloquial idioms characterize much of the poetry of our moment, it is not as though the formal dimensions of poetry have gone unexamined. Our scribes have given us examples galore of exotic verse forms. The sonnet sequence, the haiku sequence, the sestina, the cento, the dialogue, the crown of sonnets, the pantoum, the villanelle, the prose poem, the abecedarius and even a double abecedarius: all have put in appearances in this anthology series. It may also be said that groups of American poets have been and continue to be almost obsessively committed to formal causes: the revival of past models of rhyme and meter, or the search for a measure to take the place of iambic pentameter, or the development of new constrictive verse forms like those generated by the Oulipo, or the relentless impulse to foreground language as the medium of communication and distortion.

The more significant of the problems Tocqueville predicted for the fine arts in a democratic state is a tendency to widen the aesthetic impulse but weaken its quality. It cannot be denied that we no longer conceive of lyric poetry as strictly a solitary and self-taught act but rather as one that can be taught, encouraged, quickened into being, a collaborative and even group activity. Poetry serves self-expression, narcissistic and otherwise; it also has a therapeutic application. The notion that anyone can be a poet may have a leveling effect on the art, and that is why we need not critics but editors to help us by discriminating among the contending voices and insisting on the genuine article. About critics many of us agree with Hemingway, who defined the species as "men who watch a battle from a high place, then come down and shoot the survivors." But about the need to make choices, to discriminate among the poems set before us, there can be no doubt. And I believe that the best choosers come from the ranks of the poets themselves.

This seems the right moment to acknowledge the efforts of the twenty-five poets who, in their year as guest editor, read poems by the score on an almost

---

2. Alexis de Tocqueville, *Democracy in America*, trans. Arthur Goldhammer (New York: Library of America, 2004), 533, 542.

—— *DAVID LEHMAN* ——

168

daily basis. Picking the seventy-five poems of "your" year is a demanding task, even if you don't stumble over the idea of hierarchies. You need reserves of generosity and goodwill and a feeling for the idea of community. It is possible, and the editors proved it, to be loyal to an aesthetic position and, at the same time, to strive to be ecumenical; to include your favorites but also to be able to recognize quality in a style unlike your own, from an unfamiliar voice, speaking an alien dialect.

Glen Hartley has been my literary agent since I began writing books. A lover of poetry and literature, he advised me on *The Best American Poetry* when it was little more than an idea that popped into my head as I drove on a country road between Ludlowville and Ithaca, New York, one Sunday in August 1987. This volume is dedicated to Glen, without whose advocacy and support the series would neither have come into existence nor fared so well as it has. I am fortunate, too, to have worked with talented editors at Scribner: John Glusman, who signed the book in 1987 when nobody else but Glen and I thought it had a snowball's chance in Hades; Erika Goldman; Hamilton Cain; Gillian Blake; and, since 2004, Alexis Gargagliano. One thing we learned early on was that the sheer number of poems that get published in the United States is overwhelming. In our fourth year we made the decision to exclude poems published in individual poetry collections and to choose only poems that appear in periodicals. Some great magazines ended their distinguished runs: *Partisan Review, Antæus.* New magazines sprung up: poems in the 2010 and 2011 volumes of this series were printed originally in *Conduit, Court Green, The Hat, jubilat, LIT, New Ohio Review, Open City, A Public Space, Post Road, Sentence, The Sienese Shredder,* and *Vanitas,* to cite just some that didn't exist twenty-five years ago. The perennially unsung editors of these magazines continue to be our front line; I thank them and honor them. Little has been as important in my own evolution as a poet than the friendly, attentive, and frank responses that my work has elicited from magazine editors.

The abundance and variety of the poems we have published in our twenty-five years led us to suspend our usual practice of limiting each book in the series to seventy-five poems. There are an even hundred poems in this volume. Each has the distinction of having been picked twice. The year beneath the poem designates the volume in which it originally appeared. In the back of the book, after updated biographical notes, we print the original comment, if any, that the poet made in response to my plea for some words about the composition of the chosen poem.

Robert Pinsky comes from the generation of American poets that earned the PhD rather than the MFA degree if they went to graduate school. He studied at Stanford, where he absorbed the lessons of Yvor Winters; wrote a book on Landor, another one on the situation of poetry in the year of our nation's bicentennial; and taught at Wellesley, Berkeley, and Boston University. He wrote plain-style poems, acts of moral attention devoted to subjects as vast and complicated as America, psychiatry, sadness, happiness, the design of a shirt, the human heart. When *The Figured Wheel*, comprising new and collected poems, appeared from Farrar, Straus and Giroux in 1996, the poet and critic James Longenbach said it constituted "the most scrupulously intelligent body of work produced by an American poet in the past twenty-five years." A new *Selected Poems* came out from the same publisher in 2011. Pinsky has written autobiographical poems, lyrics, intellectual investigations ("Ode to Meaning"), and poems endowed with the purpose of explaining ourselves to us. But he has not eschewed the sheer pleasure of wordplay, as in his abecedarian poems that consist of exactly twenty-six words. In the variousness of his pursuits, he has done much to challenge any limiting notion of what a serious modern poet can be and do. In addition to his poems and his essays on poetry, he produced a widely acclaimed translation of Dante's *Inferno*, wrote a book on the Bible's King David, and devised a computer interactive novel (*Mindwheel*) when the personal computer was in its infancy. He plays the saxophone, loves jazz, and has recently been collaborating with jazz musicians in the presentation of his poems. On the CD *PoemJazz* Pinsky reads thirteen of his own poems plus one by Ben Jonson while Laurence Hobgood improvises on the piano. A reviewer in the *JazzTimes* wrote that Pinsky's "performances" of his poems are, in keeping with the dictates of jazz, "rich with spontaneous touches."[3]

When he served as U.S. poet laureate for two terms during the Clinton administration, that office reached the peak of its prestige. Pinsky launched the "Favorite Poem Project," which proved immensely popular. He made frequent appearances reading poems on television on the *PBS NewsHour*. In 2001 he delivered the Tanner Lectures on Human Values at Princeton University, later published under the title *Democracy, Culture, and the Voice of Poetry*, a defense of poetry as a living art whose importance will always surpass its popularity. "Poetry reflects, perhaps concentrates, the American idea of individual-

---

3. Christopher Loudon, *jazztimes.com*, June 2012.

ism as it encounters the American experience of the mass," Pinsky writes, as neat a statement as you will find of the central paradox of our culture.

The poets assembled in this volume have written about matters of public concern: "the war," whether that means Vietnam or "Bush's War"; suicide bombers, murderous explosions, a terrorist act, a deadly oil spill, the death of the shah of Iran, the videotaped assassination of an American journalist in Pakistan. The poets have accepted the challenge to write about history in the making. To be sure, they also like to tell a story or make a prophecy, to sing the blues or a sad ballad, to contemplate desire, love, loss, nostalgia, garbage, pornography, married life, Wagner at the Met, lunch, childhood, dogs, paranoia, fathers, the end of a love affair, forgiveness, poison pen letters, and the letter "Q."

Among the miraculous inventions in Raymond Roussel's *Locus Solus* are the tableaux vivants featuring figures immobile as wax dummies in a huge glass case. The figures turn out to be dead people who revive when injected with a substance called "resurrectine," at which time they act out the greatest event in their lives. Poems are a little like that. An excellent poem of any vintage returns to life the moment somebody reads it. What we can do, in a retrospective anthology, is to bring back poems that have given pleasure to more than a few discerning readers—poems that prove, in Tocqueville's terms, that an aristocratic art form can thrive in a democratic culture.

It was his poetry that kept him going

Shelley's "Defence of Poetry" (1821) culminates in an assertion of poetry as a source not only of knowledge but of power. Shelley's claims for poetry go beyond the joy to be had in a thing of beauty or a memory-quickening spot of time. The criteria of excellence may begin with aesthetics but assuredly do not end there. Poetry is "the most unfailing herald, companion, and follower of the awakening of a great people to work a beneficial change in opinion or institution." A poem is, moreover, not only "the very image of life expressed in its eternal truth" but also, and not incidentally, a metonymy of the cooperative imagination altogether. It "is ever found to coexist with whatever other arts contribute to the happiness and perfection of man." The famous pronouncement that closes the essay—"Poets are the unacknowledged legislators of the world"—does not do justice to the poet's reasoning. The visionary power he ascribes to the poet does not translate into laws, judgments, statutes, and legislative decrees, but something that exists independently of these things just as a Platonic ideal exists beyond empirical verification. For Shelley, poetic genius lies in the apprehension of a new truth before it gains currency. Metaphor is the medium of the change; words precede concepts that prefigure deeds. Not as a lawmaker, then, but as an interpreter of sacred mysteries the poet speaks to us and to the spirit of the age. The penultimate sentence in the "Defence of Poetry" comes closer to Shelley's intention than the equally grandiloquent final clause: "Poets are the hierophants of an unapprehended inspiration; the mirrors of the gigantic shadows which futurity casts upon the present, the words which express what they understand not; the trumpets which sing to battle, and feel not what they inspire; the influence which is moved not, but moves."

Shelley has always held a great appeal for youthful idealists and Romantic rebels. At eighteen he was expelled from Oxford for writing "The Necessity of Atheism." He championed free love and eloped with a child bride. He alienated his father and jeopardized a baronetcy. He foresaw the rise of democratic rule, the overthrow of tyrants, the triumph of liberty, the liberation of the oppressed. All these things were inevitable, he said. In a long poem presenting what he called a "beau idéal" of the French Revolution, his hero and heroine escape from reactionary armies and lead a bloodless "Revolution of the Golden City."[1] Shelley envisaged a new Athens, a "loftier Argo," a "brighter Hellas," a renewal of "the world's great age."[2] His amatory philosophy can be paraphrased as "love the one you're with." He notoriously denounced monogamy:

> I never was attached to that great sect,
> Whose doctrine is, that each one should select
> Out of the crowd a mistress or a friend,
> And all the rest, though fair and wise, commend
> To cold oblivion, though it is in the code
> Of modern morals, and the beaten road
> Which those poor slaves with weary footsteps tread,
> Who travel to their home among the dead
> By the broad highway of the world, and so
> With one chained friend, perhaps a jealous foe,
> The dreariest and the longest journey go.[3]

It is a remarkable statement even for a century whose novelists subjected the institution of marriage to unprecedented scorn.

Just as Shelley's occasional outbursts of self-pity ("I pant, I sink, I tremble, I expire!") can blunt the wondrous force of his enjambed couplets, so the un-

1. In "Laon and Cythna; or, The Revolution of the Golden City," later retitled "The Revolt of Islam," Shelley's longest poem, an epic of twelve cantos in Spenserian stanzas.
2. In a chorus in "Hellas," often printed separately and identified by its first line, "The world's great age begins anew."
3. In "Epipsychidion."

savory facts of his personal life (he abandoned the young bride, who committed suicide) have acted as a check on a young poet's enthusiasm for the author of "Ode to the West Wind," "Ozymandias," and "The Triumph of Life." Among the great English Romantic poets no reputation has taken quite as bad a beating as has Shelley's. "The man Shelley, in very truth, is not entirely sane, and Shelley's poetry is not entirely sane either," Matthew Arnold wrote. Arnold was not unsympathetic. He allowed that Shelley's "charm" was genuine. In a sense Shelley was an angel, Arnold wrote, but "a beautiful and ineffectual angel, beating in the void his luminous wings in vain."

Of the power of poets to legislate or otherwise effect social change we are entitled to have our doubts. In *The Dyer's Hand* (1962), W. H. Auden wrote that Shelley's noble phrase, "the unacknowledged legislators of the world," describes "the secret police, not the poets." On reflection most of us would side with Auden on that one. The idea of poetry as an agent of widespread enlightenment seems a ludicrous claim, possible to make only in the early years of a century less downcast and dispirited than the one that followed it. The poets don't stand a chance against the Ministry of Intelligence and National Security, the Gestapo, the Stasi. The only thing these entities have in common with poets is that they are, in differing ways and for different reasons, "unacknowledged." Closer to home, poetry is tolerated but pales in power, status, and everything else to punditry of even the blandest and most conventional sort. On Capitol Hill or in Foggy Bottom, few policy makers ask themselves how their initiatives will play among the poets.

Richard Blanco, who read a poem at President Obama's second inauguration, was widely described as the youngest inaugural poet, the first who is openly gay, and the first with a strong Hispanic identity. Alexandra Petri of the *Washington Post* used "One Today," the poem Blanco delivered at the ceremony, as the signal to ask rhetorically whether poetry has breathed its last.[4] Blanco irritated Petri with the poetical phrase "plum blush" applied to dusk. He was, in her view, an example of an American dream gone awry: a man who has overcome genuine obstacles for the dubious sake of mastering an "obsolete" craft. "The kind of poetry they read to you at poetry readings and ladle in your direction at the Inaugural is—well, it's all very nice, and sounds a lot like a Poem, but—it has changed nothing," Petri writes. "No truly radical art form has such a well-established grant process." Petri recirculates the perennial grievances you hear from former English majors and others who fear the worst

---

4. Petri's post appeared on the *Washington Post's* blog on January 22, 2013, http://www.washingtonpost.com/blogs/compost/wp/2013/01/22/is-poetry-dead/.

about an art form they once loved. Contemporary poetry is "limp and fangless." It lacks an audience. It makes nothing happen. It pretends to be "radical" but isn't. It is "institutionalized" and does not exist outside academic walls. You don't get the news from poetry. ("You barely get the news from the news," Petri tartly observes.) In perhaps her most devastating line, Petri proposes an analogy between poets and postal carriers: "a group of people sedulously doing something that we no longer need, under the misapprehension that they are offering us a vital service"—a far cry from the image of the reliable postman making house calls like doctors in the last line of Philip Larkin's "Aubade." Poets and their advocates responded to Petri's post with angry denials that they are "obsolete." John Deming voiced the feelings of many when he wrote that "a very small percentage receive grants. We are here, and we plate your dinners. We teach your kids. We slave over works we know will receive no wide audience. We shoe your horses. We work in all kinds of offices. We write about all of this and none of it, and some of us do it really, really well. We find ways to make a living and still practice an art form that yields clarity and meaning. How is that not Blanco's 'American dream' in every sense?"[5]

In America we have had stereotypes of the poet as clown prince, beatnik, nervous wreck, nature-loving recluse, world-besotted aesthete. Formerly an eccentric spinster, she may now be a self-actualized role model and possibly even a concerned citizen on PBS or NPR. The poet's day job is writer in residence at the local university and, for the sake of argument, let us say she is scheduled to give a talk next week on Shelley and "The Mask of Anarchy." She has chosen the poem because of the question Alexandra Petri thought important enough to ask twice in her piece in the *Washington Post*: "Can it change anything? Can a poem still change anything?" Shelley wrote "The Mask of Anarchy" in a flash of fury after word reached him of the so-called Peterloo Massacre on August 16, 1819, when militiamen and cavalrymen, drunk and out of control, galloped full-blast, with sabers drawn, into a peaceful rally in favor of parliamentary reform. The demonstrators had assembled to protest famine, desperate living conditions, chronic unemployment. The soldiers killed several demonstrators, as many as eighteen by one count, and injured hundreds more, all of them unarmed. The lecturer explains that Peterloo, a defining moment in English history, got its name from St. Peter's Field, near Manchester, where the bloody incident took place—and because "loo" as a suffix jeered at Tory pride in Britain's military triumph over Napoleon at Waterloo. Shelley, indignant, issued a

5. John Deming's "open letter" appeared in *Coldfront* on Tuesday, January 22, 2013, http://coldfrontmag.comlnews/open-letter-to-alexandra-petri.

call to action, but a call of a curious kind. In "The Mask of Anarchy," he summons the "Men of England, heirs of Glory, / Heroes of unwritten story" to "Rise like lions after slumber / In unvanquishable number— / Shake your chains to earth like dew / Which in sleep had fallen on you— / Ye are many—they are few." And how are the "heirs of Glory" to shake off their chains? With nonviolent resistance. In the face of charging bayonets and scimitars, Shelley exhorts the "many" to keep their places and not fight back when attacked: "Stand ye calm and resolute, / Like a forest close and mute, / With folded arms and looks which are / Weapons of unvanquished war." A full century before Gandhi implemented the strategy of achieving your aims by shaming your foes, Shelley got there first. "On those who first should violate / Such sacred heralds in their state / Rest the blood that must ensue, / And it will not rest on you." Thoreau admired the poem; Gandhi quoted it often in his campaign to free India.

"The Mask of Anarchy" became a major document in the history of civil disobedience. It was a radical poem in August of 1819, that magical year of Keats's odes and Shelley's "Prometheus Unbound," and poetry retains its radical potential today in spite of the constancy of worry about its waning influence. Poetry, literature, art, even the crude art of newspaper cartoons and amateur videos cause dictators to take notice. In places where the freedoms of speech and press are tested continually, the poet, merely by speaking his or her mind, risks nasty consequences. To the honor roll of courageous authors who have suffered at the hands of governments—been exiled, censored, incarcerated, even sentenced to death—we have recently had to add the Qatari poet Muhammad ibn al-Dheeb al-Ajami, who got a life sentence for having written—and been videotaped reciting—a poem entitled "Tunisian Jasmine." The poem lauds the uprising in Tunisia that sparked the Arab Spring rebellions: "We are all Tunisia in the face of a repressive [elite]," Ajami wrote. In November 2012, the Associated Press reported on the case. "Officials" charged that the poem "insulted Qatar's emir and encouraged the overthrow of the nation's ruling system." The *Guardian* ran a fuller account. Ajami had been jailed a year earlier, in November 2011, when the video of "Tunisian Jasmine" surfaced on the Internet. He had been kept in solitary confinement since his arrest. A third-year student of literature at Cairo University, he was convicted of insulting the Gulf nation's ruler, Sheikh Hamad bin Khalifa Al Thani. The more serious charge of "inciting to overthrow the ruling system" could have led to the death penalty. The poet Andrei Codrescu—who has a poem in this edition of *The Best American Poetry*—commented on NPR with his customary bite. "The emir of Qatar is a tolerant man. He allowed *Al Jazeera*, which is based in his country, to broadcast reports of the Arab Spring as long as they didn't cover local unrest." But with brazen hypocrisy the emir "drew the line" at Ajami's criticism of the Qatari regime and other governments in the region. "Freedom is relative," Codrescu said. "In the United States, it's hard to write a poem offensive enough to get you even a few days in jail. In Vladimir Putin's Russia, the young performers of the band Pussy Riot were sentenced to two years in prison for insulting him in church. That's not bad for Russia, where in Stalin's time, a poem insulting the leader would get you executed in a jiffy." By the same logic, "if Mohammed Ajami had insulted the emir in a mosque, he might have been decapitated instead of just getting a life sentence. A ruler must draw the line somewhere."[6]

In the United States, as Codrescu noted, it is hard for a poem to get noticed, even if it does its best to give offense—but, of course, that may be an underrated virtue rather than a lamentable fact. The case of Ajami's "Tunisian Jasmine" is one extreme example of the power of poetry to disturb a tyrant's sleep. Where the freedom to speak your mind is not a novelty, the poet may have an agenda other than a political one but no less dangerous. We have galloped from analog to digital models of the universe. Some poets will continue to find inventive ways to adapt to the new paradigm; others may feel that their writing constitutes an act of nonviolent resistance—a vote for Gutenberg, the book, the old seemingly obsolete technologies of communication. V. S. Pritchett, in the introduction to an anthology of stories, wrote in 1980, "In a mass society we have the sense of being anonymous: therefore we look for the silent moment in which singularity breaks through, when emotions change, without warning, and reveal themselves." That such a breakthrough is more likely to happen in a freely written poem rather than one that has been commissioned and vetted by committee for a ceremonial purpose should not come as a surprise.

Denise Duhamel, who chose the poems for *The Best American Poetry 2013*, has appeared in the series seven times since Louise Glück and A. R. Ammons picked poems of hers in back-to-back volumes in 1993 and 1994. It would have been eight times if the editor hadn't declined to include herself: her "Ode to the Other Woman's Ass" in *Ecotone* (and reprinted on *The Best American Poetry* blog) has the traits—humor, warmth, passion, intelligence, and genuineness—that make her poems irresistible. "Exuberance is beauty," wrote William Blake. "Energy is eternal delight." Denise has as much natural

---

6. "Qatari Poet Sentenced to Life in Prison for Writing," *npr.org*, December 4, 2012, http://www.npr.org/2012/12/04/166519644/qatari-poet-sentenced-to-life-in-prison-for-writing.

exuberance as anyone practicing the art, with a seemingly unlimited amount of renewable energy. I have known and worked with Denise for many years. When a production of her play *How the Sky Fell* ran for four performances in an Off-Off-Broadway theater in 1997, I was in the cast. Over the years she and I have spent more than a few afternoons collaborating on a play, poems, or other projects. I knew we'd have fun working together, and I suspected that she would have a large appetite for the many kinds of poetry being written at the moment. But I was not prepared for her intensity of focus. No sooner did she receive a magazine than its contents were devoured and considered for an ever-growing list of poems that elicited Denise's enthusiasm. It is always difficult making cuts, but Denise's professionalism ruled the day. In the making of one of these books the production schedule requires more than one deadline. Never before in the twenty-six years of this series did I work with an editor who managed to beat every deadline along the way.

Among the poets we lost in 2012 was Adrienne Rich, who edited the 1996 volume in the series—a radical book by any standard. Adrienne included poems by high school students, prisoners in correctional facilities, outsiders of many stripes. She wanted to represent the full range of poetry written in North America while maintaining vigilance against "self-reference and solipsism." She wanted "poems that didn't simply reproduce familiar versions of 'difference' and 'identity.'" On the contrary, she wrote, "I was looking for poems that could rouse me from fatigue, stir me from grief, poetry that was redemptive in the sense of offering a kind of deliverance or rescue of the imagination, and poetry that awoke delight—lip-to-lip, spark-to-spark, pleasure in recognition, pleasure in strangeness." Rich's volume ranks among the most controversial in the history of the series. Harold Bloom took such offense that when, in 1998, he edited a retrospective collection celebrating our tenth year, he omitted any poem from *The Best American Poetry 1996* and devoted his entire introduction to an attack on that book in particular and on the literary aesthetics that inform it. Any editor would have been hurt by such an assault. Adrienne took it in stride. "I look at it as a weird tribute," she said. Adrienne's poem "Endpapers," which appeared in *Granta* and was chosen for *The Best American Poetry 2013*, concludes with these lines:

> The signature to a life requires
> the search for a method
> rejection of posturing
> trust in the witnesses

a vial of invisible ink
a sheet of paper held steady
after the end-stroke
above a deciphering flame

I have a couple of friends who left Saigon on the day the last Americans cleared out in April 1975. One of them clipped the *New York Times* obituary of Nguyen Chi Thien, who died in October 2012 at the age of seventy-three. "He was a very great Vietnamese poet," my friend said. Thien, a U.S. citizen since 2004, had lived in Santa Ana, California, since coming here. His poems, collected in *Flowers from Hell* (1996), are available in English, French, Spanish, German, Czech, Korean, and Chinese—but not in Vietnamese. "My poetry's not mere poetry, no, / but it's the sound of sobbing from a life, / the din of doors in a dark jail, / the wheeze of two poor wasted lungs, / the thud of earth tossed to bury dreams, / the clash of teeth all chattering from cold," he wrote. The "Solzhenitsyn of Vietnam," as he came to be known, did not evacuate Saigon in 1975. He stayed and cast a fearless eye on the injustices of the Communist regime. Three times Thien was arrested. He did a long stretch in Hoa La Prison, the infamous "Hanoi Hilton." Of his six years there he had to spend three in solitary confinement. He had access to no books. Worse, he lacked a writing implement and the paper on which to write. He suffered from tuberculosis and was prone to respiratory illnesses. The conditions for even the healthiest prisoner were inhumane. The hunger was constant, the summer sun unforgiving, the winter cold almost unendurable. There were times when the guards chained Thien naked in his cold cell. Nevertheless he wrote. He marked the days with poems, seven hundred of them in all; he composed them, worked on them entirely in his head, and then committed them to memory so effectively that when the time came he was able to write them out for publication—to the wide acclaim they deserved even apart from the miracle of their composition. Not until 1995 was Thien permitted to leave Vietnam. By then the evidence of his heroism was irrefutable. It was his poetry that kept him going, poetry that sustained and nourished him. In a prison camp in 1976 he wrote, "I have only poetry in my bosom, / And two paper-thin lungs / To fight the enemy, I cannot be a coward. / And to win him over, I must live a thousand autumns!"

In the antagonism between science and the humanities

M aybe I dreamed it. Don Draper sat sipping Canadian Club from a coffee mug on Craig Ferguson's late-night talk show. "Are you on Twitter?" the host asks. "No," Draper says. "I don't"—and here he pauses before pronouncing the distasteful verb—"tweet." Next question. "Do you read a lot of poetry?" The ad agency's creative director looks skeptical. Though the hero of *Mad Men* is seen reading Dante's *Inferno* in one season of Matthew Weiner's show and heard reciting Frank O'Hara in another, the question seems to come from left field. "Poetry isn't really celebrated any more in our culture," Don says, to which the other retorts, "It can be—if you can write in units of 140 keystrokes." Commercial break.

The laugh line reveals a shrewd insight into the subject of "poetry in the digital age," a panel-discussion perennial. The panelists agree that text messaging and Internet blogs will be seen to have exercised some sort of influence on the practice of poetry, whether on the method of composition or on the style and surface of the writing. And surely we may expect the same of a wildly popular social medium with a formal requirement as stringent as the 140-character limit. (To someone with a streak of mathematical mysticism, the relation of that number to the number of lines in a sonnet is a thing of beauty.) What Twitter offers is ultimate immediacy expressed with ultimate concision. "Whatever else

Twitter is, it's a literary form," says the writer Kathryn Schulz, who explains how easy it was for her to get addicted to "a genre in which you try to say an informative thing in an interesting way while abiding by its constraint (those famous 140 characters). For people who love that kind of challenge—and it's easy to see why writers might be overrepresented among them—Twitter has the same allure as gaming." True, the hard-to-shake habit caused its share of problems. Schulz reports a huge "distractibility increase" and other disturbing symptoms: "I have felt my *mind* get divided into tweet-size chunks." Nevertheless there is a reason that she got hooked to this "wide-ranging, intellectually stimulating, big-hearted, super fun" activity.[1] When, in an early episode of the Netflix production of *House of Cards*, one Washington journalist disparages a rival as a "Twitter twat," you know the word has arrived, and the language itself has changed to accommodate it. There are new terms ("hashtag"), acronyms ("ikr" in Detroit means "I know, right?"), shorthand ("suttin" is "something" in Boston).[2] Television producers love it ("Keep those tweets coming!"). So does Wall Street: when Twitter went public in 2013, the IPO came off without a hitch, and the stock climbed with the velocity of an over-caffeinated momentum investor eager to turn a quick profit.

The desire to make a friend of the new technology is understandable, though it obliges us to overlook some major flaws: the Internet is hell on lining, spacing, italics; line breaks and indentation are often obscured in electronic transmission. The integrity of the poetic line can be a serious casualty. Still, it is fruitless to quarrel with the actuality of change, and difficult to resist it profitably—except, perhaps, in private, where we may revel in our physical books and even, if we like, write with pen or pencil on graph paper or type our thoughts with the Smith-Corona manual to which we have a sentimental attachment. One room in the fine *Drawn to Language* exhibit at the University of Southern California's Fisher Art Museum in September 2013 was devoted to Susan Silton's site-specific installation of a circle of tables on which sat ten manual typewriters of different makes, models, sizes, and decades. It was moving to behold the machines not only as objects of nostalgia in an attractive arrangement but as metonymies of the experience of writing in the twentieth

---

1. Kathryn Schulz, "Seduced by Twitter," *The Week*, December 27, 2013, 40–41.
2. Katy Steinmetz, "The Linguist's Mother Lode," *Time*, September 9, 2013, 56–57. Jacob Eisenstein, a computational linguist at Georgia Tech, is quoted: "Social media has taken the informal peer-to-peer interaction that might have been almost exclusively spoken and put it in a written form. The result of that is a burst of creativity." The assumption here is that the new is necessarily "creative" in the honorific sense.

century—and as invitations to sit down and hunt and peck away to your heart's content. Seeing the typewriters in that room I felt as I do when the talk touches on the acquisition of an author's papers by a university library. It's odd to be a member of the last generation to have "papers" in this archival and material sense. Odd for an era to slip into a museum while you watch.

You may say—I have heard the arguments—that the one-minute poem is not far off. Twitter's 140-keystroke constraint—together with the value placed on being "up to speed"—brings the clock into the game. Poetry, a byte-size kind of poetry, has been, or soon will be, a benefit of attention deficit disorder. (This statement, or prediction, is not necessarily or not always made in disparagement.) Unlike the telephone, the instruments of social media rely on the written, not the spoken word, and it will be interesting to see what happens when the values of hip-hop lyricists and spoken-word poets, for whom the performative aspects of the art are paramount, tangle with the values of concision, bite, and wit consistent with the rules of the Twitter feed. On the other hand, it is conceivable that the sentence I have just composed will be, for all intents and purposes, anachronistic in a couple of years or less. Among my favorite oxymorons is "ancient computer," applied to my own desktop.[3]

In his famous and famously controversial Rede Lecture at Cambridge University in 1959, the English novelist C. P. Snow addressed the widening chasm between the two dominant strains in our culture.[4] There were the humanists on the one side. On the other were the scientists and applied scientists, the agents of technological change. And "a gulf of mutual incomprehension" separated them. Though Snow endeavored to appear even-handed, it became apparent that he favored the sciences—he opted, in his terms, for the fact rather than the myth. The scientists "have the future in their bones"—a future that will nourish the hungry, clothe the masses, reduce the risk of infant mortality, cure ailments, and prolong life. And "the traditional culture responds by wishing the future did not exist."

The Rede Lecture came in the wake of the scare set off by the Soviet Union's

---

3. "Even the best computer will seem positively geriatric by its fifth birthday." Geoffrey A. Fowler, "Mac Pro Is a Lamborghini, But Who Drives That Fast?" *Wall Street Journal*, January 15, 2014, D1.

4. The 1959 Rede Lecture in four parts was published as *The Two Cultures and the Scientific Revolution*. An expanded version conjoining the lecture with Snow's subsequent reflections (*A Second Look*) appeared from Cambridge University Press in 1964.

launch of Sputnik in October 1957. There was widespread fear that we in the West, and particularly we in the United States, were in danger of falling behind the Russians in the race for space, itself a metaphor for the scientific control of the future. For this reason among others, Snow's lecture was extraordinarily successful. Introducing a phrase into common parlance, "The Two Cultures" reached great numbers of readers and helped shape a climate friendly to science at the expense of the traditional components of a liberal education. Much in that lecture infuriated the folks on the humanist side of the divide.[5] Snow wrote as though humanistic values were possible without humanistic studies. In literature he saw not a corrective or a criticism of life but a threat. He interpreted George Orwell's *1984* as "the strongest possible wish that the future should not exist" rather than as a warning against the authoritarian impulses of the modern state coupled with its sophistication of surveillance. Snow founded his argument on the unexamined assumption that scientists, in thrall to the truth, can be counted on to do the right thing—an assumption that the history of munitions would explode even if we could all agree on what "the right thing" is. For Snow, who had been knighted and would be granted a life peerage, the future was bound to be an improvement on the past, and the change would be entirely attributable to the people in the white coats in the laboratory. Generalizing from the reactionary political tendencies of certain famous modern writers, Snow floated the suggestion that they—and by implication those who read them—managed to "bring Auschwitz that much nearer." Looking back at the Rede Lecture five years later, Snow saw no reason to modify the view that intellectuals were natural Luddites, prone to "talk about a pre-Industrial Eden" that never was. They ignored the simple truth that the historian J. H. Plumb stated: "No one in his senses would choose to have been born in a previous age unless he could be certain that he would have been born into a prosperous family, that he would have enjoyed extremely good health, and that he could have accepted stoically the death of the majority of his children." In short, according to Snow, the humanists were content to dwell in a "pretty-pretty past."

In 1962 F. R. Leavis, then perhaps the most influential literary critic at Cambridge, denounced Snow's thesis with such vitriol and contempt that he

---

5. I take the term "humanist" to cover historians and philosophers, literary and cultural critics, music and art historians, professors of English or Romance languages or comparative literature or East Asian studies, classicists, linguists, jurists and legal scholars, public intellectuals, authors and essayists, most psychologists, and a great many other academics across the board: very nearly everyone not committed professionally to a career in one of the sciences or in technology.

may have done the humanist side more harm than good. "Snow exposes complacently a complete ignorance," Leavis said in the Richmond Lecture, and "is as intellectually undistinguished as it is possible to be." Yet, Leavis added, Snow writes in a "tone of which one can say that, while only genius could justify it, one cannot readily think of genius adopting it."[6] Reread today, the Richmond Lecture may be a classic of invective inviting close study. As rhetoric it was devastating. But as a document in a conflict of ideas, the Richmond Lecture left much to be desired. Leavis did not adequately address the charges that Snow leveled at literature and the arts on social and moral grounds.[7] The scandal in personalities, the shrillness of tone, eclipsed the subject of the debate, which got fought out in the letters column of the literary press and was all the talk in the senior common rooms and faculty lounges of the English-speaking world.

The controversy ignited by a pair of dueling lectures at Cambridge deserves another look now not only because fifty years have passed and we can better judge what has happened in the intervening period but because more than ever the humanities today stand in need of defense. In universities and liberal arts colleges, these are hard times for the study of ideas. In 2013, front-page articles in the *New York Times* and the *Wall Street Journal* screamed about the crisis in higher education especially in humanist fields: shrinking enrollments at liberal arts colleges; the shutting down of entire college departments; the elimination of courses and requirements once considered vital. The host of "worrisome long-trends" included "a national decline in the number of graduating high-school seniors, a swarm of technologies driving down costs and profit margins, rising student debt, a soft job market for college graduates and stagnant household incomes."[8] Is that all? Hardly. There has also been a spate of op-ed columns suggesting that students would be wise to save their money, study something that can lead to gainful employment, and forget about majoring in modern dance, art history, philosophy, sociology, theology, or English unless they are independently wealthy.

The cornerstones of the humanities, English and history, have taken a

6. F. R. Leavis, *The Two Cultures? The Significance of C. P. Snow* (Cambridge: Cambridge University Press, 2013).

7. For more on the affair, and an especially sensitive and sympathetic reading of Leavis's "relentlessly withering" attack on Snow, see Stefan Collini, "Leavis v. Snow: The Two-Cultures Bust-Up 50 Years On," *Guardian*, August 16, 2013, http://www.theguardian.com /books/2013/aug/16/leavis-snow-two-cultures-bust.

8. Douglas Belkin, "Private Colleges Squeezed," *Wall Street Journal*, November 10, 2013.

beating. At Yale, English was the most popular major in 1972–73. It did not make the top five in 2012–13. Twenty-one years ago, 216 Yale undergraduates majored in history; less than half that number picked the field last year.[9] Harvard—where English majors dwindled from 36 percent of the student body in 1954 to 20 percent in 2012—has issued a report on the precipitous drop. Russell A. Berman of Stanford, in a piece in the *Chronicle of Higher Education* ominously entitled "Humanist: Heal Thyself," observed that "the marginalization of the great works of the erstwhile canon has impoverished the humanities," and that the Harvard report came to this important conclusion. But he noted, too, that it stopped short of calling for a great-books list of required readings. My heart sinks when I read such a piece and arrive at a paragraph in which the topic sentence is, "Clearly majoring in the humanities has long been an anomaly for American undergraduates."[10] Or is such a sentence—constructed as if to sound value-neutral and judgment-free in the proper scientific manner— part of the problem? The ability of an educated populace to read critically, to write clearly, to think coherently, and to retain knowledge—even the ability to grasp the basic rules of grammar and diction—seems to be declining at a pace consonant with the rise of the Internet search engine and the autocorrect function in computer programs.

Not merely the cost but the value of a liberal arts education has come into doubt. The humanists find themselves in a bind. Consider the plight of the English department. "The folly of studying, say, English Lit has become something of an Internet cliché—the stuff of sneering 'Worst Majors' listicles that seem always to be sponsored by personal-finance websites," Thomas Frank writes in *Harper's*.[11] There is a new philistinism afoot, and the daunting price tag of college or graduate education adds an extra wrinkle to an argument of ferocious intensity. "The study of literature has traditionally been felt to have a unique effectiveness in opening the mind and illuminating it, in purging the mind of prejudices and received ideas, in making the mind free and active," Lionel Trilling wrote at the time of the Leavis-Snow controversy. "The classic

---

9. "Major Changes," *Yale Alumni Magazine*, January–February 2014, 20.

10. Russell A. Berman, "Humanist: Heal Thyself," *Chronicle of Higher Education*, June 10, 2103, http://chronicle.com/blogs/conversation/2013/06/10/humanist-heal-thyself/.

11. Thomas Frank, "Course Corrections," *Harper's*, October 2013, 10. The editorial writers of the *New York Post* (February 22, 2014) begin a *defense* of the liberal arts with "the nightmare scenario for many parents of college students. Suzie comes home from her $50,000-a-year university to tell you this: 'Mom and Dad, I've decided I want to major in early Renaissance poetry.'"

defense of literary study holds that, from the effect which the study of literature has upon the private sentiments of a student, there results, or can be made to result, an improvement in the intelligence, and especially the intelligence as it touches the moral life."[12] It is vastly more difficult today to mount such a defense after three or more decades of sustained assault on canons of judgment, the idea of greatness, the related idea of genius, and the whole vast cavalcade of Western civilization.[13] Heather Mac Donald writes more in sorrow than in anger that the once-proud English department at UCLA—which even lately could boast of being home to more undergraduate majors than any other department in the nation—has dismantled its core, doing away with the formerly obligatory four courses in Chaucer, Shakespeare, and Milton. You can now satisfy the requirements of an English major with "alternative rubrics of gender, sexuality, race, and class." The coup, as Mac Donald terms it, took place in 2011 and is but one event in a pattern of academic changes that would replace a theory of education based on a "constant, sophisticated dialogue between past and present" with a consumer mindset based on "narcissism, an obsession with victimhood, and a relentless determination to reduce the stunning complexity of the past to the shallow categories of identity and class politics. Sitting atop an entire civilization of aesthetic wonders, the contemporary academic wants only to study oppression, preferably his or her own, defined reductively according to gonads and melanin."[14]

In the antagonism between science and the humanities, it may now be said that C. P. Snow in "The Two Cultures" was certainly right in one particular. Technology in our culture has routed the humanities. Everyone wants the latest app, the best device, the slickest new gadget. Put on the defensive, spokes-

---

12. Lionel Trilling, "The Two Environments: Reflections on the Study of English," *Beyond Culture* (1965; rpt. New York: Harcourt Brace Jovanovich, 1978), 184. See also Trilling's lucid account of the Leavis-Snow controversy in the same volume, 126–54.

13. "In according the least legitimacy to the word 'genius,' one is considered to sign one's resignation from all fields of knowledge," Jacques Derrida said in 2003. The very noun, he said, "makes us squirm." At the same time that academics banished the word, magazines such as *Time* and *Esquire* began to dumb it down, applying "genius" to all manner of folk, including fashion designers, corporate executives, performers, comedians, talk-show hosts, and even point guards who shoot too much (Allen Iverson, circa 2000). See Darrin M. McMahon, "Where Have All the Geniuses Gone?," *Chronicle Review*, October 21, 2013, http://chronicle .com/article/Where-Have-All-the-Geniuses/142353/.

14. Heather Mac Donald, "The Humanities Have Forgotten Their Humanity," *Wall Street Journal*, January 3, 2014, http://online.wsj.com/news/articles/SB10001424052702304858 104579264321265378790.

persons for the humanities have failed to make an effective case for their fields of study. There have been efforts to promote the digital humanities, it being understood that the adjective "digital" is what rescues "humanities" in the phrase. Has the faculty thrown in the towel too soon? Have literature departments and libraries welcomed the end of the book with unseemly haste? Have the conservators of culture embraced the acceleration of change that may endanger the study of the literary humanities as if—like the clockface, cursive script, and the rotary phone—it, too, can be effectively consigned to the ash heap of the analog era?

There is some resistance to the tyranny of technology, the ruthlessness of the new digital media. And in the incipient resistance, there is the resort to culture as we traditionally knew it—the poem on the printed page, the picture in the gallery, the concerto in the symphony hall. "There is no greater bulwark against the twittering acceleration of American consciousness than the encounter with a work of art, and the experience of a text or an image," Leon Wieseltier told the graduating class at Brandeis University in May 2013. Wieseltier, the longtime literary editor of *The New Republic*, feels the situation is dire. "In the digital universe, knowledge is reduced to the status of information." In truth, however, "knowledge can be acquired only over time and only by method. And the devices that we carry like addicts in our hands are disfiguring our mental lives." Let us not be so quick to jettison the monuments of unaging intellect. "There is no task more urgent in American intellectual life at this hour than to offer some resistance to the twin imperialisms of science and technology."[15]

One thing you can count on is that people will keep writing as they adjust from one medium to another, analog to digital, paper to computer monitor. Upon the appearance of the 2004 edition of *The Best American Poetry* (ed. Lyn Hejinian), David Orr wrote that the series stands for "the idea of poetry as a community activity. 'People are writing poems!' each volume cries. 'You, too, could write a poem!' It's an appealingly democratic pose, and it has always been the genuinely 'best' thing about the *Best American* series."[16] Is everyone

15. Leon Wieseltier, "Perhaps Culture Is Now the Counterculture," *The New Republic*, May 28, 2013, http://www.newrepublic.com/article/113299/leon-wieseltier-commencement -speech-brandeis-university-2013.

16. David Orr, "The Best American Poetry 2004: You, Too, Could Write a Poem," *New York Times Book Review*, November 21, 2004.

a poet?[17] It was Freud who laid the intellectual foundations for the idea. He argued that each of us is a poet when dreaming or making wisecracks or even when making slips of the tongue or pen. If daydreaming is a passive form of creative writing, it follows that the unconscious to which we all have access is the content provider, and what is left to learn is technique. It took the advent of creative writing as an academic field to institutionalize what might be a natural tendency in American democracy. In the proliferation of competent poems, poems that meet a certain standard of artistic finish but may lack staying power, I cannot see much harm except to note one inevitable consequence, which is that of inflation. In economics, inflation takes the form of a devaluation of currency. In poetry, inflation lessens the value that the culture attaches to any individual poem. But this is far from a new development. Byron in a journal entry in the early 1820s captured the economic model with his customary brio: "there are *more* poets (soi-disant) than ever there were, and proportionally *less* poetry."[18]

Another thing you can count on: at seemingly regular intervals an article will appear in a wide-circulation periodical declaring—as if it hasn't been said often before—that poetry is finished, kaput, dead, and what are they doing with the corpse? Back in 1888, Walt Whitman read an article forecasting the demise of poetry in fifty years "owing to the special tendency to science and to its all-devouring force." (Whitman's comment: "I anticipate the very contrary. Only a firmer, vastly broader, new area begins to exist—nay, is already formed—to which the poetic genius must emigrate.")[19] In his introduction to *The Sacred Wood* (1920), T. S. Eliot ridiculed the kind of argument encountered in fashionable London circles of the day. Edmund Gosse had written in the *Sunday Times*: "Poetry is not a formula which a thousand flappers and hobbledehoys ought to be able to master in a week without any training, and the mere fact that seems to be now practiced with such universal ease is enough to prove that something has gone amiss with our standards." Here is Eliot's paraphrase of the Gosse argument: "If too much bad verse is published in London, it does not occur to us to raise our standards, to do anything to educate the poet-

---

17. Madeline Schwartzman, an adjunct professor of architecture at Barnard College, is stopping someone on the subway every day and asking the person to write a poem on the spot for "365 Day Subway: Poems by New Yorkers." Heidi Mitchell, "Artist Solicits Poetry From Other Subterraneans," *Wall Street Journal*, February 1–2, 2014, A15.
18. Byron, "Detached Thoughts" (October 1821 to May 1822), in *Byron's Poetry*, ed. Frank D. McConnell (New York: Norton, 1978), 335.
19. Whitman, "A Backward Glance O'er Travel'd Roads" (1888), in *Walt Whitman: A Critical Anthology*, ed. Francis Murphy (New York: Penguin, 1969), 110–11.

asters; the remedy is, Kill them off." (Eliot also asks: "is it wholly the fault of the younger generation that it is aware of no authority that it must respect?")[20] On occasion the death-of-poetry genre can produce something useful; Edmund Wilson's essay "Is Verse a Dying Technique?" comes to mind. But today you are more likely to find "Poetry and Me: An Elegy."

In its July 2013 issue, *Harper's* published a typical example of the genre, Mark Edmundson's "Poetry Slam: Or, the Decline of American Verse."[21] The piece by an older academic bewailing the state of something he calls "mainstream American poetry" and praising the poetry he loved as a youth is embarrassing for what it reveals about the author, who is out of touch with the poetry in circulation. And then "mainstream American poetry" is poor turf to stand on: Would you offer a course with that label? Would anyone want to fit into such a category? The professor's chief complaint appears to be that "there's no end of poetry being written and published out there," and though he knows he shouldn't generalize, he will do just that and say that today's poets lack ambition—"the poets who now get the balance of public attention and esteem are casting unambitious spells," which is at least a grudging acknowledgment, if only by virtue of the metaphor, that our poets remain magicians.

When such a piece runs, the magazine subsequently prints a handful of the letters the offending article has provoked. Of the three letters that *Harper's* saw fit to print in its September 2013 issue, one writer was vexed that Edmundson had focused "almost exclusively" on white males. A second thought it a shame that the author had overlooked the work of hip-hop lyricists (he mentioned Kendrick Lamar and Nas). The third letter was written by Harvard Professor Stephen Burt, an assiduous critic and reader. He pointed out that there is "something bullying" in the call for "public" poetry. Whose public, he asked: "A public poem, in Edmundson's view, might be an interest-group poem whose collective has a flag." Attacks on contemporary American poetry such as Edmundson's "have been made for centuries" and are best seen as "screeds [that] create an opportunity for those of us who read a lot of poetry to recommend individual poets as we come to poetry-in-general's defense."[22]

Each year in *The Best American Poetry* we seize that opportunity and ask a distinguished poet to glean the harvest of poems and identify the ones he or she thinks best. Terrance Hayes has undertaken the task with vigor and inventive-

---

20. Eliot, *The Sacred Wood* (1920; rpt. London: Methuen, 1960), xv.

21. Mark Edmundson, "Poetry Slam: Or, the Decline of American Verse," *Harper's*, July 2013, 61–68.

22. *Harper's*, September 2013, 2–3.

ness. A native of South Carolina, Hayes went to Coker College on a basketball scholarship, studied the visual arts, and wrote poetry on the side. An instructor directed him to the MFA poetry program at the University of Pittsburgh, where he studied with Toi Derricotte and joined Cave Canem, the organization that has done so much to nourish the remarkable generation of African American poets on the scene today. Terrance won the 2010 National Book Award for his book *Lighthead* (Penguin). His poems—which have appeared seven times in *The Best American Poetry*—reflect a deep interest in matters of masculinity, sexuality, and race; a flair for narrative; and a love of verbal games as the key to ad hoc forms and procedures. I was thrilled when Hayes told me that the first book of poems he ever acquired was the 1990 edition of *The Best American Poetry*, Jorie Graham's volume, and that he owns all the books in the series. When I asked him to read for the 2014 book, I had in front of me the winter 2010–11 issue of *Ploughshares*, which Hayes edited. In his introduction, he wrote about a notional three-story museum, the "Sentenced Museum," which resembles an inverted pyramid with the literature of self-reflection on the ground floor, the language of witness one flight up, and a host of "tangential parlors, wings and galleries" on the third and largest floor. I remember reading the issue and thinking, "as an editor, he's a natural."

As ever, this year's volume includes our elaborate back-of-the-book apparatus. To the value of the comments the poets make on the work chosen for this book, the poets themselves attest. In the 2013 edition, Dorianne Laux comments on her "Song." "Death permeates the poem, which wasn't apparent to me until I was asked to write this paragraph."

———————

It used to be the death of God that got all the attention—God whose decomposing corpse made the big stink. Was it, in the end, Nietzsche, Freud, *Time* magazine, or the masses (who preferred, in the end, other opiates) that did Him in? I can't say, but I take solace in knowing that there are, besides myself, other holdouts refusing to suspend their belief. Meanwhile, the subject has receded to the terrorism and fundamentalism pages of your newspaper, and the focus has long since shifted to literature. The death of the novel worried all-star committees for years. There was a split decision that satisfied no one, and now, with Updike dead and Roth retired, a new consensus is starting to form around the notion that the TV serial as exemplified by *The Sopranos, Mad Men, Breaking Bad, House of Cards*, and *Homeland* has supplanted not only the novel but also the movie as a mass entertainment form—one that can aspire to be both wildly popular and notably artistic, as the novel was at its best. The past tense in that last clause makes me sad, though I have the seen the future and it is even more enthralling than Galsworthy's *Forsyte Saga* given the Masterpiece Theater treatment with Damian Lewis as Soames.

As to poetry, is it dead, does it matter, is there too much of it, does anyone anywhere buy books of poetry? The discussion is fraught with anxiety and perhaps that implies a love of poetry, and a longing for it, and a fear that we may be in danger of losing it if we do not take care to promote it, teach it well, and help it reach the reader whose life depends on it. Will magazine editors continue to fall for a pitch lamenting that poetry has become a "small-time game," that it is "too hermetic," or "programmatically obscure," lacking ambition and public spiritedness? The lack of originality is no bar. Think of how many issues of finance magazines are identical in their contents year after year. Retire at 65. Insider tips from the pros. What to do about bonds in 2014 "and beyond." Why it makes dollars and sense to "ditch cable." Or consider the general audience magazine, editors of which will not soon tire of running articles that contend that a woman today either can or cannot "have it all." I am so sure that death-of-poetry pronouncements will continue to be made that I am tempted to assign the task as a writing exercise. It's an evergreen.

───── INDEX OF NAMES ─────

Aaratani, Mariko, 55
Adams, Jim, 58
Adorno, Theodor, 76–77
Aeschylus, 129
Ajami, Muhammad ibn al-Dheeb al-, 176–77
Alexander, Elizabeth, 137
Ali, Muhammad (Cassius Clay), 55
Allen, Donald M., 81, 92
Allen, Woody, 82
Alvarez, Julia, 137
Amichai, Yehuda, 78
Amis, Martin, 53–54
Ammons, A. R. "Archie," 32, 45, 93, 125,
    163; death of, 74–75; as guest editor, 23,
    29, 44, 177; prime of, 24, 43
Angelou, Maya, 21–22, 49, 58
Anjuman, Nadia, 112
Arensberg, Walter Conrad, 146n1
Arnold, Craig, 63–64
Arnold, Matthew, 81; "Dover Beach" by, 164;
    parodies of "Dover Beach" by, 114–17,
    119; on Shelley, 127, 174
Ash, John, 2
Ashbery, John, 17, 65, 111–12, 126, 163; as
    guest editor, 2–3, 5, 19, 29, 44; influ-
    ences on, 93–94; praise for, 45, 72, 111;
    prime of, 24, 43
Ashton, Sally, 144
Atwood, Margaret, 29
Auden, W. H., 45, 77–78, 93, 128–30, 149,
    151; *The Dyer's Hand* by, 120–21, 124–
    25, 174; influence of, 163–64; on poetry,
    19, 46–47, 94, 147, 174; on poets, 13, 95,
    124–25; uses of poetry by, 27, 57, 65

Baker, Nicholson, 140–42
Barańczak, Stanisław, 38
Baraka, Amiri, 84–85, 137
Barr, John, 65
Bastian, Michael, 106
Bate, Walter Jackson, 46, 163
Beatty, Warren, 54

Belieu, Erin, 160n2
Belitt, Ben, 67n2
Benac, Nancy, 137
Benigni, Roberto, 56
Ben-Lev, Dina, 51
Berman, Russell A., 185
Bernstein, Charles, 49
Berryman, John, 164
Beyer, Lisa, 80
Billington, James, 110
Birkerts, Sven, 60, 78
Bishop, Elizabeth, 3, 18, 142, 149–50
Black, Roy, 22
Blackmur, R. P., 131
Blagg, Max, 22
Blake, Gillian, 169
Blake, William, 162, 164, 177
Blanco, Richard, 174–75
Bloom, Harold, 72; as guest editor, 45–47,
    159, 166; on literary influence, 45–46,
    109, 163–64; on Rich's guest-edited
    edition, 60, 178; on strangeness in poetry,
    152, 154
Bly, Robert, 72; as guest editor, 59, 78, 109,
    116, 164
Bogan, Louise, 150
Bogdan, Tom, 65
Boller, Diane, 99
Boss, Todd, 160
Bowers, Neal, 96–97
Bowman, Catherine, 99
Bradford, Barbara Taylor, 17
Brawne, Fanny, 143
Brehm, John, 116–17, 164
Bringhurst, Robert, 149
Brodsky, Joseph, 15, 41
Brooke, Rupert, 72
Brooks, David, 88
Brooks, Gwendolyn, 22
Brown, Stephanie, 161
Bryant, William Cullen, 93
Buchwald, Christoph, 62

Bukowski, Charles, 32, 56
Burt, Stephen, 143, 189
Bush, Laura, 86
Byron, Lord, 89, 128, 188

Cahill, Jennifer, 32
Cain, Hamilton, 169
Calvocoressi, Gabrielle, 144
Campion, Jane, 143
Carroll, Lewis, 113
Carruth, Hayden, 78
Carter, Helena Bonham, 88
Carter, Jimmy, 14, 20
Cattrall, Kim, 72
Cavafy, C. P., 27
Cavanagh, Clare, 38
Chang, Jennifer, 164
Chaplin, Charlie, 133–35
Charisse, Cyd, 143
Clark, Tom, 116
Clifton, Lucille, 56
Clinton, Bill, 50, 58, 137
Clinton, Hillary, 50
Codrescu, Andrei, 176–77
Cohen, Patricia, 123–24
Coleridge, Samuel, 104, 108, 147–48
Collins, Billy, 87, 137, 164; fight over publication of work by, 66, 109; as guest editor, 111–12; as poet laureate, 78–80, 84, 98–99, 109; popularity of, 108–10
Comden, Betty, 143
Connelly, Michael, 32–33
Cooper, Wyn, 27
Cope, Wendy, 113
Cornell, Joseph, 15
Crain, Caleb, 123
Crane, Hart, 45, 132–35, 151, 162
Creeley, Robert, 29, 81
Creighton, Al, 62
Crow, Sheryl, 27
cummings, e. e., 47, 93–94
Cummins, James, 144
Cuomo, Mario, 102

Dash, Jacqueline, 67n2
Deming, John, 175
Dern, Laura, 106
Derricotte, Toi, 190
Derrida, Jacques, 186n13
Devaney, Tom, 160
Dickey, William, 41
Dickinson, Emily, 86, 89, 132, 149; influence of, 10, 52, 151; uncanny in poems of, 153–54

Dickman, Matthew, 160n2
Dietz, Maggie, 99
Di Piero, W. S., 144
Donne, John, 65
Dorn, Edward, 116
Doty, Mark, 60, 161–62, 164
Dove, Rita, 60; as guest editor, 67, 74, 78, 109, 167; as poet laureate, 67, 74
Dowd, Maureen, 58, 65
Drummond de Andrade, Carlos, 78
Duchovny, David, 72
Duhamel, Denise, 117, 177–78
Dunn, Stephen, 78, 149
Dwyer, Joanne Dominque, 149
Dylan, Bob, 64n1

Eakin, J. Michael, 88
Edmundson, Mark, 189
Edson, Margaret, 65
Eisenstein, Jacob, 181n2
Eliot, T. S., 27, 38–39, 54, 93, 135–36; criticism and, 128, 131, 162; as modernist, 142, 148; New Criticism of, 45, 100, 105; parodies of poems by, 113–14; on poetry, 138, 147, 188–89; uses of poetry by, 66, 88
Ellerström, Jonas, 62
Ellis, Rosemarie, 99
Emerson, Ralph Waldo, 41, 45, 52, 124, 130, 132
Emanuel, Lynn, 167
Epstein, Larry, 144
Epstein, Rob, 150
Erdich, Louise, 21
Euripides, 129

Faludy, György, 119
Fein, Esther B., 17
Feldman, Alan, 164–65
Feldman, Irving, 29
Fenton, James, 163
Ferguson, Gus, 62
Fitzgerald, Edward, 58
Forster, E. M., 164
Franco, James, 150
Freud, Sigmund, 188
Friedman, Jeffrey, 150
Frost, Robert, 47, 73, 147–49, 151; honors for, 83–84; popularity of poetry by, 22, 66, 93; strangeness in poetry of, 154–55
Funkhouser, Christopher, 137

Gall, Carlotta, 112
Gandhi, 176

Gardinier, Suzanne, 60
Gardner, Helen, 135
Gargagliano, Alexis, 169
Geier, Thom, 112
Gerstler, Amy, 145
Giacchetto, Dana C., 73
Ginsberg, Allen, 27, 29, 39, 41, 64, 150, 166–67
Gioia, Dana, 15, 78, 81, 86–87, 100
Gizzi, Peter, 51
Glück, Louise, 24, 29, 98; as guest editor, 19–20, 44, 78, 177
Glusman, John, 3, 169
Goldbarth, Albert, 165
Goldman, Erika, 169
Gore, Al, 54
Gosse, Edmund, 188–89
Graham, Jorie, 29; as guest editor, 7–8, 19, 44, 190
Greacen, Amy Glynn, 164
Green, Adolph, 143
Greland, Gerald, 138
Gross, Terry, 109
Gunn, Thom, 105
Guriel, Jason, 128–29

Hall, Donald, 29, 81, 87, 126, 165; denying death of poetry, 131–32; as guest editor, 5, 19, 44, 163
Hamill, Sam, 86
Hamm, Jon, 138
Hammerstein, Oscar, II, 118–19
Hannah, Daryl, 73
Harden, Marcia Gay, 74
Hardy, Thomas, 94
Hartley, Glen, 3, 169
Harwood, Stacey, 144
Hass, Robert, 29, 117, 126, 150; as guest editor, 73–74, 78, 97–98, 109, 164; as poet laureate, 48, 67, 73–74
Havel, Václav, 10, 88–89
Hayes, Terrance, 165, 189–90
Hays, K. A., 160n2
Hazlitt, William, 148
Heaney, Seamus, 2, 31–32, 72, 159
Hecht, Anthony, 116
Hecht, Jennifer Michael, 144
Hejinian, Lyn, 97–98, 105, 187
Hemingway, Ernest, 11
Henley, W. E., 81
Herbert, George, 81
Hershon, Bob, 161
Higgins, George, 90
Hirsch, Edward, 87, 108

Hirshfield, Jane, 55, 160n2
Hirson, David, 65
Hobgood, Laurence, 170
Hollander, John, 29; as guest editor, 50–51, 78, 109, 164
Holman, Bob, 32, 137
Holtzman, Elizabeth, 22
Hong, Anna Maria, 149
Hopkins, Gerard Manley, 130
Housman, A. E., 65
Howard, Richard, 39, 81, 149; as guest editor, 28–29, 44, 166
Hughes, Langston, 86
Hughes, Ted, 48, 66
Hunt, Helen, 72
Hussein, Saddam, 106

Jackson, Janet, 22
Jackson, Phil, 73
Jacoby, Susan, 123–24
Jaffee, Marc, 98
Jarrell, Randall, 92, 94, 147, 154–55
Jewel, 56–57
Johnson, Kent, 60
Johnson, Samuel, 149
Jolie, Angelina, 134
Jonson, Ben, 170
Judd, Ashley, 72

Kassube, Angella, 160
Kaufman, James, 105
Keats, John, 73, 93, 128, 143, 153, 176; as Romantic, 109, 151
Keillor, Garrison, 99, 108; poetry used by, 70, 109; reviews of anthology by, 100–103
Kelley, Aimee, 100
Kelly, Gene, 143
Kennedy, Jackie, 27, 80
Kennedy, John, 137
Kenner, Hugh, 135
Kierkegaard, Søren, 127–28, 131
Kilmer, Joyce, 73
Kinnell, Galway, 164
Kipling, Rudyard, 72
Kirby, David, 138, 145
Kirsch, Adam, 78
Kizer, Carol, 87
Klatt, L. S., 160n2
Kleinzahler, August, 100–102
Kline, Kevin, 81, 116
Knott, Bill, 40
Koçak, Orhan, 62
Koch, Kenneth, 29, 89, 101–2
Komachi and Shikabu, 55

Komunyakaa, Yusef, 28, 70, 137; as guest
   editor, 87, 89
Krause, Peter, 106
Krist, Gary, 64
Kubrick, Stanley, 76
Kunitz, Stanley, 78, 109

Lahr, John, 65
Lamb, Christina, 112
Langenbach, James, 160n2
Larkin, Philip, 37, 142, 175
Lauer, Brett Fletcher, 100
Lauterbach, Ann, 60
Laux, Dorianne, 190
Lawrence, D. H., 45
Lazarus, Emma, 90–91
Leavis, F. R., 183–87
Lehrer, Jim, 70
Leibowtiz, Herbert, 69
Lennox, William J., Jr., 89
Levin, Gerald, 82
Levin, Ira, 80
Levis, Larry, 41
Lewinsky, Monica, 50, 57–58, 72
Le Zotte, Ann Claremont, 51
Lilly, Ruth, 87–88, 100
Lincoln, Abraham, 137
Liptak, Adam, 88
Liston, Sonny, 55
Logan, William, 132–34
Longenbach, James, 170
Longfellow, Henry Wadsworth, 73
Lopate, Leonard, 109
Lopez, Jennifer, 107
Lowe, Bridget, 160n2
Lowell, Robert, 66–67
Lummis, Suzanne, 87
Lumsden, Roddy, 159

Mac Donald, Heather, 186
MacLeish, Archibald, 137, 148
Malley, Ern, 60, 146
Marquis, Don, 1, 44
Marvell, Andrew, 164
Masefield, John, 57
Mason, David, 164
Maugham, Somerset, 112
McCartney, Paul, 72
McChrystal, Stanley, 143
McClatchy, J. D., 60, 100
McCullough, David, 65
McDonald, Cherokee Paul, 22
McEwan, Ian, 116–17
McGreevey, James, 84–85

McHenry, Eric, 78
McHugh, Heather, 29, 117–18, 165
McInerney, Jay, 53
McManus, James, 87
McVeigh, Timothy, 80–81
Melville, Herman, 89
Merrill, James, 24, 29, 43, 45, 150, 163
Merwin, W. S., 24, 29
Millard, Charles, 73
Millay, Edna St. Vincent, 73
Milton, John, 11, 28, 93, 109, 163
Miłosz, Czesław, 78
Monroe, Harriet, 87
Moody, Rick, 58
Moore, Archie, 55
Moore, Clement, 73
Moore, Marianne, 47, 49, 78, 150
Moritz, A. F., 159
Moss, Heather, 90
Moss, Thylias, 60
Motion, Andrew, 66
Moyers, Bill, 31, 70
Muldoon, Paul, 104–5, 126, 164
Mura, David, 60
Murray, Les, 132
Muske, Carol, 60
Muske-Dukes, Carol, 87

Nash, Ogden, 73
Nelson, Maggie, 78
Nemerov, Howard, 50
Neruda, Pablo, 56, 67n2, 72
Newman, Ted, 137
Nieman, John, 105–6
Nieto, Dona, 72–73
Nietzsche, Friedrich Wilhelm, 73
Nikolopoulos, Angelo, 164
North, Charles, 150
Noyes, Alfred, 73

Obama, Barack, 137–38, 174
Ochester, Ed, 108
O'Donnell, Rosie, 106
Offen, Ron, 66–67
O'Hara, Frank, 17, 106, 118; *Mad Men*'s
   allusions to, 138–39, 180; on poetry, 132,
   150–51
O'Neal, Shaquille, 73
Orbach, Jerry, 112
Orem, Laura, 144
Orr, David, 187–88
Orwell, George, 76
Osborne, Robert, 143
Osen, Frank, 138

Ostriker, Alicia, 78
O'Sullivan, Leanne, 159
Owens, Wilfred, 89

Padgett, Ron, 165
Palmer, Melissa, 73
Palmer, Michael, 132
Paltrow, Gwyneth, 56
Pankey, Eric, 160n2
Parcells, Bill, 65
Parker, Dorothy, 27
Parsons, Carol, 87
Pater, Walter, 148–49
Paz, Octavio, 57
Peacock, Molly, 81, 159
Pearce, Guy, 88
Pelosi, Nancy, 143
Perloff, Marjorie, 60
Pessoa, Fernando, 60, 165–67
Petri, Alexandra, 174–75
Petroni, Michael, 88
Piercy, Marge, 22
Pinsky, Robert, 29, 50, 78, 81; "Favorite
   Poem Project" of, 48–49, 70, 99; as guest
   editor, 170–71; as poet laureate, 48–49,
   67, 83, 99
Pinter, Harold, 86
Plath, Sylvia, 48
Plumb, J. H., 183
Poe, Edgar Allan, 27, 49, 73
Pollitt, Katha, 144
Pope, Alexander, 151
Pound, Ezra, 45; modernism and, 141–42,
   148; on poetry, 47, 63, 147
Powell, Colin, 89
Previn, André, 143
Pritchett, V. S., 177
Putin, Vladimir, 177
Putnam, Phoebe, 144

Quindlen, Anna, 28

Raab, Lawrence, 77
Radosh, Daniel, 57–58
Rakosi, Carl, 98
Ransom, John Crowe, 135
Read, Herbert, 60
Reagan, Siobhan, 32
Rector, Liam, 85
Reed, Henry, 113
Remnick, David, 55
Resnikoff, Charles, 22
Reugebrink, Marc, 63
Revell, Donald, 60

Rich, Adrienne, 24, 29, 87, 132; as guest
   editor, 33–34, 44, 60, 178
Richards, I. A., 143
Ricks, Christopher, 64n1, 135–36
Riding, Laura, 47
Rilke, Rainier Maria, 72, 124
Rimbaud, Arthur, 74
Roberts, Julia, 72
Robinson, Edwin Arlington, 78, 137
Roosevelt, Franklin Delano, 137
Roosevelt, Theodore, 137
Rourke, Mickey, 22
Roussel, Raymond, 171
Ruefle, Mary, 150
Rushdie, Salman, 73

Sappho, 31
Sarafpour, Behnaz, 89
Sartorius, Joachim, 63
Saul, Lewis, 144
Schmidt, Michael, 63
Schulman, Grace, 29
Schulz, Kathryn, 181
Schwartzman, Madeline, 188n17
Seidel, Frederick, 117
Selby, Don, 99
Serwer, Andrew, 65
Sexton, Tom, 80
Shakespeare, William, 87, 162; influence of,
   11, 50; uses of poetry by, 56, 58, 70, 73
Shankar, Ravi, 74
Shapiro, Alan, 162
Shapiro, Harvey, 86
Shaw, Fiona, 39
Sheehan, Julie, 165
Sheen, Charlie, 56
Shelley, Percy Bysshe, 45, 90, 148, 164,
   175–76; in defense of poetry, 127, 172–74
Shepherd, Reginald, 60
Shoemaker, Jack, 63
Sieiferle, Rebecca, 74
Silano, Martha, 165
Silton, Susan, 181–82
Silverblatt, Michael, 109
Simic, Charles, 29, 126; as guest editor, 15,
   19, 33, 44, 78, 108
Sisskind, Mitch, 144
Smith, Robert, 106
Smith, Stevie, 32
Snow, C. P., 182–87
Sondheim, Stephen, 119
Sophocles, 129
Soto, Gary, 137
Southwick, Marcia, 51

Sparrow, 29–30
Springsteen, Bruce, 56
St. John, Davis, 29, 87
Stein, Gertrude, 124, 148
Stepanek, Mattie, 80
Stephen, J. K., 113
Stevens, Wallace, 45, 47, 71, 81, 109, 144,
    151; defining poetry, 6, 148; on poetry,
    65, 112, 128, 150, 155; uses of poetry
    by, 50, 56
Stimpson, Catharine, 144
Stone, Ruth, 90
Stoppard, Tom, 65
Strand, Mark, 24, 29, 56, 138, 160n2; as
    guest editor, 12, 19, 44; uncanny in
    poems of, 160–61
Susanna, Alex, 62–63
Sweeney, Matthew, 159
Swenson, May, 162
Swift, Daniel, 78
Swift, Todd, 144
Szymanska, Adriana, 62
Szymborska, Wisława, 37–38

Tarantino, Quentin, 143
Tate, James, 29, 40–41, 44, 78, 163
Tempelsman, Maurice, 27
Tennyson, Alfred, Lord, 81
Thani, Hamad bin Khalifa Al, 176–77
Than Shwe, 145–46
Thien, Nguyen Chi, 179
Thomas, Dylan, 39, 93
Tichý, Miroslav, 142
Tocqueville, Alexis de, 167–68
Tomkiw, Lydia, 150
Tranter, John, 159
Travis, Robin, 57
Trillin, Calvin, 106
Trilling, Lionel, 115–16, 131
Trzeciak, Joanna, 38
Tucker, Ken, 144, 150
Turner, Brian, 117
Twain, Mark, 84, 118

Untermeyer, Louis, 93–94
Updike, John, 108–9

Van Doren, Mark, 152, 154
Vendler, Helen, 31, 81, 94–95, 110–11
Villepin, Dominique de, 89
Violi, Paul, 51, 138, 161

Wagoner, David, 29, 136, 160n2, 165
Wai, Saw, 145–46
Walcott, Derek, 2, 18
Walker, Alice, 137
Warren, Rosanna, 133
Webb, Charles Harper, 87
Weiner, Matthew, 139, 180
Wendell, Turk, 72
Wenderoth, Joe, 117
Wetzsteon, Rachel, 144, 156
Whitman, Walt, 23, 52, 84; on becoming a
    poet, 152–53; honors for, 50, 86; influ-
    ence of, 10, 165–67; on poetry, 151, 188;
    uses of poetry by, 45, 50, 58, 73
Wieseltier, Leon, 187
Wilbur, Richard, 24, 29, 31, 86, 138n4, 149,
    154, 156, 160n2
Wilde, Oscar, 15, 45, 54, 66, 121, 128n2
Williams, C. K., 132
Williams, Oscar, 94
Williams, William Carlos, 22, 45, 47, 164
Wilner, Eleanor, 64n1
Wilson, Edmund, 15, 129–30, 189
Wiman, Christian, 103
Wimbrow, Dale, 65
Winch, Terence, 144
Winfrey, Oprah, 80
Winters, Yvor, 170
Wordsworth, William, 104, 109, 113, 124;
    influence of, 103, 164; on pleasure of
    poetry, 110, 118; on poetry, 136, 147;
    popularity of poetry by, 45, 72; as Ro-
    mantic, 148, 154
Wright, Charles, 125–26, 165
Wright, Franz, 105
Wylie, Elinor, 93

Yamaguchi, Kristi, 55
Yasusada, Araki, 59–60
Yeats, William Butler, 45, 73, 93, 143
Yost, Chryss, 99
Young, Kevin, 60, 100, 155–56

Zapruder, Matthew, 165
Ziegler, Anna, 90